DIPLOMATIC CHANNELS

By the Same Author

Tricks of the Trade

The Rise, Decline and Future of the British Commonwealth

The Jamdani Revolution

Towards the New Horizon: World Order in the 21st Century
(with James B.L. Mayall)

Fiction

The Ugly Ambassador

Guesswork

The Eccentric Effect

The Invisible African

DIPLOMATIC CHANNELS

KRISHNAN SRINIVASAN

Maulana Abul Kalam Azad
Institute of Asian Studies,
Kolkata

MANOHAR
2012

First published 2012

ISBN 978-81-7304-968-2

Published by
Ajay Kumar Jain *for*
Manohar Publishers & Distributors
4753/23 Ansari Road, Daryaganj
New Delhi 110 002

Typeset by
Kohli Print
Delhi 110 051

Printed at
Salasar Imaging Systems
Delhi 110 035

For

GOPAL GANDHI
ROGER HERVEY
RUDRANGSHU MUKERJEE

With Salutations

Diplomacy is like playing on a chessboard where the pieces have been left behind from a half-finished game started by others

Contents

Preface

This book consists of two monographs and some articles that have previously been published. 'Retrospection' is an account of my tenure as foreign secretary and was written in January 1996, ten months after I had demitted office. It is reproduced here without any change except for the addition of the summary and endnotes. 'Non-alignment Revisited' tries to place the Indian version of non-alignment in perspective, putting forward the view that after Nehru's death stripped away its idealism, it was, shorn of the bombast, a strategy first of realism and later of opportunism. India's definite tilt towards the Soviet Union for reasons of practicality from 1964 to 1984, was scarcely concealed by the facade of non-alignment. The published articles are reproduced in the hope that they have a more durable value than that provided in the pages of a newspaper.

My sincere thanks to Aveek Sarkar, publisher of the ABP Group, for permission to reprint some of the several articles which have appeared in *The Telegraph* over the years. My thanks also to Ravindra Kumar, managing director and editor of *The Statesman*, for use of 'Caste and the Creamy Layer' and 'No Tears for Muammar Gaddafi' published in his newspaper. 'Gupta's Monologues' first appeared in *Gentleman,* Mumbai. My gratitude to N.G. Satish, Anirudh Chari and Hari Vasudevan for their valuable advice, and to Brinda, Maggie, Liz and Rohan for their tacit encouragement.

KRISHNAN SRINIVASAN

RETROSPECTIONS

THIS period of 1994/5, when I was the Foreign Secretary, anticipated many issues whose consequences would dominate international affairs and Indian foreign policy in the coming years. Indian economic liberalization, though nascent and proceeding in slow deliberate stages, began to attract the attention of the world's larger economies. Bilateral ties with Islamabad were becalmed and remained in that state for the next five years. For the first time ever, Pakistan's efforts to have Indian policy in Kashmir discussed and condemned at the United Nations were frustrated. A fresh start was initiated towards ending the insurgency and unrest in Kashmir by restoring the democratic process to that state. The United States was repeatedly warned about the growing threat from the Taliban and chose to look the other way. Relations with post-Soviet Russia were slowly rebuilt by virtue of a series of important agreements. An office with diplomatic status was opened in Taiwan, and a 'Look East' policy came into being, though it was not yet termed as such. India formally announced its intention to seek permanent membership of the United Nations Security Council. North Korean aspirations to becoming a nuclear-weapon and missile power sparked widespread concern, and led to efforts to cap its development of weapons of mass destruction.

I was the Foreign Secretary of India from February 1994 to March 1995. This was a duration of only thirteen months, but it was an important period of transition, and the harbinger of significant trends for the future. It was a time of transition, when India emerged from grave financial and communal crises to being a country that began to attract widespread international attention for its political resilience and economic potential.

My tenure was dominated by three main factors – arms control, in the overall context of relations with the USA; economic liberalization, with the main interest focused on the developed and investment-inclined industrialized countries, and Pakistan, with Kashmir as the top priority.

During this period, the President was Sankar Dayal Sharma, the Vice-President K.R. Narayanan, the Prime Minister P.V. Narasimha Rao, and the Minister of External Affairs Dinesh Singh. During my last few days in office, Dinesh Singh was replaced by Pranab Mukherjee. The Chairman of the Foreign Affairs Committee in Parliament was A.B. Vajpayee, a former foreign minister and leading member of the main opposition party, the BJP.

In this time, President Shankar Dayal Sharma[1] made only one visit abroad during which I accompanied him. I was of little assistance since I fell ill on the flight to Sofia in Bulgaria with a strange combination of malaria and pancreatitis. I struggled through my briefing for him and the press on board the aircraft, and in great pain attended his speech to the Bulgarian parliament and his meeting with President Zhelev, but could not continue. I was then taken to a clinic in Sofia with excruciating pain in the small of my back. In the clinic, language problems proved to be an obstacle, with a mixture of Bulgarian, Russian and German serving as inadequate channels of communication, and I was subsequently moved to the Cromwell Hospital in London for a week before my return to New Delhi. I found a large bouquet of flowers, with the name of Narasimha Rao as the sender, at the hospital waiting for me when I woke up – a kind and thoughtful gesture by the prime minister's personal staff, since I doubt whether it would ever have occurred to Narasimha Rao himself.

When receiving visitors in Rashtrapati Bhavan, President Sharma resorted to the old strategm of having a hard cushion on his chair which raised his height to some level higher than their's. This could have been because of a hernia problem that he had surgically operated upon towards the end of 1994, but he continued the practice of sitting on the high cushion even after the operation had been successfully performed. It was probably due to this medical problem, or a prostate, that during the Bulgarian visit referred to earlier, he suffered from incontinence and consequent embarrassment to himself and spectators alike during an outdoor wreath-laying function in Sofia.

Sharma liked to have a retinue of silent admirers by his side on formal occasions, to whom he would nod and smile when he felt a particularly felicitous remark by himself needed to be noted by the onlookers. He had a mumbling, indistinct manner of speech, causing his scarcely comprehending foreign visitors much bewilderment. He was in the habit of lecturing his politely-smiling guests on Indian civilization and its historically tolerant nature, with not altogether accurate historical allusions to Christianity, Islam and Judaism. He chose the most unimaginative bric-à-brac to be given as presentation gifts to his guests and visitors, and deliberated at length and agonisingly, surrounded by his bemused household staff led by the Military Secretary biting his tongue, before making his final choices.

On a one to one basis, Sharma was more restrained, genial and down to earth. He liked to hear gossip about ministers. Prime Minister Narasimha Rao was wary of Sharma and kept his distance. The prime minister did not welcome Sharma's forays into diplomacy, tried to discourage Sharma's foreign visits, and to render them as non-substantial as possible without actually opposing Sharma's wishes. The prime minister particularly resented Sharma's desire to be accompanied by large numbers of ministers and parliamentarians on such journeys, though he lacked the courage or inclination to confront the president on this point. Sharma indulged in this largesse at governmental expense partly to maintain a base in Parliament in the hope of running for a second term, and partly because he felt strongly that a person's worth was judged by the quality of his entourage. He wanted to be regarded as a Platonic scholar-statesman, wanted to address parliaments, meet intellectuals and be recognized as a savant. Both Sharma and Narasimha Rao shared an unstated yearning, in this respect, to be equated with Jawaharlal Nehru and Indira Gandhi. Rajiv Gandhi was never mentioned.

K.R. Narayanan[2] was more urbane, more affable, sharper, and had a better knowledge, especially of the East, than all the other top leaders, but, encouraged by his wife, he had an exaggerated notion of his importance and protocol status. He had been a humdrum professional diplomat with leftist inclinations who had been looked upon kindly and advanced by Mrs Gandhi and her close associates. He was well thought of in political and diplomatic circles, and attempted to craft new ideas into his speeches, though he rarely came up with anything memorable. He had his likeable side despite a naive vanity and vaunting ambition, because he was one of the very few Indian leaders of that time who was reasonably well read.

Raja Dinesh Singh[3] suffered a stroke a few weeks after I took over as foreign secretary. He was very happy to be back in the External Affairs Ministry and had hoped to be assertive, but foreign affairs had changed in the several decades since he was last in that office, though he had himself not changed with the times. He was very poorly read and did not absorb ideas through conversation. He spoke in set pieces, which were shallow and often mawkishly sentimental. After his stroke, when he could scarcely walk and could speak only with the greatest difficulty, he ceased to be a factor in the ministry and was excluded from not only the preparations but even as a physical presence during Narasimha Rao's foreign tours. He understandably became intensely suspicious of the two ministers of state, R.L. Bhatia[4] and Salman Khurshid,[5] whom he thought were undermining him in public and private, and began to suffer from paranoia. He wanted to be kept informed and consulted so that he was not upstaged, but he was unable to assimilate any information and became increasingly confined to his residence. He suffered both physically and psychologically, became depressed, fearful, morose and lachrymose. His mind wandered as he became more and more introverted. Long silences during conversations with him became commonplace, and in the end, I had as unobtrusively as possible to speak to visitors on his behalf like a ventriloquist, even at a particularly uncomfortable conference with the troika of European Community foreign ministers at Brussels.

Dinesh Singh always saw himself as being in the cabinet as a counterweight to Minister of Human Resources Arjun Singh, who was regarded as being opposed to Narasimha Rao on behalf of Sonia Gandhi. Dinesh Singh no doubt clung to office in the hope of making a medical recovery, but his several sycophantic doctors were more at fault in misleading him in that expectation. He felt let down by Narasimha Rao since he began to be rigorously excluded from any meetings with the prime minister. When he tried to speak in cabinet, Narasimha Rao would brusquely interrupt him and give the floor to some other minister. He had become superfluous to everyone but the foreign secretary, who had to console, comfort, counsel and act as his minder and psychiatrist, and make him feel an essential part of the ministry. I was told by his household that my visits every few days to his home were eagerly looked forward to by him and made him feel better in body and mind. These visits were not easy to make, as much as I liked him for his courtesy and his considerable charm, of which by the end only the tatters remained.

The two ministers of state were feeling their way throughout this time. They did not take sufficient advantage of Dinesh Singh's absence from Parliament to make a name for themselves, because R.L. Bhatia, by far the lesser mortal in understanding and exposition, took it upon himself as the 'senior' junior minister, to answer as many of the parliamentary questions as he could, albeit in a halting and unconvincing manner. Bhatia was a journeyman, wrongly placed in the External Affairs Ministry. He was strongly given to better ties with Pakistan and the former Communist bloc. To supplement his frequent hints at a close acquaintance with the one-time Russian spymaster Yevgeny Primakov,[6] he tried at times to promote the initiative of an India-Russia-China axis;[7] at other times an India-China-Iran grouping. He tried to put in play some of his shadowy back-channels with those countries, but nothing useful ever came of them, and, overall, his diplomatic perceptions were juvenile.

Salman Khurshid was more than capable and intelligent, but he did not take the necessary pains to master any subject, though he was certainly by far the best face and voice of the ministry at that time. He was at his best on Kashmir, but one topic, however, important and brilliantly presented, could not represent a minister's complete repertoire. Both ministers of state, but especially Bhatia, tried on occasion to meddle in personnel matters, and these efforts called for evasive or blocking action.

Narasimha Rao,[8] as the first non-Nehru/Gandhi Congress prime minister apart from Shastri,[9] felt especially vulnerable within his own party to the charge of betraying Nehruvian socialism and the traditional foreign policy ideals of the Congress party; the more so, since when he was sworn in as prime minister, he was not even an elected member of either House of parliament, having been denied a nomination by Rajiv Gandhi.

Relations between Narasimha Rao and Sonia Gandhi are difficult to describe; non-existent would probably be an accurate description. Sonia was a rather remote, very dignified and correct presence at formal functions, but was never approached for friendly conversation by Narasimha Rao. They both kept their distance and their separate private space from each other. Narasimha Rao probably regarded her as a critical observer of all his actions, and that she considered him an unworthy successor of the Nehru-Gandhi inheritance. How she regarded him is not known, but there was clearly no love lost between them.

Narasimha Rao received a briefing by the concerned officials before his foreign visits both in New Delhi and on arrival in the foreign country. It was important for the foreign secretary to take the floor as soon as possible, because otherwise the prime minister's Principal Secretary A.N. Verma, or some ministers, or our local ambassador, would intervene on some trivial subject and the whole exercise would be diverted on a disastrous tangent. Narasimha Rao was exceptionally nervous about relations with the USA. He knew the importance of our relations with that country and that the liberalization policy initiated by himself and Finance Minister Manmohan Singh[10] depended to a great extent on the USA. But he was unsure of himself, perhaps felt inadequate to handle President Clinton, and had to steer a deft course between nationalist aspirations in the security field and the need to keep the USA in friendly and positive play. Among the powerful states in the international community, Narasimha Rao best knew the background in regard to Russia, though he was relatively unfamiliar with the new leadership of Yeltsin and Chernomyrdin. The briefing papers prepared for Narasimha Rao's visits to the USA and Russia were voluminous and masterpieces of their kind, but were little consulted or of any practical use in reality. Nevertheless, they would make excellent historical records if ever published. Some of the conceptual papers prepared on these two big powers by the ministry were quite excellent in terms of contemporary history and analysis.

The access I had to Narasimha Rao varied. In brief, I could see him when it was necessary, but it was sometimes only for a few minutes sandwiched between two of his other engagements. On one occasion, I had to squeeze into his car from the airport to his office-cum-residence at Race Course Road to obtain a hearing. None of the Indian prime ministers after Jawaharlal Nehru have been capable of organizing their time properly. Seeing the prime minister for the required duration became ever more difficult as his domestic political problems increased. Despite his Quintus Fabius Maximus reputation, and the short time that was invariably at my disposal, I managed to extract decisions from him even on some sensitive subjects. On the celebration of the Dalai Lama's birthday in India, issues on the Sino-Indian and Sino-Bhutan borders, permission for the newly-discovered Karmapa in Tibet to assert his claim to the Rumtek monastery in Sikkim, the question of a visitor's visa to Taslima Nasreen, the self-exiled writer from Bangladesh, the award of the Nehru Prize for International Understanding to Aung San Suu Kyi and on other matters, Narasimha Rao gave quick decisions when presented with the clear options, often in the teeth of contrary advice from the military or intelligence. It was easier, however, to obtain decisions from him privately than in a group meeting, where he would attempt to appear magisterial or intellectual, and invariably ended by procrastinating. The files I sent him came back quickly enough. The only time I greatly upset him was when I sought to anticipate our protocol reactions to the impending death of Deng Xiaoping[11] – possibly, like many others, he did not want to look mortality in the face.

Narasimha Rao had considerable respect for some former members of the foreign service, especially retired officials like N. Krishnan[12] and Muchkund Dubey.[13] He also thought it prudent to take views from politicians, retired diplomats, non-resident Indians of varying talents and capabilities, the occasional swami, and many others who rarely had anything much to contribute. He received unattributed notes from diverse sources such as the Srichand and Gopichand Hinduja brothers in London urging various courses of action in foreign affairs. Nothing was done to pursue any of this advice, though it wasted everyone's time. Narasimha Rao liked to be his own inscrutable man. He was, in essence, a cold fish. He had no evident personal attachments and no warmth. All politicians use people, but his was an even more than normally cynical disposition. Those who counted on being remembered, or on reciprocal admiration, were certain to be sorely disappointed. He went through the civilities perfunctorily and with no interest in his surroundings. As a personality, he was already dead to the world. Given an opportunity, he spoke disparagingly about most of his ministers, but would still not delegate any authority. Such a sense of humour as he possessed was surprisingly childish; so the rare jokes that he made invariably had an edge to them.

Narasimha Rao was, therefore, the opposite of charming. A poor conversationalist, he liked it best when playing the intellectual. His favourite on-stage declamation was about Indian individualism and nationalism and their derivation, the Partition of India, the character of the Indian subcontinent, and the interlinkage of religion and politics. He delivered this narration, unsolicited, to a baffled Chinese Foreign Minister Qian Qichen, and again to the Frenchman Alain Juppe, and I am reliably told, he did the same thing when he and Clinton had a one-to-one meeting in the Oval Office at the White House. So much for the Foreign Office's briefing papers for such meetings! It is hard to say what impact these philosophical monologues had on their audiences. Clinton must have thought about the inscrutable East, and Qian about the deviousness of the Indian mind; and both about the propensity of Indians to deliver lectures to others. Juppe, being French and therefore more theoretically-minded, was perhaps more impressed.

Relations with the major powers naturally dominated the work of the ministry. The USA was interested in expediting India's economic liberalization due to the Clinton agenda of the American economy first and last, his desire to open markets, to conclude the Uruguay Round and to consolidate relations with the world's fastest growing economies. At the same time, the USA was concerned about a possible Indo-Pakistani conflict, especially with the use of modern technology, whether nuclear or missiles. The Americans wanted to prevent the deployment or the diversion of such weapons, using the precepts of the Non-Proliferation Treaty and the Missile Technology Control Regime. They were not as much concerned with a settlement of Indo-Pakistani issues as with keeping the lid on them, and they backed away from direct involvement in the Kashmir question after the new Assistant Secretary of State for South Asia, Robin Raphel,[14] grossly overplayed her hand in the first few months after taking office. This resulted in less pressure and a more even-handed approach politically on the part of Washington, but a greater degree of energetic involvement in the arms control area. In particular there was a strenuous effort to draw India and Pakistan into a 7-nation or a 9-nation multilateral discussion on the subject. They felt such a gathering would be a better forum to bring pressure to bear on India and Pakistan towards bilateral negotiations, and to promote vertical and horizontal non-proliferation and non-deployment. Their idea was to assemble the five permanent members of the UN Security Council, also, of course, the five nuclear weapon powers, plus India and Pakistan; or the five permanent members together with the two front-running potential permanent members of the Security Council, namely, Japan and Germany, plus India and Pakistan in forums for negotiation.

The USA had concluded with ample justification in the months before I took over as Foreign Secretary, that India had in fact agreed to the holding of such discussions. Several countries had conducted separate bilateral, but obviously coordinated, disarmament talks with New Delhi, among them Britain, Germany, Japan, Russia, France, and of course, the USA in the persons of Lynn Davis and Bob Einhorn. Now Washington was convinced with good reason that India had clearly indicated that it was prepared to expand these bilateral discussions into a multilateral forum, and the records indeed supported this assumption. It was left to me in the ministry to back-pedal and take preventive action.

After a discussion in New Delhi with US Deputy Secretary of State Strobe Talbot, Narasimha Rao agreed to pay an official visit to the USA on the assurance that he would not be pressurized over the issues of Kashmir, human rights or arms control. The US wanted this visit to take place to keep themselves as a player in the subcontinent after several barren years during and after the Gulf War, when there had been precious little dialogue of any kind. They pressed for a getting-to-know-you visit, and they thought that Narasimha Rao was a person they could do business with, due to the opening up of the Indian economy. Narasimha Rao also agreed with Strobe Talbot, whom he found particularly persuasive – 'not like the usual American', he opined – that the Indians and Americans could engage in 'quiet diplomacy' on the possible options of the 5 plus 2 or the 7 plus 2 negotiating formulas. His brief to his designated confidant N. Krishnan, whom he selected to lead a four-member Indian side to the talks in a hotel in London, was to see that the proposed forum was widely expanded in such a way as to cover all the leading countries in the Asian region and the nuclear-weapons-capable countries the world over, on the argument that discussions on arms control in modern times could not be confined within national or even continental boundaries. In effect, the Indian concept would make the proposed forum a sort of mini-Disarmament Conference that would include countries like Israel and Iran that the USA would have no reason to welcome at such a gathering. It would have become a conference on general and complete disarmament rather than a meeting to badger India and Pakistan, and a forum where the USA and other nuclear-weapon powers would find themselves on the defensive. This Indian line would not have come as any surprise to Washington, since I had earlier indicated our new position to Robin Raphel, but the Americans hoped that Talbot had prevailed on Narasimha Rao to change his mind, and they remonstrated that we had gone back on the assurances my predecessor had given to them previously. The 'quiet diplomacy' talks did not remain quiet. Perhaps leaks took place from the ministry that was always prone to be leaky; perhaps a female member of the Indian delegation was spotted by a journalist in London without any plausible explanation as to her presence there. In any event, there were many questions raised in the press and the Parliament, and this added fuel to the already highly combustible atmosphere in which Narasimha Rao made his visit to Washington.

Narasimha Rao had been intensely agitated before and during his Washington visit. This may be the right time to rectify a particular false rumour. I was widely reputed in New Delhi circles to have walked out of a meeting taken by the prime minister at his Race Course Road office in preparation for his US visit, but the facts are less spectacular. A gathering was arranged with about a score of secretaries of various departments with Narasimha Rao, and when he arrived, he testily asked what the purpose was of such a gathering and why I had arranged it. I replied equally icily that the meeting was not organized by the MEA and that we had received notice of it from the prime minister's office, like everyone else that had been asked to be present. I added that had my ministry organized it, we would not have done it in such a fashion. Both the prime minister and I then calmed down, but everyone else in the room was taken aback. The meeting proceeded, and needless to say, with such a large gathering in attendance, nothing at all consequential was achieved.

Narasimha Rao was well aware, as all Indian prime ministers before and after him, that there was no 'national consensus' either in India or in the USA on how to deal with the other country. He feared that there would accordingly be trouble with the parliament and the media on whatever the outcome of his visit. This was at the heart of India's problem with America; both countries were intensely self-righteous. Both wanted from the other various assurances that the other would not and indeed could not give. India wanted America to respect it as a great democracy and world power, whose views and interests had to be taken into account. It wanted the moral support and economic backing of the United States, but at the same time wanted that country to keep out of the politics of the Indian subcontinent. The United States was willing to concede a certain primacy for India in South Asia, but wanted India to abjure the use of nuclear weapons and missile technology, and open up its markets at a much faster pace. It wanted India to recognize that Kashmir was an unresolved problem that needed to be settled promptly and peacefully with Pakistan. The Indian public was enthused about all things American, but the government was deeply Nehruvian in its suspicions. The American public knew little about India and cared less, and their government oscillated between involvement and indifference, both of which fuelled New Delhi's mistrust.

In Washington itself, Narasimha Rao made a reasonable address to Congress, very much a set piece, but his lack of personality was not up to spontaneous meetings with the media or influential Congressmen, and therefore, as a public relations exercise, the visit was a non-event. Our new economic policies, however, helped to burnish the Indian image in Congress, the big business houses, and with the overseas Indians in America. On the margins of the visit, I met an old college friend, American Ambassador Anthony Quainton,[15] who advised me that India should not deviate from the Clinton line – 'it's the economy, stupid!' – which was a trump card in the USA. Nothing else, according to him, mattered to the Washington establishment.

During the Oval Office talks with Clinton, Narasimha Rao found little to say and lapsed into silence. Clinton waxed fluently and eloquently on Germany and Japan's economic and political problems, and how he had concentrated on America's small and medium businesses. It was only small talk at the highest level. Then the rest of us left Narasimha Rao and Clinton to spend almost one hour together privately. Lunch followed, which was dominated by Senator Daniel Patrick Moynihan[16] with his acerbic wit. Narasimha Rao again lapsed into a moody silence. Our Ambassador S.S. Ray[17] and Finance Minister Manmohan Singh attempted some interventions but sounded stilted. Clinton gave his next Ambassador to India, Frank Wisner, who was present, a big build-up.

The talks Narasimha Rao had with Clinton achieved little, but the joint statement between the two sides revealed no sign of any American pressure on Kashmir or arms control. Attempts by us to link the possible Comprehensive Test Ban Treaty and Fissile Material cut-off treaties with a time-bound programme for the total elimination of nuclear weapons were rejected by the Americans. Nevertheless it was a reasonable and up-beat iteration of Indo-American relations at that time, with a good deal of convergence on world issues like population, human rights and environment, apart from economic liberalization, and it was welcomed in India even by those sceptics who peered closely between the lines for any hidden concession to the Americans. In a way, this was Narasimha Rao's greatest diplomatic triumph. Dealing with the USA over this period was the area in which the External Affairs Ministry performed at its best.

For the time being, the proposed 5 plus 2 and 7 plus 2 forums were forgotten, but Narasimha Rao nevertheless decided to give the intermediate range missile, a so-called technology demonstrator called Agni, a pause in its trials. The development of India's missile programme was then being fashioned by A.P.J. Abdul Kalam,[18] the chief scientific adviser to the prime minister. The short-range vehicle-mounted mobile ballistic missile Prithvi, whose serial production was of great concern to the Americans and the Pakistanis, however, completed its tests and was, in effect, quietly deployed with the Army. The Americans must have known about this, as indeed they did about the arrival and imminent deployment of three dozen M-11 Silk-worm Chinese missiles, then unloaded and lying in Pakistani ports, into the Pakistan Army, which we brought forcefully to their notice. Like the three monkeys, the Americans when told of facts running counter to their current policies – the Taliban, missiles, nuclear transfers – problems all originating in Pakistan – they just rolled over and played possum.

The Americans could do little about the Prithvi, which became a big issue with its then imminent deployment. They tried to interest India in a voluntary adherence to the discipline of the MTCR without actually being admitted to its membership as a missile country, and there was a discussion for the first time with the MTCR troika in New Delhi. But there was no common ground to be reached, because it was never clear to us what benefit we would derive from any such self-denying ordinance, since we were self-sufficient in missile technology and material and were not sharing such technology either in missiles or nuclear matters with other countries. In other words, we were thus effectively already following the provisions of the NPT and MTCR. The self-sufficiency of India in these strategic areas, of albeit localized importance, made it almost impossible for the USA to apply the kind of pressure on India that they would have dearly liked. And because they were constrained as far as India was concerned, they felt themselves equally restrained when it came to the notoriously un-self-sufficient Pakistan, in the interests of 'even-handedness' as they saw it.

On return to New Delhi from Washington, Narasimha Rao

wished to invite Clinton to be our guest of honour at the 1995 Republic Day, and for me to enquire about his availability. I passed on the invitation informally first on the phone through Strobe Talbot to test the waters. Talbot checked with Clinton, and phoned back to say that the president could not accept it for the year 1995. A separate invitation was also extended to Mrs Hillary Clinton[19] (she did come, along with her daughter Chelsea), and there were visits in quick succession by Energy Secretary O'Leary, Defence Secretary Perry and Commerce Secretary Brown. I heard that Clinton apparently complained jokingly: 'suddenly all my Cabinet Members want to go to India', and amazingly very quickly, after talking about nothing for years, we started talking about everything with the Americans, including naval exercises and defence technology imports; and the Americans made no complaint when we imported enriched uranium from the Chinese to keep the Tarapur reactor running. The formal burial of the Indo-American agreement for the supply of fuel to Tarapur, which had long been in disuse anyway, was not an occasion for friction, but for a proforma re-statement without debate of the Indian and American positions at the IAEA in Vienna.

A far greater challenge to the USA than India at this time was North Korea, which refused to permit IAEA inspections of two undeclared nuclear-related sites, announced its withdrawal from the NPT in 1993 (later rescinded), and by mid-1994 was poised to move to production of weapons-grade plutonium. In December 1993, the IAEA's Director-General, Hans Blix, said he could no longer give assurances that North Korea was not producing nuclear weapons, and the IAEA referred the matter of non-access to the UN Security Council, whereupon Pyongyang said it would declare war if sanctions were imposed on it. The US, under great pressure from public opinion at home, agreed to deploy Patriot missiles in South Korea and held joint military exercises with the South Koreans. But throughout the crisis, the USA sought to avoid any escalation that might again involve Chinese intervention, and after former President Jimmy Carter visited Pyongyang and the death of Kim Il-sung in June 1994, an Agreed Framework was signed in October between USA and North Korea. This accord provided for North Korea to shut down the Yongbyon plant and cease plutonium production, while the US would help to construct two light-water reactors to help North Korea's energy problems, and also supply half a million tonnes of heavy fuel oil annually until the construction of the reactors was completed. Because of continued domestic opposition in the US, the reactors and the delivery of fuel fell totally behind schedule and it looked as if Washington was reneging on its commitments. If Kim Jong-il 'Baby Kim',[20] who took over from his father, was anything like the so-described 'Great Leader' Kim Il-sung, I was sure that the non-implementation of the Framework would neither be forgiven nor forgotten in Pyongyang, and this would be a new crisis waiting to explode.

In 1994, at the UN General Assembly, India made its first formal announcement of its candidature for a permanent seat on the UN Security Council.[21] So incidentally did Japan. Both countries also were then, not coincidentally, starting to campaign against each other for a non-permanent seat on the Council. I was unable, during a visit to Tokyo for this purpose, to prevail on the Japanese *Gaimusho* to allow India the priority to precede it, although they had been on the Council more recently than us. Having failed to break the deadlock, the talks in Tokyo were largely spent in speculating on the character of Kim Jong-il, which was of great interest to us because the Japanese knowledge of North Korea was intimate and far superior to ours – though even they admitted to being baffled by Baby Kim.

The visits Narasimha Rao made to Germany and Britain in February and April 1994 respectively, were much more relaxed in comparison to his Washington visit. Our main objective was to interest the two Western economies in India's economic reforms, for which there was already considerable enthusiasm in those countries; and in the case of Germany, to unlock the barriers which it, like several other industrialized nations, had set up during the Gulf War to exports of lethal stores to regions assessed as war-prone. Various aspects of India's armaments industry, especially the main battle tank, were being severely jeopardized by these haemorrhages. Some of these problems were overcome, and relations with both countries improved. Both British and German ministers started to visit India in numbers, and non-official contacts, especially in the trade sector, developed rapidly. Narasimha Rao's lack of charisma cost us less in the European public relations environment than in the American one, where the medium was the message. Both countries, however, along with France, pressed India very hard in regard to their commercial interests, and Indian trade circles complained that efforts like the Indo-British 'partnership initiative' and the Indo-German consultative group produced conclusions that favoured our partners and not ourselves. It was true that Indian political spokesmen were always less than robust in promoting our business interests, and this was not only a cultural problem. Perhaps the unsavoury interplay of the politician and businessman in India, and the long-running Rajiv Gandhi Bofors scandal had something to do with it.

During the visit to London, the newly-opened Nehru Centre was officially inaugurated. Gopal Gandhi,[22] the director of the cultural centre, had assembled a stellar cast of British dignitaries and intellectuals connected with India but Narasimha Rao seemed overawed by the occasion and was embarrassingly tongue-tied. Narasimha Rao got along well, however, with John Major, prime minister of the United Kingdom, a man easy to get on with, who was largely supportive of Narasimha Rao at crucial times like the demolition of Babar's mosque by the BJP at the end of 1992. With Helmut Kohl, Federal Chancellor of Germany, there was no particular warmth between the distinctly non-vegetarian Kohl and the frugal Narasimha Rao, but there was a mutual convenience to be exploited.

Narasimha Rao's visit to Russia in August 1994 found the prime minister much more at ease, though he was not yet on personal terms with President Boris Yeltsin or Premier Victor Chernomyrdin. The US visit was now behind him, and the agenda for India was relatively simple – to revive the former Soviet-Indian special relationship to the maximum extent possible. For its own reasons, which had much to do with a nationalistic Duma and the rise of Vladimir Zhirinovski,[23] its difficulties with Japan and possible NATO Eastward expansion, Islamic revival in Central Asia and especially Chechnya, and the need to find markets for its languishing industrial and ordnance factories, this view was to an extent reciprocated by Moscow.

Dozens of agreements were signed both during this visit and the return one made by Chernomyrdin to New Delhi a few months later, which removed the chill with Russia that had arisen after the break up of the USSR in 1991. The most significant of these agreements were the continuation of support by Russia to the Indian Air Force, and Moscow's concurrence to provide seven cryogenic rocket engines for our Geo-Stationary Launch Vehicle despite the Americans bearing down hard on the Russians with the argument that this transfer was covered by the Nuclear Suppliers Group ban on dual use technology. Apart from Russian help to build the cryogenic rockets, additional technology for India's space programme would be provided. Talks were taking place in utmost secrecy on collaboration for a nuclear-powered submarine for the Indian Navy. A Declaration on the Protection of the Interests of Pluralistic States was signed, an excellently phrased philosophical statement on the nature of a democratic, pluralistic, multicultural, mutilingual and multiracial State and the need to protect its unity. It also contained mutual respect for the territorial integrity of the other signatory as defined in their respective constitutions, and embodied in this Declaration was a commitment to cooperate in Central Asia that had recently emerged as a political no-man's land between Kashmir and South Russia. Commercial, scientific and cultural underpinnings were attempted to be put in place, but it was obvious that even if there was the will in Moscow – and there certainly was such a desire among the old-school politicians and academics and scientists but not among the new breed of politicians or the younger generation – there was no money in either country for extensive programmes manifesting goodwill and brotherhood as there had been in the erstwhile Soviet Union days.

Premier Victor Chernomyrdin was a cool and canny aide to Yeltsin, who, in the formal meetings did not seem to be nearly as eccentric or dictatorial towards his colleagues on his side of the table as his reputation had led one to believe. Yeltsin and Chernomyrdin chatted amiably with each other throughout a banquet in honour of Narasimha Rao in the Kremlin, with the orchestra playing an occasional Indian film song, the only time when the Indian prime minister seemed to jolt awake momentarily and display some animation.

During the talks, the Russians were friendly but definite. They wanted Aeroflot rights to Bombay, and they wanted a treaty on the protection and guarantee of investment. Andrei Kozyrev, the foreign minister, was distant and uninterested; it did not appear that relations with developing countries were any priority for him, a trait that he shared with his predecessor Eduard Scheverdnadze and his American counterpart Secretary of State Warren Christopher. A matter that exercised the Indian Parliament and media greatly was whether new Russia had changed sufficiently from the former Soviet Union to sell weapons to Pakistan. At the official level to us, they said no. At Yeltsin's level to Narasimha Rao, likewise. At other political levels, there was a less clear response, probably reflecting a debate within Kremlin circles. But during this period, there were no such sales.

At a reception at the Embassy during the visit, I encountered Mikhail Gorbachev,[24] a lonely and isolated figure in a crowded and animated setting. Then and now, irrespective of his popularity elsewhere, and especially in the West. In Russia, he seemed to be ostracized for undermining first the power, and then the existence, of the former Soviet Union.

I went with Narasimha Rao to Oman in the summer of 1994. Oman had always shown a remarkable propensity to take a strikingly independent line from the other Arab countries, and its ties with India historically were very strong – the Sultan's grandfather is buried in Bombay – and Oman had invested heavily in India's energy sector. A fertilizer plant in Oman and a marine pipeline to India's west coast, both based on Omani natural gas, were under serious consideration. It was exceptionally hot in Muscat, the scorching sun overwhelming the air-conditioning of the cars. Narasimha Rao was kept waiting in the guesthouse for about an hour by Sultan Qaboos before his audience, which understandably did not lift his spirits, and made his entourage extremely nervous as they drifted away one by one from his sullen and taciturn presence. Our indefatigable and bold ambassador, Ranjit Gupta, valiantly kept the prime minister company for a while, but even he was eventually rebuffed by Narasimha Rao's sour mood. However, Narasimha Rao's eventual meeting with Qaboos turned out to be a great success – the prime minister was captivated by the style, pragmatism and studied attentions of the bearded bachelor Ruler. The mood of the whole visit lightened. A grand luncheon banquet in the Sultan's palace was followed by Narasimha Rao walking out to see the sea for all of fifteen seconds before the burning sun became too much for him to bear. The joint statement was prepared with considerable ease.

It became the practice for a large number of heads of Indian business houses to accompany the prime minister abroad. This new development was possibly started by German Chancellor Helmut Kohl, who came to India with a huge delegation of German businessmen and stayed with them in a hotel, on the flimsy ground that Rashtrapati Bhavan did not have a bed big enough for his bulky frame – an excuse that caused eyebrows to be raised and not only at the president's house. But it was felt politic to allow Kohl to have his way and develop fellow feeling after hours with his business cronies for his own purposes. Needless to say, considering the nexus between business circles and politicians in India, this concept of joining the prime minister on visits abroad was embraced with considerable eagerness by the business associations, who vied with one another to field groups to accompany the prime minister on his state visits, and to organize splendidly lavish events in their margins. Whether any real business accrued as a result of such excursions, or whether the deals concluded had been stitched up well in advance of the announcements during the visit, was a matter best left uninvestigated. But the reality was that fraternal relations between the businessmen in India and our own political leaders were further enhanced.

I visited Hawaii with Deputy Chief of Mission Kanwal Sibal[25] towards the end of 1994 after my visit to the UN General Assembly. We called on the admiral in-charge of the US Pacific Command and were given a strategic lecture by him with a 30-minute power-point presentation. At the conclusion of this exercise, I had to point out that we were surprised that he had made no mention of China, without consideration of which there could hardly be an overall strategy by any country in the Pacific region. It was plain to deduce that the United States regarded China as little other than a large and promising market. We could not share such a benign optimism.

Narasimha Rao had visited China in 1993, a year before I

became the foreign secretary, when a number of useful accords had been reached. There was scope to enhance trade and scientific cooperation – the sale of enriched uranium for Tarapur was an outcome of this. The problem of the border remained, in all the three sectors, the East, Central and West, and there had been minor Chinese intrusions on our territory. In the East, the Chinese had encamped ten years back at Sumderong Chu well inside what we claimed as our territory, and where, here and at another place also in the Eastern sector called Namka Chu (or Che Dong as the Chinese termed it) our two armies were confronting each other across a narrow distance, constituting a potential flashpoint. In New Delhi, before I left for Beijing for the border talks, at a meeting convened by the prime minister in his Parliament House office with the chief of army staff present, we agreed that we could offer to take the first step to withdraw unilaterally in a phased manner, with each stage of withdrawal being matched by the other side, but we were naturally anxious to determine in advance where both sides would end up in their final deployment. Ideally, we wanted the Chinese to withdraw to the high watershed to the north, or what we considered to be the international border, Zanglung in the case of Sumderong Chu and Thagla in the case of Namka Chu. We were ourselves prepared to withdraw to a defensible ridge further South, thereby creating a no-man's land in between.

I then visited Beijing for the talks lasting over two days, and put forward our propositions for the two pockets of controversy. The Chinese were first caught off balance, and then, after a considerable pause for reflection, responded that we must take the initial step, because, in their opinion, we were in the wrong to be there in the first place. And they added that we should then leave it to their good judgement as to what they would do next. They concluded meaningfully that we would not be dissatisfied with the outcome. We replied that this was unacceptable; their reply was vague and not good enough. But this was the beginning of the solution to the close confrontation flashpoints; it was the first time we had spelled out how we could achieve, to mutual advantage, the demilitarization of those dangerous areas, and created the basis of a future agreement.

It is to Narasimha Rao's credit that he accorded us the go-ahead to make our proposals. If the Indian public, egged on by the ultra-nationalists in politics and the media, had known we had agreed to take the first step in withdrawal in what was regarded as India's own territory, there would have been a very emotional and adverse reaction. But Narasimha Rao was ready to take such risks, and felt sure enough that confidentiality would be maintained, though Army Headquarters, even more than the Ministry of External Affairs, was always prone to excessive leaks. It was also prone to adopt macho stances that could not be supported by the Army's inherent capacity. But on India's north-east border, the Army obviously felt that discretion was the better part of valour, and they could not afford to make the errors of judgement of 1962. We went on to conclude, without too much of a problem, draft agreements with the Chinese on military and air flight movements near the border, a schedule of confidence-building meetings on the border between the two armies, and some new cross-border trading routes at Nathu La and Shilpi La between India and Tibet. We also suggested that we would be amenable to an additional border trading post in the Ladakh sector.

During this entire period, the question of the Dalai Lama, his growing international prestige and popularity, and his stay and activities in India, caused the Chinese the liveliest concern. When we talked to them about Kashmir, they countered by talking about the Dalai Lama. We held to the position that they should understand and accept that the Dalai Lama was a religious figure immensely respected in India, and that we would continue to treat him as such. To deflect Chinese criticisms, we pointed out that they had engaged in talks with the Dalai Lama's representatives themselves. We hinted heavily that they were better off with the Dalai Lama in India than if he had lived in the West. We delayed our support to them on a European Community sponsored draft resolution on Tibet in the Geneva Commission on Human Rights until their diplomatic representations became more and more anguished. Those who like to claim that the Chinese do not care about criticism of their human rights record are totally mistaken. The Chinese are ready to pay a high price to avoid censure, and regularly do so to the Americans and Europeans, though their opening gambits and diplomatic demarches are invariably shrill and threatening.

We decided to open an office in Taiwan headed by a retired diplomat, V.C. Khanna, who spoke Chinese but had never been posted as our ambassador in Beijing. The office was in all respects under the External Affairs Ministry, financed by us and reporting to us, but it would not issue visas and for the sake of cover – little more than a transparent fig leaf, really – would be considered an office of one of our commercial parastatal organizations. We prepared the ground by broaching the subject very gently, and I finally passed on Khanna's name to my Chinese opposite number during a formal dinner for Qian Qichen at Hyderabad House in New Delhi. He was non-committal – we could hardly expect them to acquiesce in any case – and interpreting lack of comment as approval, we went ahead. Taipeh at first was adamant that both our office and their's in New Delhi should have the authority to issue visas, which they wanted to interpret as an attribute of sovereignty. But they did not have a strong hand to play, and eventually had to yield ground on the issue.

With increased repression in Tibet by the Chinese, and notwithstanding the active discouragement and interdiction by Kathmandu, there was a constant stream of Tibetan refugees arriving in India via Nepal, a stream which became a minor flood during the Dalai Lama's *Kalachakra* sermons in Bodh Gaya. Although the understanding was that the Tibetans would go back home the way they came after the public audience, many of course did not return and merged into the ranks of the exiles in India. This caused the liveliest concern among our intelligence agencies, and I warned the Dalai Lama of the dangers of spies and agents provocateurs working for China among these devotees. I suggested to His Holiness that the Tibetan influx be vetted for its authenticity. The Dalai Lama was taken aback and adamant in his refusal: 'was India becoming a prisoner of war camp?' he asked me excitedly. The great man, despite the threat to his person and his cause, would not accept that the end could justify the means. We compromised with the conclusion that the Dalai Lama's establishment in Dharamshala would inform us if it had any suspicions about any individual newcomer. I knew, and no doubt the Dalai Lama did too, that Indian intelligence would not be content with this solution, and would find ways to subject the pilgrims to close scrutiny.

Relations with Pakistan, like relations with the USA, were a constant and pressing preoccupation throughout this period. Too many politicians, academics and media people in India had made these two topics a life-long obsession and career to allow them to recede into the background. It ill sits in our mouth to complain about any other country hyphenating India and Pakistan, when we in India ourselves cannot rid ourselves of the Pakistan fixation.

This was the period of the apogee of the nexus between the Pakistani military and the *jehadist* groups in Kashmir which had started in 1989/90 with the almost complete breakdown of governance in that State. The last round of talks with Pakistan at foreign secretary level had taken place in Islamabad just before I took over, and there had then been an understanding that the talks would continue, and there had been an exchange of non-papers to define the positions on each side. The non-papers covered a range of subjects; the Sir Creek boundary, the Tulbul navigation project, the reconvening of the Joint Commission, the Siachen glacier, proposals to make the Line of Actual Control less tense, and so on. Very soon, however, Pakistan Foreign Secretary Shariyar Khan's publicly-declared opinion that the talks had been constructive were brushed aside in Islamabad by the politicians of the ruling Pakistan Peoples Party, who vetoed the idea of any further meetings. For India's part, we said we were ready to discuss all aspects of the Kashmir question; but that the accession of the whole of the State to India was not open for negotiation. So the proposed talks at best would be jaw-jaw instead of war-war, and at worst a restatement of all the barren and acrimonious debates between the two countries that had been well rehearsed *ad nauseam* over the decades. Pakistan thought the whole exercise was side-stepping the central issue of the future of the political disposition of Kashmir. They continued to foment trouble in the State with scarcely-concealed infiltration of militants and arms, and declared that the Simla Agreement of 1972 did not preclude a reference to international opinion. So for the first time ever, they sponsored a draft resolution against India on Kashmir in the UN Commission on Human Rights[26] in Geneva in spring 1994.

Both countries sent heavyweight delegations to Geneva, necessitated by domestic opinion, hoping that the responsibility for a possible defeat in the voting would be spread among all political parties and shades of opinion. In Geneva, both countries launched an NGO war against each other. Whereas for some time past, Pakistan had been nurturing NGOs for just such an eventuality, we were caught on the wrong foot and had to make a start in a field we knew little about. The only two Indian NGOs accredited to the United Nations were a rather obscure Delhi-based non-aligned research body called the Research and Information Service, and the other, the All-India Women's Conference. Both countries lobbied members of the Commission in their capitals. Telegraphic traffic increased dramatically. Delegations in Geneva exchanged barbed words. Most other countries must have felt a strong sense of *déjà vu* after some weeks of this strife. They must have said to themselves, a plague on both your houses.

We felt indignant that we were obliged to descend to the level of the Pakistanis and playing into their hands, since one of their prime objectives has invariably been that they should cut India down to the same size as themselves and establish a bogus parity. When you stoop to bandy words with someone lesser than you, the whole world sees you both as equal. The number of votes in favour of Pakistan's draft resolution was always going to be small; our reckoning was that our's would be somewhat higher – something like 7 for us against 4 for Pakistan, with all the rest, constituting the huge majority of members, abstaining. Iran offered its good offices to negotiate the text of a compromise resolution that would be agreeable both to Islamabad and New Delhi. This proposal was conveyed to me over the telephone by our ambassador to the UN when I was attending a meeting in the room of the prime minister's Principal Secretary Amar Nath Verma, and I had summarily turned it down in the hearing of several witnesses.

In the final week or so before the time for a vote, Narasimha Rao became very shaky. Was there some other way out? he asked me anxiously. Could we agree to a chairman's statement? A Special Rapporteur? N. Krishnan was in New Delhi by chance, and when he came to see me, I went over the ground with him. A man himself given to a surfeit of circumspection, he agreed in the end that it would be a close-run thing, but that we had to brazen it out. He met Narasimha Rao privately a few days later and told him so. That helped to stiffen Narasimha Rao's spine, but in a larger group meeting shortly before the vote, with Minister of State Bhatia also present, Narasimha Rao was still extremely nervous. I assured him that the numbers were on our side. He looked very dubious, but mercifully allowed matters to take their own course.

On the day of the vote, given the time difference between New Delhi and Geneva, I was sitting in my office late at night alone except for my colleague Secretary Salman Haidar[27] when, coming to the end of our patience, we restlessly put through a call to our Ambassador Satish Chandra in Geneva to find out what was going on. The vote was taking place later than we had expected, and the tension was mounting unbearably. Satish Chandra's secretary said he would pass on our enquiry to our delegation to the United Nations at the Palais de Nations. A return call came through around 10 p.m. Indian time. The Pakistanis had unconditionally withdrawn their draft, the very first time we had rolled them back on Kashmir with international opinion on our side, though in fact only by a handful of votes in our favour. Though the draft resolution never came to a vote, it was the first time since the Security Council debates in the 1960s on Kashmir that Pakistan had raised this question at the United Nations. Our success was therefore a heady moment, but I was surprised by the national jubilation with which Atal Behari Vajpayee[28] and Salman Khurshid were received at the airport when they returned from Geneva.

Iran absurdly tried later to take credit for Pakistan's withdrawal. The Iranian diplomats in the foreign ministry at Tehran had tried to frighten me during my visit there by hinting darkly that the tally would favour Pakistan, an assessment I heard with incredulity. I left them in no doubt that we did not agree and would not compromise. Iran then had no option but to try to influence Islamabad to withdraw, since they did not want to be seen as voting for Pakistan. They wanted to play a role in India, and among the Shias in Kashmir in particular, and a publicly partisan pro-Pakistan position would jeopardize that possibility. China also used its influence with Pakistan; Beijing was moving towards a neutral position on Kashmir, not least because of the fear of the virus of Islamic extremism threatening their far Western approaches.

Our respite with Pakistan's international campaign on Kashmir was, however, short-lived. They tried to resurrect the matter in ECOSOC, then in the 1503 Geneva Committee on Contributions, and then, picking on references to Kashmir in Boutros Ghali's Report of the UN Secretary-General to the General Assembly in September 1994, they introduced a draft resolution against India in the General Assembly's First Committee backed up by a 'Kashmir Committee' of the Organization of Islamic Conference consisting of Senegal, Turkey, Saudi Arabia and Pakistan. This Committee was not of great help to Pakistan because the members did not engage themselves in lobbying for the draft, but only in testing the waters, and eventually advised Pakistan to withdraw after numerous postponements of the voting. The Turkish ambassador in New Delhi relayed to us his New York colleague's description of the Pakistani members of the Kashmir Committee as 'terrorists', so obsessed had they become on sponsoring an anti-Indian resolution.

Our networking of friendly countries and the neutralizing of Pakistan's likely supporters had been effective. On my reckoning, we would have won any vote at the UN with plenty to spare. Few countries, other than Pakistan's most fervid backers, wanted to get on the wrong side of India. Most countries were sick and tired of the repeated raising of Kashmir by Pakistan and wanted to find a way to rebuff them. And the intricacies and passions connected with the Kashmir question deterred any but the most hardy or thin-skinned countries from getting too deeply involved.

As a lobbying exercise, we had conducted a textbook campaign. Both Houses of Parliament passed unanimous resolutions drafted in the External Affairs Ministry, reaffirming our traditional position on Kashmir, to make it clear we had all-party democratic support for our stand. Prior to the 15 August 1994 Independence Day function on the Red Fort ramparts, I slipped into Narasimha Rao's notes for the prime minister's traditional speech a rhetorical rebuttal of Prime minister Benazir Bhutto's[29] frequent iteration that Kashmir was an unfinished business of the Partition. This was to the effect that the only unfinished business of Partition was the resumption to India of the Pakistani-occupied part of the State. As a fail-safe, I also gave Narasimha Rao a pithy brief on how to deal with any press questions on our reaction in case Pakistan, by some extraordinary and unanticipated mischance, should win the UN vote. We left the lobbying with foreign capitals, by and large, to our diplomatic missions rather than sending out costly and often counter-productive political envoys – which is what the Pakistanis had done. We made haste to open diplomatic relations on a concurrent basis with each one of the several countries that had recently gained independence and joined the United Nations. We dispatched a few diplomatic envoys who knew their business and the local languages both from headquarters and foreign posts to the less-travelled capitals. I once went on a hectic round trip that took me for a day each – sometimes only a few hours – to Oman, Jordan, Syria, Lebanon, Egypt, Turkey, the Czech Republic, Russia and Japan before I left for New York and the UN. Every chance I could, I stopped for a day at one or other of the Gulf States. I was on personal phone-call terms with my counterparts in as many foreign offices as possible. Some of them returned my visits to them by coming to New Delhi. We encouraged groups of ambassadors stationed in New Delhi to visit Kashmir and, within the constraints on free movement imposed by the insurgents, got them to see whom they wanted. Of course, the role of the United States was in a special category, and needed to be dealt with differently.

Kashmir was an internal domestic problem but it was clear that we could not keep the international wolf from the door, and more particularly the NGO interest, unless some major steps were taken domestically to address international concerns. To move the government machine at home was a Herculean task, given Narasimha Rao's reluctance to push the Kashmir governor, retired Army General K. Krishna Rao, beyond a point. And that point, to Krishna Rao, supported by the Intelligence Bureau, was that the insurgency situation in the State remained too precarious for any sort of peace initiative on our part. My counter-strategy was to call back to New Delhi our Ambassador to the United Nations Hamid Ansari[30] and our High Commissioner to Pakistan Satinder Lambah[31] before the start of the United Nations General Assembly. Then I made the rounds of the leading political players in the capital along with both of them. With Chinmaya Gharekhan[32] having retired, Ansari and Lambah were among the most brilliant Indian ambassadors of my time, but would be highly placed on the all-time list of diplomatic representatives of any country.

The three of us began by enlisting the support of the junior Home Minister Rajesh Pilot,[33] then the person with the greatest foresight on Kashmir in the government, Home Secretary K. Padmanabhiah and the Research and Analysis Wing Secretary Ajit Syali, to the release of the leading dissidents in Jammu & Kashmir held under security provisions. These were Messrs Lone, Gilani and Shabir Shah, who had become the focal points of international NGOs' humanitarian interest. We also extracted the agreement of the Home Ministry and the Intelligence Bureau to the release of dozens of other lesser known detainees held without trial under suspicion of terrorist activities. Home Minister S.B. Chavan[34] was less than enthusiastic, but indicated reluctantly that he would go along. He was also eventually persuaded that the democratic process needed to be restarted in the State. Then we tackled Narasimha Rao, who was willing to abide by the advice of the Home Ministry on the releases of the detainees, and agreed that we could see Chief Election Commissioner T.N. Seshan about the possibility of holding fresh elections in Kashmir. Narasimha Rao further agreed that we could negotiate with the International Committee of the Red Cross for its possible access to Kashmir in its humanitarian capacity, and that if we could arrive at a satisfactory dialogue with Amnesty International, that NGO could be allowed to visit the State also. Seshan needed little persuasion. He agreed to start the process for elections immediately with a revision of the State's electoral roll.[35] The strongest card that our small pressure group had to play at all our meetings was that the defeat of Pakistan at Geneva had demoralized the militants in Kashmir, and this positive trend would be reversed if Pakistan could garner international support for a resolution against us at the United Nations in New York due to our lack of democratic transparency in Kashmir.

At our initiative, Narasimha Rao convened a meeting on Kashmir to take place on a Saturday night to which nearly everyone who had a role to play in the State was summoned and was present, except for Chavan who was detained in Bombay. After a slow start, with Governor Krishna Rao saying his usual prolix piece, followed by some discursive discussion, Narasimha Rao suddenly and unexpectedly flew into a furious temper, declaiming almost hysterically that he would never surrender the gains made by Nehru and Indira Gandhi. The context was not clear, but the outburst could have been triggered by my pointing out the fragile international position that India would find itself in, if we did not show any forward political movement in the State. In any event, Narasimha Rao fixed me in his baleful sights throughout his fulmination. The meeting was rocked to its heels by Narasimha Rao's angry outburst, but that was only the start of the drama. Rajesh Pilot, to his undying credit, broke the mounting tension by interrupting the prime minister in his tirade, and shouted him down with a screaming outburst of his own, to the effect that he was being marginalized and sabotaged in his efforts in the State by Krishna Rao, and that the present *status quo* in Kashmir served no purpose. As dramatic theatre, it was grand opera. In the end, everyone filed out dazed and shell-shocked, wondering what had actually transpired and what, if anything, had been achieved. It was nearly 11 o'clock at night, and we had started at 8.30 p.m. No decisions had been taken. But the important thing was none of the steps that we had painstaking put together had been overturned either, and the long road towards the resumption of a political process in Kashmir started at that point. The three of us, Ansari, Lambah and I, repaired to my residence, confused at the outcome of our efforts, but elated at the same time. We realized we had been present at a momentous passage of arms, and also that we had played a major part in shaping the way of things to come. Narasimha Rao's Principal Secretary A.N. Verma, habitually surly and silent during such meetings, recognized the coup that we in the External Affairs Ministry had engineered from within the system. He was less than pleased, but there was nothing he could do after the event to turn the tide.

On a private basis, I kept US Ambassador Frank Wisner and the British High Commissioner Nicholas Fenn informed about the pending releases of detainees, the decision to make arrangements with the ICRC to visit Kashmir (an idea first suggested by the Americans) and steps to proceed with elections to a State Assembly. I went from the United Nations to Washington to see Peter Tarnoff, the political under secretary and my US counterpart, and challenged him to oppose the idea of future elections in Kashmir, pointing out that a negative vote against India at the UN would only stimulate militant activity and render futile the democratic steps the Indian government was trying to take. In fact, the decisions taken by us had put the US and Pakistani governments in a considerable quandary, because they could not be seen to be rowing against the tide of democratic processes and greater openness in Kashmir. Pakistan accused us of deviousness and hypocrisy, saying we would never follow through once the United Nations voting was over. Robin Raphel's phone conversation with Monju, the US ambassador in Islamabad, which we came to hear about from a phone intercept, said it all, and was a study in frustration for the State Department's putative leading policy maker on the subcontinent. She had pressed for a US affirmative vote for the Pakistan resolution, she told Monju, but had been blocked by the 'higher-ups'. This knowledge gave us considerable satisfaction. So did a meeting between Pranab Mukherjee, standing in for Dinesh Singh, and Deputy Secretary of State Strobe Talbot at the UN in New York. He disagreed, Talbot told us, with almost everything the Pakistanis had told him, and thought he would agree with almost everything he heard from us.

We had ourselves moved an innocuous-sounding draft resolution in the UN First Committee, referring to various previous public pronouncements by the US, Russia and China, on the desirability of the complete elimination of nuclear weapons, and urging the nuclear weapon powers to arrive at a fixed time-frame in which to do so. This caused acute embarrassment to the United States at a time when they were pressing for a resolution favouring the CTBT, and they sent senior arms control expert John D. Holum to New Delhi to urge us to desist, though we had found some co-sponsors of our resolution by that time. Our ambassador in Washington, S.S. Ray, unaware as usual of the larger picture, and our need to have a chip to bargain with the Americans, sent fevered and ignorant messages to Narasimha Rao as the State Department proceeded to press down on him very hard. We eventually withdrew our draft, pointing out loftily that we were willing to help out the US in their concerns, and we would expect them in reciprocity to have the same attitude towards us when it came to our concerns. I had to explain to a bemused Narasimha Rao, who had seen Ray's frantic cables, what it was all about. Priding himself on being a subtle and devious latter-day Chanakya, Narasimha Rao was slow in detecting such tactics when used by others.

The Indian Foreign Office during this extremely fraught period was fortunate in that it was left to function with the minimum of political interference. Dinesh Singh was ill and getting worse. Bhatia knew his limitations sufficiently well to leave matters to the foreign service, and Khurshid was kept busy doing what he liked best and did best, which was to canvass other delegations on Kashmir at the UN in New York. The broad strategy was therefore left in my hands. In a replay of what had happened at the Commission on Human Rights in Geneva earlier that year, the vote in the First Committee on the Pakistan-sponsored resolution started to get repeatedly postponed at Pakistan's own request, and Narasimha Rao became increasingly agitated. The political consequences of a defeat at the United Nations again began to dawn on him, encouraged by the Cassandra voices of some of his ignorant and over-excitable informants and non-officials whom he had dispatched to join our delegation at the UN General Assembly. At a meeting round his Cabinet table at Race Course Road – the very same venue where we had had the fateful Kashmir meeting some weeks earlier – I again had to reassure the prime minister that we appeared to be in a comfortable position, and the numbers that we could identify were in our favour. For the second time that year, I stuck my neck out, and this time there was no N. Krishnan to give the prime minister confidence and moral support. Narasimha Rao looked at me dubiously, said nothing, and asked me for speaking notes on what to tell the media in the event of either success or failure. The Parliamentary Foreign Affairs Committee members were also sceptical. Were we doing enough? they asked. Why had the parliamentarians not been asked to lobby hither and thither in world capitals? I assured them that their assistance was not necessary. Time would soon tell whether my presumption was justified.

I heard the news of Pakistan's withdrawal from Hamid Ansari in the very early hours one morning Indian time when I phoned his car phone as he was driving home in the evening from the United Nations building. 'Mr Foreign Secretary – ', he began in a tired but happy manner, and I knew at once that we had won again. I was subsequently amazed that none of the Pakistani ministers and officials involved had been asked to resign. I do not think the Indian Parliament and media would have been so benevolent if we had lost a vote to Pakistan in the UN. Despite the early hour, I quickly phoned Narasimha Rao, Dinesh Singh, Bhatia and Pranab Mukherjee. I gave Dinesh Singh letters of thanks to send to our ambassadors. The Parliamentary Standing Committee gave me an ovation when they convened at my request to listen to our report. Our public posture, authorized by Narasimha Rao, was in a studied low key, thanking those who had supported us, including those in the Organization of Islamic Conference – a dig at Pakistan – and reaffirming our constant desire for friendship with Pakistan. This approach earned us more friends. The public and media were more restrained this time than they had been after Geneva; possibly they had got used to triumphing over Pakistan. I was often asked by baffled Indian journalists how we had managed to overcome such incredible odds.

A Pakistani spokesman later said that they had decided not to proceed with their draft resolution at the UN because of 'procedural difficulties'. Indeed it is true that we had some procedural ammunition up our sleeve if by mischance a draft resolution had come before the General Assembly after being passed by the First Committee, but this had been discussed only in the narrowest circle and at high levels in the ministry, and we had not determined any final strategy on how to use our intended stratagem. But clearly Pakistan had some inkling of what we might be up to – was there a mole in our Foreign Office? – although the real reason for their withdrawal was without question that they had not found enough support, and could not have carried the day.

We had not yet done with Pakistan on Kashmir at the United Nations that year. Jamshed Marker, the Pakistan ambassador, had drawn the attention of the Security Council, of which Pakistan was a non-permanent member at that time, to Kashmir as a potential breach of peace and security. We were drawn into another round of lobbying, this time only with the Council's fifteen members. We had to face the difficult question of whether the new Russia would give us the benefit of the traditional Soviet veto in our favour if the worst came to the worst. Sergei Lavrov,[36] the Russian ambassador at the UN, was ambiguous. Our ambassador in Moscow Ronen Sen[37] was certain, on the other hand, that instructions had been sent to Lavrov to use his veto. My personal relations with Alexander Chernysev, the Russian deputy minister-in-charge of South Asia, became a matter of importance, since we were unsure, to say the least, of Russian Foreign Minister Kozyrev. Time passed slowly, as the Presidency of the Council rotated month after month. The deadline was the 31 December 1994 when the Pakistanis would leave the Council and their malign influence would thereafter be severely diminished. The USA held the Presidency of the Council a month before the end of the year, followed by the United Kingdom. The American month passed; so did the next, and we were home and dry. The council president from the United Kingdom, David Hannay, who handled the letter from Marker, insisted on being irritatingly 'even-handed' and conducted some low-key consultations, but finally did not take matters further.

Pakistan had been repeatedly wrong-footed by us during this period, and they did not help their case by stone-walling on our repeated proposals for talks, not even to deal with day-to-day matters of concern to the citizens of both countries, like visa matters and border crossings. While the USA promoted, and occasionally even financially sponsored, 'track two' non-official dialogues of high-minded citizens from both countries, and tried to expand this forum to include Kashmiris from both sides of the line of actual control, at the Pakistan government level, the official position remained one of no contacts. Talks with Pakistan were good for India because of the pressure on Kashmir. For the identical reason, Pakistan was not in the least interested. My talks in the middle of the year with my Pakistani counterpart, Foreign Secretary Najmuddin Sheikh, in Dhaka at the SAARC foreign ministers meeting led to nothing, as did my fleeting encounters with him in the margins of a Commonwealth senior officials meeting in Islamabad. He was evasive and avoided even purely social contact, but we agreed on a few procedural matters, like preventing expulsions of diplomats from each other's country from becoming a propaganda spectacle. But such agreements could not be sustained, given the atmosphere prevailing in the two countries, and because these expulsions were a reflection of the tit-for-tat rivalry between the intelligence operatives of the two countries, who saw advantages in maximum publicity. The Pakistanis, with some justification, saw little to gain from bilateral meetings that would not deal with the core issue as they saw it, of the status of Kashmir, and they were smarting from their foreign policy defeats during the year in multilateral forums. But their reluctance to talk to us was a setback to their own efforts to secure international support, and they could count on few foreign friends at the end of the day.

In reality, as I emphasized in New Delhi to the ambassadors of the five Security Council permanent members, there was no likelihood of any major armed clash between India and Pakistan, though the US tried from time to time to play up this prospect to give themselves more leverage in the arms control issues. As in the case of the Indo-Chinese border, there were many fail-safe mechanisms in place to damp down any accidental flare-up from getting out of hand. And neither side saw any benefit from a large-scale clash, which would be short-lived in time and probably inconclusive. It would lead to the involvement of outsiders, which would automatically imply a less than optimal solution for both India and Pakistan, because there would necessarily have to be an element of compromise. It would lead to the collapse, at least in the short-term, of the economic reforms that both countries were trying, with some measure of success, to introduce. But the level of aggravation for us from Pakistan always remained high.

We tried our best, but could not prevent, the Pakistanis closing our Consulate in Karachi in November 1994 in retaliation for the voluntary withdrawal of the Pakistani Consulate in Bombay in the previous March because the Pakistanis could not find any office accommodation. It is true that after the Bombay blasts in March 1993 perpetrated by Dawood Ibrahim and Tiger Memon in retaliation for the Babri Masjid demolition, landlords were disinclined to accomodate the Pakistanis, and the Jinnah House issue in Bombay remained deadlocked in the courts with Jinnah's grandson, Nusli Wadia, asserting his legal claim to the property. Besides this, the aggressive surveillance of our diplomats and other staff members in Pakistan, always objectionable, reached totally unacceptable heights.

The Indian north-eastern states were in a situation of continuous disaffection and militancy, either declared or simmering. The Chinese had long ceased to interfere in that area openly, but there were now other inimical players, including Burma, Pakistan and Bangladesh. There were also the evils of rampant corruption, the drugs culture, unemployment and AIDS. It was hard to ignore the fact, though our politicians did just that, that for India, if matters did not improve, the north-east would be a far greater injury to national unity in the long term than even Kashmir. Twice, a meeting on the north-east with all the top politicians and officials assembled, to be addressed by Home Secretary K. Padmanabhiah, had to be deferred at the last moment because the prime minister was otherwise too preoccupied to attend. The political will to confront and get to grips with the problems in that highly sensitive part of India were just not apparent, possibly because there was no unwelcome international attention directed to this region of India.

The question of river waters and assistance to militants in India played a major role in our relations with Bangladesh, Bhutan and Nepal. Narasimha Rao was insistent that there should be no agreement with Bangladesh on releases of the Ganges River in the dry season, and it was after months of effort that I managed to persuade him to let me try, in confidential talks with my counterpart in Dhaka, Osmani, to link a Ganges settlement with matters of concern to us like transit and Bangladesh's covert assistance to militancy in our north-east states. The first round of talks with Osmani in New Delhi unfortunately proved to be the last, because I was unable to return his visit. Nevertheless, it was clear that Dhaka's idea of linking the issues was one in which the sequencing of India's concerns would come long after what Dhaka wanted on the Ganges waters, and would, as we knew from previous bitter experience, probably be a non-starter once the Bangladeshis had got what they wanted.

With Myanmar, we had to find a line between widespread parliamentary and public support for Aung San Su Kyi and her followers in the National League for Democracy, and a reasonable relationship with Yangon to assist us to suppress unofficial cross-border trade and militant support to the insurgents in our north-east. Under the influence and promptings of K.R. Narayanan and veteran journalist Nikhil Chakravarty, Su Kyi was awarded one of India's leading prizes, the Jawaharlal Nehru Award for International Understanding, but the announcement was, at my intervention and with the approval of Narasimha Rao and Narayanan, kept secret until we had conveyed advance information about the award to the Burmese authorities. They received the news in Rangoon in peevish silence. Some cross-border trade and transportation agreements were developed with Myanmar, though the need for nearly 100 per cent Indian financing for infrastructure projects like road-building made progress much slower than was desirable.

With Bhutan, we concluded negotiations for the second stage of the Chuka hydroelectric project, which would be an important source of power supply to India, as well as earning considerable revenues for Bhutan. We continued to advise King Jigme Singe Wangchuk on his border with China, though the lack of tension on our own border with China lent less immediacy to this advice.

Our aim was that the Chumbi Valley separating Sikkim and Bhutan should not in any eventual agreement between Bhutan and China be broadened or deepened, which would make the Siliguri 'chicken's neck' for Indian access to our north-east even more vulnerable. There were plenty of historical arguments for the King to use with the Chinese, and many of them had been earlier ferreted out by S.N. Rao of the Historical Division and myself from the India Office archives in London. But the King seemed rather more anxious to accommodate the Chinese, though this would be at our expense. His real anxieties were to prevent Chinese activities in his kingdom that would weaken his absolute though benign monarchy, and he was quite willing to pay a price to the Chinese to be left in peace. The King was also unwilling to help us with Bodo insurgents using the jungles in southern Bhutan for sanctuary, but he wanted us to resettle in India several thousand Bhutanese of Nepali origin who had been ethnically cleansed from Bhutan. All these differences took place, of course, while we were publicly professing the greatest mutual affection and support.

In Nepal, the Congress alliance of the squabbling Ganesh Mansingh, G.P. Koirala and K.P. Bhattarai was ousted by the Communists. In the first discussions in New Delhi with the new government, we made some concessions on trade and transit, but they were never to be put into practice since the Communists quickly fell to another Congress grouping under Premier S.B. Deupa. Despite their election rhetoric, the communists did not seek an amendment to the Indo-Nepal Treaty of the late 1940s. In fact, they found it hard to define what they found wrong with it, considering that it gave the Nepali people such enormous, and often non-reciprocal, privileges in India. The so-called (and wholly outdated and unutilized) security clauses regarding mutual consultation in the case of attack may have galled the nationalists, but they must have realized that to unravel one part of the Treaty would lead to the unravelling of the whole. We had to placate the Nepalis, and also encourage them at the same time to co-operate with us to check the rampant use of the open border between India and Nepal by smugglers, insurgents, crooks and militants of various kinds. Cooperation in river waters progressed at a snail's pace, with flood control, irrigation and power generation on Pancheswar, a joint river on Nepal's western border with India, showing the greatest promise.

Relations were often bedeviled by our police forces from the northern Indian states repeatedly crossing the border into Nepal in hot pursuit of petty criminals without the knowledge of the Nepali authorities or for that matter even our own Home Ministry. On one occasion, the Delhi Police went in hot pursuit of suspected miscreants who fled across the open border to Nepal, and our policemen were apprehended red-handed in Kathmandu by the Nepalis. Unlike the customary blank denials and specious claims that our police were 'on holiday', the courageous and imaginative Home Secretary, N.N. Vohra,[38] decided to make a clean breast of it, and after consultation with him, I instructed our ambassador in Nepal to tender an unqualified apology to the Nepalis. The subsequent reading out of our apology in the parliament in Kathmandu helped to smooth things over and saved us many consequential problems.

With Sri Lanka, the replacement of President Premadasa by Chandrika Kumaratunga and the egregious Hameed as foreign minister by Lakshman Kadirgamar proved a welcome change. The outcome of Hameed's earlier visit to India had been confined to a plea to us, usually petulantly and offensively made, to lower the Indian duty on cloves. When Kadirgamar came, the discussions were more meaningful and cooperative. One of the rare occasions when I saw Narasimha Rao betray any pleasurable reaction was when Kadirgamar handed over a personal letter to him from Chandrika Kumaratunga's mother, Mrs Bandaranayake.[39] The LTTE's involvement with Rajiv Gandhi's murder gave the two countries a common enemy, and led directly to vastly improved relations between us, though New Delhi had always to keep a sharp eye on pro-LTTE sympathizers in Tamil Nadu. Repatriation of Sri Lankan refugees in India went much more slowly than we would like, due to the continued fighting between Colombo and the Tamil Tigers.

The Maldives and India were involved in a bizarre sex and spy scandal in south India, allegedly involving women from Maldives and Indian scientists from the Indian Space Research Institute.

In the end, the investigations by the Central Bureau of Investigation uncovered very little, but there was obviously more to it than met the eye, considering that when President Gayoom of Maldives was first shown the diary of one of the Maldivian *femmes fatales* by a special envoy we sent to Male for this purpose, he refused to be debriefed privately without any others present, and showed no great surprise at the diary's contents – hardly the reactions of someone who might be nervous to learn about something he did not know previously.

Throughout this time, the government in Kabul was led by President Rabbani, who was busy, along with the Tajik Ahmed Shah Masood, in repelling Gulbuddin Hekmatyar who was based in Pakistan, while the Uzbek warlord Rashid Dostum was content to consolidate his power centre in Mazaar-e-Sherif. Rabbani made overtures to New Delhi, because Hekmatyar was widely seen as Pakistan's man. These included appeals for arms, and facilities for Ariana Airways at Delhi Airport. We sent humanitarian assistance in the form of tea and medicines in separate consignments to as many major warlords as possible and promised technical assistance to Rabbani, although, with Kabul Airport closed, the transportation problems were acute. To Dostum, Masood and Ismail Khan, the only access was through Uzbekistan or Iran. Rabbani posted an ambassador in New Delhi and we planned to reopen our mission in Kabul, especially after noting that relations between Kabul and Islamabad had come under severe strain. The rise of the Taliban movement, sponsored by Pakistan's Home Minister Nasiruddin Babar and the Inter-Services Intelligence, and permitted by Benazir Bhutto, was watched by us, and Rabbani and Iran, with great unease. The Saudis were believed to be switching their support from Hek-matyar to the Talibans, and judging from the Delphic responses of US Ambassador Frank Wisner in New Delhi to my pointed queries, the Americans may have not been a disinterested party either. I repeatedly brought the looming Taliban menace to Wisner's notice, at which he claimed total ignorance and had no comment to offer.

Iran tried to strengthen its relations with India, but only on their own terms. They spuriously acted out the part of an honest broker with Pakistan during the Geneva UN Human Rights Commission, a role that totally lacked any credibility. They worked through persons like R.L. Bhatia in the ministry to promote themselves as part of an anti-hegemonic troika of Iran, China and India. They sought technology from India to maintain their Russian submarines, and in the nuclear and space fields, to which we responded coolly and cautiously. They tried to interest us in road-rail transit routes to Central Asia and in a natural gas pipeline across Pakistan, or alternatively, a marine pipeline, to India. To a great extent, and for various reasons, all these proposals fell on barren soil. We were suspicious of their speaking in two voices, one in New Delhi, and a vastly different one in Islamabad. We looked warily at their assiduous cultivation of the Shia community in India, and felt uneasy about their true intentions in Kashmir. We fully understood the mutual gains possible in economic cooperation, but each one of the proposals we made for practical cooperation seemed to be confronted with insuperable procedural and other difficulties in Tehran. Letters of intent remained intentions only; contracts never seemed to come our way despite our competitive bids. Large potential joint projects like a power plant or fertilizer plant never seemed to get off the ground. The authorities in Tehran were both unwilling and unable to extend any assistance to break this deadlock of Iranian rejection and non-cooperation. After one particularly non-productive joint commission meeting in New Delhi, the London-based Hinduja brothers, who enjoyed some influence in Iran, proposed to bring Bhatia and Foreign Minister Ali Akbar Velayati together in Hyderabad House in New Delhi to have what was supposed to be a post-prandial heart-to-heart talk about mutual suspicions and frustrations. The intention was to closet Velayati plus one aide and Bhatia and myself in a small room for an intimate off-the-record discussion. The attempt came to grief, since Velayati had, probably deliberately, omitted to brief his subordinates, and the large crowd of persons from the Iranian delegation who swarmed into the room made the search for a genuine and frank discussion impossible. We therefore wasted our time by ending up exchanging useless platitudes of mutual goodwill.

The State of Israel had been recognized by India with full

diplomatic relations in 1992. Several agreements had been signed, and there was useful cooperation in the scientific field, and some promise of access to military technology that we could not obtain from elsewhere. Narasimha Rao was mistaken in his exaggerated fears that the Muslims of India would prefer to keep Israel at arms length even after opening full relations with them, and the burgeoning Oslo peace process helped us in pressing ahead. But the Israelis had an uncompromising bilateral agenda when it came to political and diplomatic support. We were disappointed that they were not interested in a joint and principled stand on the NPT renewal which was to come up in 1995, and despite Shimon Peres'[40] personal sympathies, it was clear that their officials wanted to bargain their support to us on Kashmir against our position on the various draft resolutions against Israel which were then still common currency in the United Nations. They were difficult people to deal with, heavily laden with too much gravity and self-righteousness, coupled with a total absence of any sense of humour, and the Palestinian Authority had my sympathy in having to deal with them. The Israelis wanted our help with Iran in looking for one of their missing pilots, and with Bangladesh in opening diplomatic ties; we were not able to do much for them in either case.

Negotiations with the Israelis were invariably tiresome because their negotiators were thuggish, unyielding and unprepared for any compromise. The other most frustrating interlocutors were the Chinese. When dealing with the Chinese, one had to be prepared for endless repetitions and reiterations of narrative with no hint of forward or even sideways movement. It was necessary to be careful to present one's points of view in one's own personality, and not to be drawn into copying their system of stylized and mesmeric repetitions that are tiring in the extreme. Making a few concrete proposals and insisting on a specific response proved to be a better method. With the Americans, if the bottom line was clearly indicated, they did not create any major problem, but their first priority always seemed to be the opening up of the Indian market. For example, we spent considerable exertions on matters like the Indian import duties on walnuts from California because the State Department had convinced our Ambassador S.S. Ray that the support of members of Congress from California was crucial to the fostering of good relations between India and the USA. With the Russians, if agreements were decided upon in advance by the sherpas at lower level, the leaders themselves did not create any last minute difficulties.

The South African democratic and multi-racial revival took place in 1994. I suggested that Narasimha Rao might declare a national holiday on the occasion of President Nelson Mandela's inauguration. This was opposed by the ever-cautious Finance Minister Manmohan Singh, who happened to be present when I was speaking to the prime minister, on the grounds that Indians benefited from too many holidays already. But a decision was taken on illumination of public buildings, resolutions of felicitations in both Houses of Parliament which were drafted in the ministry, and President Nelson Mandela to be invited as chief guest at our Republic Day celebrations in January 1995.

Singapore President Goh Chok Tong visited India and showed great enthusiasm for bilateral cooperation, especially in relation to an IT 'Park', a new airport in Bangalore, and the setting up of a new private airline; a collaboration between Singapore Airlines and Tatas. The Singapore delegation positively bubbled with innovative proposals, both economic and cultural; technical manpower, and also political in the form of more proximate links with ASEAN. This visit by Goh, the second in 1994, and Singapore's manifest determination to enhance political and economic ties with India, marked a new beginning for India's closer ties with South-East Asia, which became later known as the 'Look East' policy.[41] Singapore was willing to help India with an entré to ASEAN and the 'structural dialogue' partnership began. Goh saw India as a priority partner for Singapore while welcoming China's rise. In a telling phrase, Goh a year before had described India as Singapore's second wing, with China being the first, to give it a strong lift. But unlike Lee Kuan Yew, now his country's so-called Minister-Mentor, his successor tended to play down any theories of India as a balancing factor with China, because Singapore now felt China was unstoppable, and it was better for ASEAN to have both India and Japan on board because the USA would one day withdraw from East Asia and go home.

The NPT Review Conference was scheduled for the United Nations in New York in April 1995, at which we declined having observer status. Nevertheless, we wished to have a first-hand account of the meeting, and I requested the Rajiv Gandhi Foundation to seek NGO observer accreditation. I obtained Narasimha Rao's approval to send Krishna Rasgotra[42] as the Rajiv Gandhi Foundation's representative to the Conference at the ministry's expense. As it turned out, after I had retired, he was not sent, for whatever reason, and the NPT was renewed indefinitely and without any change to the text.

We were in the process of negotiating our entry to the Chemical Weapons Convention, an exercise largely left to the Department of Chemicals under the Ministry of Petroleum and Chemicals. Many inter-departmental meetings and conclaves of the Committee of secretaries had been held, and Notes for the Cabinet had been prepared and approved. But suddenly one afternoon, Naresh Chandra,[43] a relatively incognito secretary in the Prime Minister's Office who, I had thought, dealt primarily with advising Narasimha Rao on matters relating to the demolished Babri Masjid, enquired about the position in regard to the Convention as if it was the first time he had ever come to hear about it. When I told him how far the matter had progressed in the Department of Chemicals, he seemed very distraught and asked me to send him all the files we had on the subject; the rest he would obtain from the Department of Chemicals directly. Someone in the hierarchy with more knowledge than I had on the state of our chemical weapons research had obviously belatedly woken up and alerted the prime minister, who had passed on the task of damage mitigation to Naresh Chandra.

The Protocol division of the ministry noticed that a particular senior diplomat from one of our neighbouring countries was importing large quantities of electric and electronic goods, far in excess of what could be his personal requirements. The customs and revenue authorities were asked to investigate the matter and they traced the items to a storage facility rented by this diplomat, from where the items were sold on the open market. The

Chief of Protocol was authorized by me to ask the High Commissioner concerned for the immediate removal of this diplomat from India, or alternatively, to allow him to face prosecution. The High Commissioner first pleaded his subordinate's innocence, and then asked for more time for an investigation by himself. We remained adamant. Then the High Commissioner came to see me and informed me in confidence that the guilty diplomat was in fact a senior intelligence official, and his being declared *persona non grata* would have a serious negative bearing on our bilateral relationship. I responded that I was willing to take a chance on that, and if the person was not removed at once, we would impose a stringent time limit, after which we would withdraw his diplomatic status. Finally the High Commissioner, who was by this time quite overwrought, sheepishly admitted that he had little control over this intelligence official and was fearful of the consequences to himself if he took any action against him. In other words, after first making a threat, it now became an appeal to our compassion. I was unmoved. The matter concluded with the errant diplomat's removal without any impact on our bilateral relations, or, as far as I know, any effect on the High Commissioner's future career.

Since many years back, the Pakistan government had engaged the services of one or more public relations firms in Washington to reinforce their arguments on Capitol Hill, and to counter other influential lobbyists. Our ambassador in Washington, S.S. Ray, made persuasive appeals to the prime minister and the ministry to do likewise. The embassy was asked to short-list potential applicants, and the one led by David Springer met with the approval of both the External Affairs Ministry and the Finance Ministry, which was kept closely involved with the decisions taken. The cost was less than half a million dollars a year, the contract was subject to short-term periodical reviews, and it was made a condition that the principals of Springer's firm should pay a visit to India to appreciate our concerns at first hand. This was the first time in any foreign country that the Government of India had engaged a foreign firm of lobbyists to promote our interests.

The setting up of the Aspen India chapter was the result of

overtures made in 1994. The idea was first broached to me that year in Washington by the then head of the Aspen Institute in USA at an event during the official visit of Narasimha Rao. The president of Aspen told me that his group had a tie-up with Italy and a few other European countries, and was interested in doing something similar with India because of the intellectual resources of our country. I welcomed this approach to strengthen Indo-US civil society ties. As a follow-up, I was then invited, as a kind of test-run, to attend an intellectual event which took place in Aspen, the ski resort in Colorado from which Aspen USA takes its name. I did this in 1995, shortly after I demitted charge as foreign secretary, since I did not feel it was proper to participate while I was still working with the government. Further talks about a possible Indian chapter of Aspen took place at that venue, where I was the only Indian present, and it was assumed by Aspen USA that I would continue to play some role to facilitate Aspen's connections with India. I was asked which Indian body would best serve as a counterpart to Aspen USA. I suggested a few organisations, and among those on my list was the Confederation of Indian Industry. On my return to India, I spoke to Tarun Das,[44] the director-general of the CII, about this opportunity and asked him if there would be any interest in the CII in such a joint venture. If an Aspen India chapter is eventually established in India, I do not doubt that my role in its creation would be rapidly forgotten.

During my time as foreign secretary, the Cabinet Secretaries were first Zafar Saifullah and then Surendra Singh. Saifullah had an incisive intellect, and when he summarized or analysed a discussion, he was impressive. The secretary of the Research and Analysis Wing dealing with foreign intelligence was Ajit Syali, for whom I had a great deal of respect, and with whom the Ministry was able to work extremely smoothly. The Directors of the Intelligence Bureau were first V.G. Vaidya and then Dinesh Pathak. Both were under the handicap of serving too many quarrelling masters in the Home Ministry, and had the further disadvantage of losing credibility by formulating opinions on inadequately processed and unverified raw material. They achieved a measure of success in apprehending some enemy operatives and terrorists, and I took some pride in informing the British High Commissioner in 1994 that the Indian police had arrested near Delhi the British-born terrorist Omar Sheikh,[45] who had kidnapped a group of Western tourists. But in the conduct of foreign policy, the influence of the Intelligence Bureau was negligible, and on domestic issues like Kashmir, they were more an obstacle to be overcome than an asset.

TV coverage at that time was still in its infancy, although a few anchors, especially Karan Thapar of HTV and Ashis Ray of CNN-Asia, took keen and intelligent interest in foreign affairs. I tried to keep the print media up to date on the important issues and build an image for the ministry of substance rather than the internal manipulation that had prevailed in previous years. Each month I held a press conference, on the record, for correspondents attached to the ministry. Despite my efforts to inform the media about India's position on many world issues, the only subject that seemed to energize the media was Pakistan. Almost each month I had a lunch for six to eight editors or senior columnists. I met the foreign press representatives accredited to India on a couple of occasions, but did not find those gatherings sufficiently productive either for myself or for them. The only lively meeting with this last group was before Narasimha Rao's trip to Washington, when the foreign press corps thought the prime minister was in for a very hard cross-examination from Clinton, and could not understand why I did not share their pessimism.

About fifty heads of Indian Missions were posted or transferred during this period. This was because there had been a long hiatus in the approval of deployments before my taking over as foreign secretary. I tried to keep the chain of postings up to date, and sent in a list of proposals every two months or so. There would be incalculable delays with the prime minister before it came back. The political appointees I would discuss beforehand with Narasimha Rao. I pondered long over each proposal, whether at head of Mission or other levels. I tried to be just and that justice was also seen to be done. Dinesh Singh asked for four specific postings of personnel to be implemented, and Narasimha Rao took personal interest in three. They had their way, as they were entitled to.

The Policy Planning unit of the ministry was encouraged, and it produced a stream of papers for the first time, which were circulated to other ministries including the prime minister's office. I requested the length of these to be limited to one, or one and a half, pages like the documents circulated by the Intelligence Bureau and the RAW, which stood a much better chance of being read because of their brevity. I was anxious to raise the morale of our passport offices, to get better premises for them, and to reduce the backlog in the issue of passports. A table-top book about the buildings and art objects owned by the ministry was published, and a history of the Foreign Service was commissioned from a retired head of the Historical Division. The committee dealing with the acquisition of art objects for our Missions was reactivated, as was the Foreign Service Wives Association, both of which had become moribund.

Needless to say, not everything that could be done was done. Not everything that should have been done was done either. On the whole, however, much that was good was done and Indian foreign policy and the Ministry of External Affairs were the stronger for it.

January 1996

NOTES

1. S.D. Sharma, president of India, 1992–7. Died 1999.
2. K.R. Narayanan, president of India, 1997–2002. Died 2005.
3. Dinesh Singh, external affairs minister, 1969–70 and 1993–5. Died 1995.
4. R.L. Bhatia, later governor of Kerala and Bihar.
5. Salman Khurshid, later full cabinet minister under Manmohan Singh, 2011.
6. Yevgeny Primakov, later prime minister of Russia.
7. The Indian-Russian-Chinese triangle was, according to our Ambassador Ronen Sen, looked upon with favour by Moscow.
8. P.V. Narasimaha Rao, prime minister, 1991–6. Died 2004.
9. L.B. Shastri, prime minister, 1964–6. Died 1966.
10. Manmohan Singh, finance minister, 1991–6; prime minister 2004 to date.

11. Deng Xiaoping, paramount Chinese leader, 1978–92. Died 1997.
12. N. Krishnan, Indian ambassador to the UN in New York and later the head of the Rajiv Gandhi-sponsored Africa Fund to assist the front-line countries against apartheid in South Africa.
13. Muchkund Dubey, foreign secretary 1990–1.
14. Robin Raphel, then assistant secretary in the State Department dealing with South Asia
15. Anthony Quainton, sometime US ambassador to Nicaragua, Kuwait and Peru.
16. D.P. Moynihan, ambassador to India 1973–5. Died 2003.
17. S.S. Ray, chief minister, cabinet minister, governor and ambassador. Died 2010.
18. A.P.J. Abdul Kalam, president of India, 2002–7.
19. Hillary Clinton, later US secretary of state, 2009 to date.
20. Kim Jong-il, died 2011, succeeded by Kim Jong-un, his third son.
21. Narasimha Rao had earlier flagged our qualifications to be a permanent member at the UN Security Council in 1992 when heads of government had participated in a special session of the Council.
22. Gopal Gandhi, former member of the Indian Administrative Service, subsequently ambassador to South Africa, Sri Lanka and Norway, and governor of West Bengal.
23. Vladimir Zhirinovski, ultra-populist and ultra-nationalist politician.
24. Mikhail Gorbachev, general-secretary of the Soviet Communist Party from 1985 to 1991, and the last head of state of the USSR.
25. Kanwal Sibal, foreign secretary, 2002–3.
26. The UN Commission on Human Rights at that time comprised 53 members elected by ECOSOC.
27. Salman Haider, then the second seniormost official in the ministry, and later foreign secretary, 1995–7.
28. Atal Behari Vajpayee, then chairman of the Parliamentary Standing Committee on External Affairs. Later prime minister 1998–2004.
29. Benazir Bhutto, prime minister of Pakistan 1988–90 and 1993–6. Died 2007.
30. Hamid Ansari, later vice-president of India, 2007 to date.
31. Satinder Lambah, later ambassador to Russia and Germany.
32. Chinmaya Gharekhan, ambassador to the UN, later Butros Ghali's chef du cabinet and then UN secretary-general's representative in Gaza.

33. Rajesh Pilot's promising political career was cut short in a fatal car crash in 2000.
34. S.B. Chavan, home minister, 1991–6. Died 2004.
35. Elections were eventually held in the State of Jammu & Kashmir in 1996.
36. Sergei Lavrov was my counterpart in the Russian Foreign Ministry before he became ambassador to the UN in New York. Subsequently foreign minister of the Russian Federation.
37. R. Sen, later ambassador to Germany, high commissioner to the United Kingdom and ambassador to the USA.
38. N.N. Vohra, later principal secretary to the prime minister and governor of Kashmir.
39. Srimavo Bandaranayake, prime minister of Sri Lanka 1960–5, 1970–7, 1994–2000. Died 2000.
40. Shimon Peres, then foreign minister of Israel. Later prime minister and president.
41. Goh's visit marked the start of the 'Look East' policy, though the term had not been coined at that time.
42. M. Rasgotra, foreign secretary, 1982–5.
43. Naresh Chandra, later governor of Gujarat and ambassador to USA.
44. Aspen India was eventually established 10 years later, in 2004. Tarun Das continues to be associated with Aspen India with the title of Trustee.
45. Ahmed Omar Saeed Sheikh was in an Indian prison until, in 1999, the Vajpayee government exchanged him and other prisoners in Afghanistan for the release of a hijacked Indian plane. He then played a part in the kidnapping and murder in 2002 in Pakistan of journalist Daniel Pearl, and is still in a Pakistani prison.

NON-ALIGNMENT REVISITED

I. THE AGE OF IDEALISM

ACCORDING to the historian Frederick Halliday, modern history can be separated neatly into the following partitions: the first Cold War was from 1946 to 1953, Antagonism from 1953 to 1969, Détente from 1969 to 1979 and the second Cold War from 1979 to 1987 – in other words, until after the arrival of Gorbachev in 1985.[1] The alternative narrative of segregating Indian post-Independence foreign policy into three segments – pre-1964 ending with the death of Jawaharlal Nehru; 1964 to 1989 being the periods of Indira Gandhi, the Janata government and Rajiv Gandhi; and the post-1990 and post-Cold War period – equally facile and over-simplified as it might be, nevertheless well serves the purpose of defining the Indian policy of non-alignment into the same three periods, each comprising, first, the formulation, and later the distinct mutations of both the doctrine and its application.

In essence, non-alignment's ideological moorings began, lived and died with the idealism of Jawaharlal Nehru. And ironically, the coming into being of the Non-Aligned Movement heralded the beginning of the end of the hey-day of non-alignment as a policy. The period from 1964 to the end of the Cold War was fundamentally one of realism and pragmatism, and found India moving ever closer into the orbit of the Soviet Union. Non-alignment rhetoric came to life only during the various meetings of the Non-Aligned Movement and that too, heavily tinted with the Soviet Union's colouring. The period after the Cold War, with the demise of the Soviet Union, left India temporarily without moorings in an unfamiliar international environment, but it recovered remarkably quickly to adjust itself to a period of opportunism, in the sense of seeking and exploiting opportunities, whether in the manner of its attraction to the USA as an asset in resisting the predicted rise of China, or in reviving ancient ties with East and South-East Asia in the form, if not the substance, of a 'Look East' policy. Some of the early improvizations that characterized Indian foreign policy during Nehru's time returned, though without his inimitable charm and flair, to sustain Indian diplomatic flexibility, and give it advantage as the country's economic situation improved sufficiently to be described in the first decade of the twenty-first century as an 'emerging' power. But this last phase also marked a far cry from the original principles of non-alignment.

The impulse to be defined by exceptionalism has marked the history of many countries that believe in their manifest destiny. Henry Kissinger described American exceptionalism as messianic and that of China as based on culture.[2] Exceptionalism, by implication, denotes innate superiority, and in India's case it refers to intellectual or cerebral superiority. The Indian nationalist movement with its stress on Indian self-reliance, however utopian, did certainly nurture a feeling of Indian exceptionalism, though this was partially offset by the desire to be universalist and receptive to outside influences. M.K. Gandhi had said 'I do not want my house to be walled in on all sides and my windows to be stuffed. I want the cultures of all the lands to be blown about my house as freely as possible. But I refuse to be blown off my feet by any.' This contradiction was never reconciled, and 'this dichotomy,' writes Swapan Dasgupta, 'is a feature of the Hindu way of thinking'.[3] Within India, life has been shaped by the belief that India, and India alone, with its abundant wisdom and mental faculties, knows best, and a fierce sense of beleaguered national pride turned Indians from being modestly self-confident to being nervously prickly – a constant feature of Indian diplomatic representatives that detracted considerably from the well-founded arguments they often adduced. The Indian diplomat Subimal Dutt, who occupied many important positions, bewailed this attitude in his diary entries:

> When shall we cease thinking that other countries are falling head over heels to win our support? We have a sense of superiority complex . . . we adopt a sanctimonious attitude.[4] Why should we take upon ourselves the duty of advising Egypt continuously and even to the minutest detail? Ali Yavar [Indian Ambassador] has become extremely conceited, regards himself as a super-Ambassador.[5]

Indian non-alignment drew considerably on this sense of exceptionalism and superiority, but it was grounded in a characteristically hazy Nehruvian vision, since he, no less than anyone else, could predict the future with any accuracy. In the final assessment of Nehru's non-alignment, it was essentially improvizational.

Jawaharlal Nehru had given indications of the notion of non-alignment on several occasions before he coined the actual phrase in 1950. That non-alignment in Nehru's conception had idealistic origins cannot be doubted. These were associated in his mind with what he saw as India's exceptional and exemplary personality and intellectual subtlety. As early as 1939, he had said that 'India will always make a difference to the world: fate has marked us for big things',[6] and in a speech to the Constituent Assembly in 1944 he declared that India must follow its own cultural pattern and have close relations with all countries; that world peace would be strengthened if India did not align itself with any group, and that the aim should be to prevent another World War. In 1946, six days after Nehru formed the national government, he said in a broadcast that 'we propose . . . to keep away from the power politics of groups aligned against one another . . . it is for this One World [tipping his hat to Wendell Willkie] that free India will work',[7] and he backed this up by sending greetings to both the USA and the Soviet Union. At the core of his concept of non-alignment was that Asia should finally take charge of its history, and that India and China were pre-ordained to be its prime movers. Indeed, he felt that independent India should assume the mantle of leadership to unite Asia.

Nehru thought that the essence of sovereignty was the right to be able to make decisions that were not subject to another authority. In this spirit, he sent ambassadors to Washington and Nanjing in China and to Moscow even before Indian Independence, and he envisaged the Asian Relations Conference that he convened in 1947, again before Indian Independence, as a practical step towards making the elusive Asian unity a reality. But that experience for Nehru proved not to be an entirely happy one. He declared that 'it is fitting that India should play her part in this new phase of Asian development . . . she is the natural centre and focal point of the many forces at work in Asia . . . and geographically she is so situated as to be the meeting point of Western and Northern and Eastern and South-East Asia'. But such views were heard with indignation by China and with alarm by the smaller nations of South-East Asia. Contrary to Nehru's expectations, this conference marked the still-birth of the Asian solidarity that its convener had so earnestly desired. In the stark light of retrospect, this gathering was not a success for India; it left no plan of action and no structure, and no coherent Asian identity emerged. On the contrary, Nehru fell into the contradictions that his idealism and lack of experience had brutally exposed. A few months earlier, Nehru had responded to a telegram of congratulations on the formation of the interim Indian government sent from Tibet, in which the message had made mention of the close and cordial relations which had existed 'between our two countries' since ancient times.[8] Among the thirty-two delegations present at the Asian Relations Conference, Tibet had its own nameplate and flag, and in the hall was hung a banner with a map of Asia showing Tibet as a separate country along with other Indian neighbours such as Afghanistan, Burma, Bhutan, Nepal and Ceylon. China duly protested at the presence of the Tibetan delegation, whereat Nehru responded ingenuously that the gathering was a non-official cultural conference and was not 'expected to consider political niceties'.[9] This unhappy predicament for Nehru was to prove a harbinger of difficulties to come.

But Nehru was not to be shaken from his view of India's larger mission in the world. 'If you peer into the future and if nothing goes wrong – war and the like – the obvious fourth country in the world is India', he said in the Lok Sabha in May 1954.[10] The ruling Indian National Congress party had endorsed his version of non-involvement in the problems of other countries at the Haripura session of the party in 1938, though, given the period, this was in the context of the forthcoming struggle between the Axis and Allies in the Second World War rather than the Cold War which still lay far ahead in the unpredictable future. Whatever the party may have agreed to, the actions of Subhas Chandra Bose and his followers did not conform to the Nehruvian path;

they obviously felt with extraordinary optimism, as did Aung San and Sukarno, that they would find the road to freedom made easier by way of Tokyo and Japanese occupation. Ideology, as opposed to idealism, played a lesser part in Nehru's make-up, and it was just as well, for it could hardly have survived the forthcoming Soviet-Yugoslav break, the Sino-Soviet split, de Gaulle's insistence on France's strategic independence in NATO, and the trans-Atlantic rupture between the USA, France and the United Kingdom over Suez. In the 1950s, India purchased arms without any ideological preferences. In 1956, Dutt captures the sense of India's options:

> [Nehru] spoke of the purchase of Russian planes. Does not want to tie himself solely to the Anglo-Americans and thereby be subject to their pressure. In an emergency Russians would give us anything. Also worried lest refusal might give bad impression about our independence to Russians. Warned him if we buy we cannot expect secret weapons from the British; also political effect and likely effect of withdrawal of US aid on our Five Year Plan. He is obviously greatly worried.[11]

Nehru was a complex personality; as a theoretician, he saw world problems as systemic and interlinked, and not in a binary mode of choosing between right and wrong. He said in 1946 that India would participate in international conferences 'as a free nation with its own policy and not merely as a satellite of another nation'[12] and as a practical man, his instructions in 1948 to Indian delegates at international meetings were to consider India's interests first, even before the merits of the case; this was the paradox of a purportedly moral orientation to foreign policy and the compulsions of the real world.

Nehru had come to high office with two-thirds of a lifetime of opposition to imperialism, colonialism and racism behind him, and he felt that the nationalism of the newly independent countries must guard against conflict, and rely instead on diplomacy and international cooperation. He held utopian ideas of hoping to transform the world political order, and these were the ideas loosely adumbrated in the 'doctrine' of non-alignment. Once the Cold War had come into being, Nehru's non-alignment policy was an implicit dependence upon the inevitability and permanence of the East-West impasse. Throughout the Cold War period, India failed to see the basic truth that the possessors of nuclear weapons were always in mortal fear of the similar weapons belonging to the opposing side, and had no desire to be the first to use them and invite retaliation. Ideologically, Nehru was agnostic, but he was conditioned by the Europe of the 1930s against fascism and totalitarianism; at the time of independence, the Western world was familiar to Indian intelligentsia, but not the Soviet Union, China or Japan. 'His intellectual endowment was exceptional',[13] wrote a contemporary diplomatic observer, and was a mixture of the emotional and intellectual that explained his tilt towards socialism and why his attitude to the West was always ambivalent. He had a propensity to equate imperialism with capitalism, which also led him into a bias against the USA. Nehru was socialistic, and so the socialist bloc of the Soviet Union would have held an automatic appeal, but he was detached enough to come down hard on the Indian communists domestically when they opposed his policies.

Non-alignment evolved in the inherently conflict-prone background of the Cold War and decolonization – the first requiring conformity and obedience, the latter being centrifugal and diverse. Nehru was disinclined to engage emotionally with either bloc, and he instinctively opposed the conformity required by them. Though India could do little about the arms race because of its own priorities with Kashmir and Goa, much of Nehru's opposition to alliances stemmed from the American arms supplies to Pakistan from 1954 and the creation of SEATO (1954) and CENTO (1956). Dutt had this to say:

> The reasons for our opposition to the Baghdad Pact – [Pakistan's] Suhrawardy and Feroz Khan Noon's fulminations against India; how NATO weapons supplied to UK and France were used against Egypt in the recent fighting in Egypt without US's consent.[14]

Washington sought to prevent Asian dominance by any single power that could pose a threat to the USA, and decided that if the 'free world' was to be protected from communism, whether of the Soviet or Chinese models, Pakistan had to be a part of the

West's strategic area and collective security mechanisms against communism. For this, it was necessary to assist Pakistan to maintain sufficient military capability in order to meet any threat and to enable it to support US interests in West and South Asia. The Americans also felt, as had Olaf Caroe of the Indian Civil Service, that it would be easier to defend their interests in the Middle East, including access to oil resources, with Pakistan as an ally. Thus Pakistan became the only country in South Asia that participated in US-led military alliances in the 1950s. For Pakistan, however, joining these alliances was not primarily to contain communism but to strengthen its defence and bargaining power against India. Both the USA and China, with or without Pakistani urging, had convinced themselves that India had hegemonic designs over South and South-East Asia, and they were determined to resist this potential threat and counter India by means of Pakistan.

Before the term 'non-alignment' was fashioned, India from 1947 to 1950 was self-admittedly neutral, and this was the phrase used as an alternative to non-alignment until the first Non-Aligned Conference in 1961. India was big enough not to suffer from the fear of isolation that prevailed among most of the other newly-independent countries, while Western lack of sympathy and support at the United Nations over Kashmir and Goa alienated Nehru and other Indian leaders further. Any alliance associated with the former colonial metropolitans would court domestic unpopularity. Although India was not able to get its independence of thought and action recognized by the leading countries of the communist bloc for several more years after 1947, Nehru nevertheless persevered. He did not wish to join any formal grouping, but had no desire to alienate the communist camp in any way. He regarded non-alignment as the solution to India's dilemma in the East-West conflict, and after the Korean War, there was a growing awareness that mere neutrality was not enough. Thereafter, cordial relations with Moscow and Beijing became central to Nehru's non-alignment, and the Panch Sheel agreement of 1954 and the Bulganin-Khrushchev visit to India in 1955 were the high-watermarks towards its accomplishment.

The close ties developed by New Delhi with the communist

bloc did not lead to any severance of ties with the West, though Nehru was hard put to justify his friendship with the communist countries to Washington. In 1956, during a visit to USA, Nehru went to considerable lengths to explain the rationale why India pursued a policy of neutrality. If a country was to be an ally of another in a defensive organization, he claimed, it must adhere to it with an appropriate military contribution. India was, however, in no position to arm itself in proportion to its population and geographical size, and thus any alignment by India with the free world would only serve to weaken rather than strengthen the alliance. This specious and apologetic defence of non-alignment by its founder inspires the belief that Nehru found it as hard as anyone else to define the concept except in the context of realpolitik. Therefore his *bona fides* were often held to be suspect. 'Indians have a tendency,' wrote Walter Crocker, 'to hold at the same time mutually incompatible positions . . . that . . . undermined, inevitably if unjustly, confidence in their authority.'[15]

In 1947, Nehru had said wryly in parliament that 'neither of the big blocs looks upon us with favour'.[16] Non-alignment, nebulous as it was, was not in itself flawed, but was eventually mismanaged by Nehru and his advisers, due perhaps to overconfidence in their intellectual abilities to manage the international situation without any compromise of lofty principle. They neglected in particular the necessity for any state without allies to be able to protect itself from external force. The elementary need for a military build-up against Pakistan and China was ignored, possibly because the army, in a throw-back to colonial times, was often seen by India's senior politicians as a somewhat adversarial element to civil society and political authority. Although Nehru dispatched the Indian Army Chief, General Cariappa, to Gandhi to assuage the latter's concerns, Gandhi continued to believe that the army had been used only for firing at Indians, and because the independence movement had been non-violent, his initial hopes were that India could avoid war altogether. If the conflict with Pakistan over Kashmir had not taken place in 1947/8, the army may well have been disbanded, and it was Kashmir that transformed the army from a colonial agency to a national one. Nehru seemed aware of this dilemma when he commented on the undesirable priority of building up the armed forces when he stated: 'Mahatma Gandhi would have taken the risk, no doubt, and I dare not say he would have been wrong.'[17] This lack of preparedness made it all the more foolhardy for India to confront the Chinese in 1962 when a negotiated settlement was still available, or at least conceivable.

The Korean War, 1950–1953

Korea enabled India to play a role of balancer by avoiding the 'needless entangling engagements' advocated in the previous century by William Gladstone. In June 1950, North Korea under Kim Il-sung invaded the South. President Truman took Taiwan under the protection of the Seventh Fleet which was deployed into the Taiwan Straits, a move that was considered by China to be an invasion of Asia. The United Nations Security Council declared North Korea the aggressor in the absence of the Soviet Union, which had absented itself from the Council in protest against the presence of Taiwan in China's rightful seat on the Council. During the first few months of the Korean War, there was hardly any reaction from China, although the US intervention in Taiwan was considered a direct threat to it. Nehru suggested the matter be resolved in the Security Council with China taking Taiwan's seat and the Soviet Union ending its boycott. Stalin accepted this proposal and the Soviet Union returned to the UN in August, but the USA refused to admit communist China. Nehru accepted the Security Council resolution denouncing North Korea as the aggressor, but claimed that joining the other 16 nations in extending military help to South Korea was beyond the Indian capacity; in reality, he was not inclined to oppose China or the Soviet Union, and there were unhealthy comparable parallels with Kashmir that must have occurred to him. India voted against the Soviet proposal to hear both North Korea and China at the Security Council. Of the Asians, the Philippines and Thailand supported the US but India, Pakistan, Burma and Indonesia stayed clear of involvement. At about this time, China started talking of liberating Taiwan and Tibet, the latter in what Zhou Enlai termed a 'sacred duty'.

With the help of Nehru, war between US and China over Taiwan was avoided; the US said that once the Korean issue was settled, it would withdraw its protection of Taiwan, and that it had no aggressive intentions against mainland China. China got the Security Council to hear its case over US aggression in Taiwan and over Manchurian airspace. US advanced north across the 38th parallel in Korea and China prepared to enter the war. Indian Ambassador K.M. Panikkar was summoned at midnight on 3 October to meet Zhou, when Nehru was thanked for his efforts for peace, but told that if the US crossed the 38th parallel, China would intervene – though Zhou also added for good measure that American troops had already crossed the line. On 8 October, the UN General Assembly in a Uniting for Peace initiative, also known as the Acheson Plan, approved a resolution that US forces under General MacArthur could cross the line to bring about Korean unification. This US-inspired resolution, on which India had abstained, was pronounced as illegal by China, and the Soviet Union declared that the General Assembly was not entitled to discuss any war settlement which had to be the exclusive preserve of the US, UK, USSR and China: Moscow believed the USA was trying by various strategems to contain the communist bloc.

At this juncture, though Chinese steps to 'liberate' Tibet had begun, it entered the Korean war. The American forces eventually went north as far as the Yalu River bordering Korea and China, and were subsequently pushed back to the 38th parallel. On 1 December Truman suggested he was thinking of using the atom bomb in Korea. When the American troops were in retreat, Truman might have used the atom bomb against China, which was an action urged by MacArthur, but Nehru warned Attlee of such a possibility, and the latter flew post-haste to Washington to discourage Truman from such a step. Washington was later to deny that any such action was ever contemplated. The Chinese were certain that if Manchuria was attacked, the Soviet Union would enter the war and a Third World War would have been the result. Nehru asked China to declare that it would not advance South beyond the 38th parallel provided the USA also agreed to respect that line. China's terms were: US withdrawal from Taiwan, its own admission to the UN, and removal of all foreign troops from Korea. There was proposed a commission of Pakistan, Thailand and the Philippines for a Korean settlement, which was rebuffed by China since Thailand and the Philippines were US allies in the war. In January 1951, Nehru at a Commonwealth heads of government meeting suggested a new conference on Korea without preconditions, though later the proposal had tacked on to it a provision for a prior ceasefire, which China rejected. India then suggested to China a qualified acceptance together with its own clarifications. USA termed the Chinese acceptance of the Indian proposal a contemptuous rejection and wanted to brand China as an aggressor; it could not contemplate any ceasefire which would seem like a defeat. On 1 February India voted against a resolution to brand China an aggressor. In April, MacArthur was dismissed, and in July 1951 China and the Soviet Union accepted the 38th parallel as the armistice line and *status quo*. An Indian medical team was dispatched to Korea at the end of the war.

The USA objected to an Indian presence in the Korean Political Conference of 1953, while Nehru suggested a neutral commission to take charge of Korean prisoners. This mechanism was important because without it, the whole armistice package may have broken down. India became chairman of the Korean Neutral Nations Repatriation Commission in 1953. Some North Korean prisoners of war were in internment in India as late as 1956 because they had no wish to go to either Korea or Taiwan. A few even stayed on permanently in India.

The Korean conflict was Indian non-alignment's finest hour. India brought initiative, courage and appeal to non-alignment, which in the early1950s had no multilateral strength of any kind. India was alone and defiant against the conventional wisdom that emanated from the great power capitals, and was in turn praised and vilified by China and the USA. India had steered a careful middle course as the 'only worthwhile neutral',[18] and Nehru's views found support from some future founder-members of the Non-Aligned Movement like Burma and Indonesia. China was happy at Nehru's insistence that China should be admitted to the UN, and his not joining Truman's desire to neutralize Taiwan with a *cordon sanitaire*.

In 1954, shortly after the Korean War, the Indo-China Geneva conference took place, after which India became the chairman of the commission to supervise and control the implementation of the Geneva accords. Indian troops assisted this work, which was outside the UN auspices. India was on all three Indo-China commissions, for the countries of Vietnam, Laos and Cambodia. Nehru had earlier rejected, as being opposed to the principles of non-alignment, a proposal by British Prime Minister Eden asking if India would join a collective pact to guarantee an Indo-China settlement. V.K. Krishna Menon, Nehru's leading assistant in foreign affairs, was his chosen instrument during the Geneva conference, and continued to be an important factor and the leading public practitioner of non-alignment in the ensuing crises in Egypt and Hungary.

Suez and Hungary

Egyptian President Gamal Abdel Nasser contracted for Soviet arms in 1955 and recognized the People's Republic of China in May 1956. These moves motivated the USA to withdrew its support to the Aswan Dam project, followed in turn by the World Bank and the United Kingdom. At first, while supporting Nasser, India lay stress on the use of the Suez Canal as an international waterway, and strove to get a workable agreement towards that goal. The British/French/Israeli attack on the Egyptian Suez Canal zone, however, took Nehru by surprise, who called it a 'dastardly action' and undermined his high opinion of the valued Commonwealth principle of consultation, though he did not withdraw India from the Commonwealth association because he knew that the people in Britain were almost solidly against their government's intervention. A UN General Assembly resolution under the Uniting for Peace formula passed a US-sponsored resolution on 2 November 1956, that provided, *inter alia*, for the first UN peacekeeping force,[19] of which India was a prominent member.

Almost simultaneously, in Hungary, Russian troops had entered the country to put down an uprising against the communist Moscow-backed government. India abstained or voted against five UN General Assembly resolutions condemning the Soviet Union, and calling for the withdrawal of its troops and holding elections under UN auspices. Later in the year, India voted for only two out of six resolutions; for cooperation by Hungary with the UN secretary-general's nominees to enter Hungary and for relief work. This seemed to expose the application of double standards by India in dealing with the West and with the Soviet Union, and domestically Nehru was assailed by Asoka Mehta and J.P. Narayan, who were hardly to be considered sympathizers of the West. K. Natwar Singh, then a young Indian diplomat in China and later to be the Indian foreign minister, wrote, 'I was deeply grieved by our official reaction to the Hungarian tragedy. In the earlier weeks we came out badly. It was the limit of double thinking. We did not know the facts; this was the lame excuse. Krishna Menon was the one who misled the prime minister.'[20]

K.P.S. Menon, ambassador to the Soviet Union and Hungary at the time, said, 'nothing has caused so much misunderstanding . . . regarding India's foreign policy than her attitude towards the Hungarian revolution',[21] and Dutt in New Delhi recorded in his diary:

> Most distressing news from Hungary. Soviet troops have reentered Hungary in large numbers and occupied airfields. Earlier reports indicated that Hungary also renounced Warsaw Pact and declared its neutrality. Soviet policy unmasking itself. Krishna Menon sought to find some explanations for Soviet action – misrepresented, etc. . . . We are still silent. No wonder many countries think we are not really neutral. . . . PM [Nehru] referred to the distressing situation in Hungary. This is the limit to which he has gone. I do feel we have not taken an objective view of events in Hungary, have been more inclined to accept Soviet version. . . . We have lost our moral prestige among many democratic countries. The Soviet government are better rascals – as rascals as the Eden government. We have condemned the latter in unmeasured language, not the former. How can we justify ourselves? I wish I could do something else than be foreign secretary. But in essentials our foreign policy is right. . . . [22] There is a large section of opinion in the country and parliament which disagrees with our lukewarm attitude on Hungary. . . .[23] I am having for the first time doubts about PM's objectivity . . . I am seriously thinking whether I should not go out of the Foreign Office.[24]

> It is obvious that Krishna Menon does not take the Soviet action in Hungary seriously... PM sent another telegram [to New York] asking him to participate in voting [rather than absent himself] and abstain. N.R. Pillai, [Secretary-General of the Ministry of External Affairs] was unhappy. He doubts whether Krishna Menon will explain our views carefully.[25]

India's position on Hungary is perhaps explained by SEATO and CENTO having been established and a less accommodating policy towards the West in Moscow. The USA's severity in dealing with the UK/Israel/France coalition was in turn possibly dictated by the need to keep its own hands free to deal with the Soviet Union. Fearing this escalation of tension, and the likelihood of a US intervention in Hungary, Nehru's apologists have reasoned that he wanted to prevent the outbreak of a hot war at any cost by giving Moscow the benefit of any doubts. On a less lofty plane, it can be argued that India had no reason to antagonize the Soviet Union when it could not get any better deal from the West. At all events, the result of Nehru's mildness towards the Soviet actions in Hungary diminished greatly the kudos gained for his non-alignment policy in the Suez crisis, Korea and Indo-China.

China

After the 1949 revolution, the communists in China regarded all non-communist countries as pro-American. Nehru had decided that as long as the Kuomintang flag flew anywhere on the mainland, he would not recognize the communist regime in China, and Ambassador Panikkar was recalled to India and sent back only after recognition. India was, in fact, the first country to recognize the People's Republic of China after Burma, because, according to Panikkar, India delayed its announcement by a few days in order to concede to Burma the privilege of being the first.

Mao Zedong regarded the leaders of the newly independent ex-colonial countries as 'running dogs of imperialism' and this characterization specifically included India's leadership. For example, a Shanghai publication wrote, 'Nehru is a rebel against the movement for national independence, a blackguard who undermines the progress of the people's liberation movement, a loyal slave of imperialism.'[26] Mao himself declared, 'sitting on the fence will not do, nor is there a third road'.[27] China saw the non-alignment of India as confusing the issue and India as a bad example to newly independent Afro-Asian countries. For the communist bloc, 'peaceful coexistence was temporary tactics; it was not an article of faith'.[28] Even 'during the honeymoon period' after the Korean War and when Zhou Enlai visited India four times from June 1954 to January 1957, 'China had certain reservations toward India'.[29]

In sharp contrast to China's views about India, Nehru held a rather romanticized view of China, an approach that represented the triumph of wishful thinking over strategic thinking. Nehru had not perceived any threat to India from China despite some mutual acrimony over Chinese actions in Tibet in 1949–50 and during the Korean War. 'Unfortunately,' wrote a diplomat in China in the mid-1950s, 'Nehru took a somewhat romantic view of Indo-China relations,'[30] and Dutt records that 'PM disinclined to listen to anything even indirectly disparaging to the Chinese.'[31] Nehru was not keen to start with China 'on the wrong foot', and was very conscious of Sun Yatsen's description of China as a hyper-colony.[32] Nehru initially followed the British line that China was no threat to India because its control of Tibet was largely fictitious, but this changed when China invaded Tibet in 1950, and Indian officials then took the position that there was a 'physical limit' as to what India could realistically do. And so the inherited British policy of support for the independence of Tibet subject to the suzerainty of China was abandoned.

Despite cautionary voices like that of Home Minister Vallabhbhai Patel, who wrote to Nehru in 1950 that 'it looks as though it is not a friend speaking in that language but a potential enemy',[33] Nehru pursued his policy of friendship with China with determination. In 1950, speaking at the committee of Parliament for external affairs, Nehru's temper flared up when asked by a member about the possibility of a Chinese attack from the north, riposting that such an attack was impossible across Tibet which was 1,200 miles wide and 12,000 feet in altitude. When he was advised against losing Tibet as a buffer state (buffer against who? he enquired sarcastically) or giving up the privileged Indian position inherited from the British in Tibet, he refused to listen, and 'in some cases was scornful of the advisers concerned and virtually reprimanded them'.[34] This self-imposed compulsion to maintain good relations with China strongly influenced India's evolving policy during the Korean War and India's non-participation at the 1951 San Francisco Conference at which most of the world agreed on a peace treaty with Japan. Before 1954, India was almost alone outside the communist bloc in championing the entry of China into the United Nations and seeking assurances from the Americans on Taiwan, but China continued to regard India with suspicion and scepticism, if not hostility.

However, Nehru might not have been as naïve as his later detractors have alleged. Speaking to US Ambassador Chester Bowles, Nehru said his views on China were very different to those of his Ambassador Panikkar. Bowles' informal notes record Nehru as telling him; 'Panikkar usually succumbed to whatever situation he was in. . . . When Commies took over, Panikkar's views as in the past had changed abruptly and today tended dangerously to idealize Chi scene.'[35] And in 1954, the same year of the first American arms sales to Pakistan, Nehru minuted that,

> It is not inconceivable that China and the Soviet Union may not continue to be as friendly as they are now. Certainly it is conceivable that our relations with China may worsen . . . Of course, both the Soviet Union and China are expansive . . . Chinese expansionism has been evident during various periods of Asian history for a thousand years or so. We are perhaps facing a new period of such expansionism.[36]

Despite whatever misgivings he may have entertained, Nehru changed his mind more than once as to whether to raise the ambiguities of the India-China boundary with Zhou Enlai before the April 1954 Indo-Chinese Agreement was signed, which incorporated the Five Principles of Peaceful Coexistence. Finally, he acted on Panikkar's advice not to mention the subject, overruling the view of G.S. Bajpai, the former and first secretary-general of the External Affairs Ministry, that India should resolve the issue before signing any agreement. Nehru made earnest efforts to assuage the fears of communist China in Burma and South-East Asia, particularly at the Bandung Afro-Asian Conference in 1955, and several growing apprehensions in India at differences on the border were minimized and suppressed until 1958 on the grounds that such differences could be exploited by the West. For the same reason, the Dalai Lama in February 1957 had been strongly dissuaded from staying back in India, and was prevailed against his own inclinations and better judgement to return to Tibet.

Nehru's hope of keeping India non-aligned made him neglect Pakistani President Ayub Khan's offer in April 1959 for a joint defence of the subcontinent against the Chinese threat. In 1961 or thereabouts, even with Pakistan at the time a close ally of the USA, China and Pakistan would begin exploring avenues of co-operation and territorial adjustments of Kashmir's northern border with China. Crypto-communists in the Indian bureaucracy like diplomat T.N. Kaul urged Nehru in 1959 to push the Dalai Lama back to Tibet to appease China and earn its goodwill as India had done once before in 1957. Nehru disagreed, but even after 1959 and the Dalai Lama's flight from Chinese-occupied Tibet, India refused to plead the Tibetan case in the United Nations, and objective assessments of India-China relations in 1959 by scrupulous officials in the External Affairs Ministry like Jagat S. Mehta were blocked by senior bureaucrats such as Foreign Secretary Subimal Dutt and not allowed to reach Nehru's desk. Dutt, however, was himself more than aware of the looming threat from China, both immediate and long-term. He noted:

> We must try and settle the dispute. The Chinese are much more determined than we; our whole system is such that in a struggle with them we are bound to lose. We must therefore try and settle. Pandit Nehru will leave a terrible legacy to posterity if he leaves the border dispute unsettled.[37] China will assume a more rigid and aggressive attitude. Shall we be able to match them? They are aggressive, determined, autocratic and authoritarian. We are slow, inefficient, divided amongst ourselves.[38]

Among the many irritants that Beijing resented in the 1960s was the assistance extended from the Soviet Union to India that China regarded as an unfriendly action and belonging to China as of right. Thus in a sense, the conflict that took place in 1962 was directed as much by Beijing at Moscow as at New Delhi – though China's revolution owed nothing to the Soviet Union, not even moral support, and China from the first resisted any semblance of domination from comradely Moscow. The Indo-Chinese border conflict of 1962 was the first challenge that India's non-aligned policy, and the newly-formed non-aligned group of countries, had to face, because it was evidence of the use of force and aggression by a major power against a non-aligned country. Non-alignment by India gave reassurance to the Soviet Union and was to be instrumental in stabilizing the bilateral relations between New Delhi and Moscow for over three decades, but as a means to an end, it collapsed with the attack by China, a country on which Nehruvian foreign policy so greatly had depended. Nehru requested the president of the United States on 19 November 1962 for direct intervention with twelve squadrons of supersonic all-weather fighter aircraft and modern radar with American personnel to provide air cover over India, though he added that any air action beyond Indian borders would be taken by Indian aircraft manned by Indian crews.[39] The urgency receded, but when the USA and Britain did not match their military assistance at that time with similar commitments for the future, India turned to an increasing extent to look for a safe anchorage with the Soviet Union, and India's ties with China until the end of the Cold War were to be hostage to the triangular interplay between the USA and China, the Soviet Union and China, and Pakistan and China. Nehru himself had to recant publicly and eat humble pie: 'We have been living in a fool's paradise,' he declared bitterly.[40]

The Soviet Union

Nehru felt that the Russians as a people were looked down upon by the West, and the Soviet Union was an outcast among nations, so he tended to sympathize and regard the socialist bloc as an equal. 'If the future is full of hope, it is largely because of Soviet Russia', he had said in 1936.[41] As in the case of China, Nehru was wrong in thinking that after the humiliations at the hands of the European powers, the communists would appreciate India's goodwill expressed through non-alignment, because, like the communist regime in China, Moscow initially looked askance at the notion of neutrality. Lenin had pronounced, 'the idea of neutralism is nothing but a mistaken and contemptible pretext', and Khrushchev, that there could be 'neutral states' but no 'neutral men'.[42]

Nehru showed a sense of urgency in opening an embassy in Moscow because the Soviet Union was then regarded by him as the epitome of anti-imperialism, but in the opinion of Moscow's leadership, India was viewed as a semi-colony and non-alignment as an imperialist device. Moscow thought the whole process of decolonization was only a charade, that the former colonies could not follow any independent policies of their own making, and were mere satellites of their previous masters. In Stalin's time, India was accordingly considered part of Western imperialism and Stalin hardly responded to Nehru's overtures, whereas 'Nehru totally misjudged Stalin'.[43] When India did not formally join Stalin's orbit, it was frozen out. The Soviet Union's supreme leader did not meet Vijayalakshmi Pandit, Nehru's sister and specially selected first envoy, even once, and she was made to feel very unhappy in Moscow. Her colleague at the Indian embassy, Rajeshwar Dayal, admits that there was no real knowledge about the Soviet Union, but only various degrees of ignorance. Ignoring Soviet press attacks on Gandhi and himself, Nehru persevered with the Soviet Union despite this initial hostility, and unlike the case of China, this time it paid rich dividends. With the break from Moscow of Tito's Yugoslavia and the death of Stalin in 1953, there came to be a perceptible change in Moscow's attitude towards India as a promising partner. In the same year, Foreign Minister Gruber of Austria requested Nehru, who was then in Switzerland, to urge the USSR to end the 4-power occupation of Austria, which had been a reluctant partner of Nazi Germany. Nehru instructed K.P.S. Menon, the Indian ambassador in Moscow, to plead with Soviet Foreign Minister Molotov to look sympathetically upon this idea, and this *démarche* by non-aligned India might well have been the first step on the road leading to the 1955 Treaty culminating in Austria regaining its full independence.

Non-alignment was made legitimate from the Soviet viewpoint by the Indian refusal to send any combat troops to Korea but only a medical team, its diplomatic recognition of China, support for China's desire to be admitted to the UN, the Geneva accords, and its refusal, along with the Soviet Union, to sign the Japanese peace treaty. In 1953, for the first time, Moscow made a friendly reference to India's efforts to end the Korean war – the first time for India, or for that matter, for any non-communist state, to be given such recognition from so important a person as the chairman of the Soviet council of ministers. Moscow began to come round to the view that coexistence was possible with states with different socio-political systems. By 1955 and the visits of Nehru to Moscow and that of Bulganin and Khrushchev to India, the Soviet Union discovered some common threads in Indian and Soviet foreign policies and the anti-imperial, anti-West potential of non-alignment. Dutt tried to identify some reasons for the warm welcome accorded to the Soviet leaders on their first visit to India in 1955:

> The majority of the people also had instinctive sympathy for USSR and their leaders – (i) communist influence within the country (ii) socialism and equity (iii) good deal for the common man. USA and other Western powers stand for haves, somehow associated with colonialism . . . I have faith in PM's judgment. No blind faith: he has proved right in (1) recognition of China (2) military blocs (3) hydrogen bombs (4) planning within the country. He knows, I am sure, what he is doing.[44]

After the Twentieth Party Congress in Moscow in February 1956, Indian foreign policy was increasingly appreciated, and non-alignment was given respectability by being accepted by one of the super-powers. In September 1957, the Soviet Union proposed a conference of the two big powers which would also be attended by some neutral countries – India, Yugoslavia, Egypt, Indonesia, Sweden and some others. Dutt states in his diary that Nehru received a long letter about the suggested summit from Bulganin:

> We are neutral but a little balanced towards the Soviets; somehow or other we incline favourably towards any approach by them – any

proposal made by them. We responded warmly to a letter from Bulganin. I have often thought over this. I think PM has convinced himself that Soviets are anxious to lessen international tension and it is the Western powers led by Dulles who are keeping the Cold War; that the various proposals made by the Soviet are not *mala fide*: at least they should be trusted. Some beginning towards a détente in the present tense relations between the USSR and the USA must be made and the Soviet proposals show a way out. On the other hand, many people in the West think that Soviets are out to convince neutral opinion of their good intentions and some [sic] or other get Nehru to endorse their stance. Soviet objective is to detach the neutral states from any possible US influence and thereby promote their influence in the world with a view to ultimate communist domination of the world. The Soviet in their own security interest will never allow people in East European states to decide by free and secret votes what form of government they would prefer to have. That is why they insist that in any settlement the socialist gains in these states must be maintained. PM believes that the only hope of these states regaining some freedom lies in the withdrawal of Soviet forces and direct control by the Soviet, and this is possible if only the existing tension diminishes and the Soviets feel secure. Therefore any measure which would reduce this tension should be welcome. An overall settlement at one step is not feasible. Make a beginning with one or two small steps, do not let negotiations get bogged in detail. Foreign ministers will get involved in arguments (with Dulles present, one can be sure of this); a summit meeting should therefore be tried.[45]

On 1 June 1957 Bulganin had told Ambassador Menon in Moscow that the Soviet Union was India's true friend and would always be with India, adding, 'neither Pakistan nor any other power can come in the way of our friendship'.[46] There was solid Soviet support to India over Goa, and Dutt records his appreciation in 1961:

Having advised all countries to settle differences peacefully, he [PM] would face accusations of double standards if the Army were to walk into Goa. This is exactly what has happened. A resolution sponsored in the Security Council by Britain, US, Turkey asking Indian forces to withdraw from Goa received seven affirmative votes but vetoed by Soviet Union. The Soviet prestige will undoubtedly go up in India. Brezhnev [Soviet President] speaking at a reception in Bombay on 17th evening gave full support to the liberation of Goa . . . on the

20th he congratulated the government and people of India on Goa's liberation.[47]

After years of initial abstention, there was also Soviet support after 1952 on Kashmir at the UN Security Council and arms aid commencing in 1961 with the supply of transport aircraft for use in Ladakh. And there was reciprocal support, though tacit, by India for Soviet action in Hungary. On the humanitarian and moral aspects of the Berlin Wall, constructed in 1961, Nehru said not a word.

It became fashionable and politically correct, if not mandatory, for Indian politicians and bureaucrats to show marked favour in private and public for the Soviet Union, which was identified as India's only friend in the UN Security Council. This was wishful thinking to some extent. Moscow, preoccupied with the Western threat, the ideological split with China and the Cuban missile crisis, had adopted a neutral or even pro-Chinese posture on the boundary dispute, and urged Nehru to accept China's proposals for negotiations without preconditions. G.S. Bajpai and Badruddin Tyabji, both Indian diplomats, advised Nehru not to over-identify India with the Soviet Union, and instead to nurture closer ties with the nations of South-East Asia. Nehru ignored these appeals and ridiculed the countries of South-East Asia that had links with the West as 'Coca Cola governments'. Dutt had much to say about these pro-Soviet attitudes in government circles:

Indira [Indira Gandhi] is extremely anti-American.[48] PM mentally is more favourably disposed towards the communist countries than towards US.[49] N.R. Pillai worried about the way we are inclining towards communists by slow but sure steps while maintaining neutrality. . . . Some of our officers and ministers . . . falling head over heels to bring Russians in a big way. KPS [Menon] – I don't know whether he has that love for communists but he is going even farther.[50] N.R. Pillai, C.S. Jha [Secretary in the Ministry] all anxious to attend to-night's reception by the Czech Ambassador . . . lest they be suspected of anti-communist leanings. . . . How demoralized we are getting. Who says we are neutral? Vice-President Radhakrishnan said to me that we are going too far in boasting communist flags, etc.; bound to have repercussions.[51] Americans are not saints. . . . But some of our own people – our representatives abroad and some officers at home – do not miss an opportunity to indulge in anti-American sentiments because they think that would please PM. If the civil service ceases to be objective how can it perform any useful function? Are we approaching a time when to be dubbed pro-American is to ruin a man's career? McCarthyism in reverse? Fortunately PM has not ceased to be objective.[52]

Western colonial rule was roundly condemned by New Delhi but colonialism had many manifestations such as the sway of the Soviet Union over the nations of Eastern Europe. This awkward truth was ignored by New Delhi with the argument that 'why should a non-aligned country ignore its interests [when] one [bloc] . . . is friendly and another hostile?'[53] 'Non-alignment would be a poor policy to adopt if it meant rebuffing friends and courting unfriendly powers', wrote C.S. Jha.[54] Dutt explains the circumstances in which close ties between India and the Soviet Union served the purposes of both countries:

The Soviet government wish to remain friendly with us despite our differences and quarrels with China. He [PM] asked me the reason. I said that they had their own difficulties with China. Although the differences are ideological they are bound to affect state relations. The Soviet Union wish to counter the spread of US influence in our country. PM agreed that with our difficulties over Goa, Indo-China border, Kashmir, we must cultivate friendship with the Soviet Union assiduously.[55]

Nehru was to claim that the Soviet Union was India's second line of defence and vice versa. In the eyes of his critics, he permitted himself great licence, knowing he could always fall back under the US umbrella in case of need, but it is doubtful if the Soviet Union was really any threat to world peace after Stalin. The Red Menace and the Yellow Peril were both always an imagined rather than a real challenge to the West.

The United States

No less than China and the Soviet Union, the United States of America saw no virtue in non-alignment in the early years of its manifestation. Secretary of State Dulles termed it 'immoral and short-sighted', and his dismissal of the policy was even more absolute than that of Stalin. Eisenhower, however, showed greater understanding, perhaps remembering that the USA had itself been non-aligned for a hundred years, and his views were to an extent reflected later by Kennedy and Johnson. Non-alignment was implicitly accepted by Kennedy in his inaugural address, which had followed its recognition by the Soviet Union under Khrushchev.

But there were difficulties in bilateral relations between India and the United States from the very outset. Washington was not used to dealing with haughty and sensitive leaders of newly-independent countries like Nehru, who visited the USA in 1949, and felt that the Americans expected acquiescence from India on all issues. During Eisenhower's presidency, American arms supplies to Pakistan began in 1954, and was always a source of bilateral friction. As Dutt writes,

> I distrust their [Communists] friendly approaches. Should we then rebuff them? If we do so, we lose friends immediately without disarming the suspicions of the other side. At the same time I dislike the US for the way they are arming Pakistan. They have been told repeatedly about Pakistan's hostile intentions towards India; how US will be unable to prevent the use of the weapons supplied by her if Pakistan decides to use them against us. . . . To hold the balance is extremely difficult. In seeking to do so, we may not acquire any fast friends; we may earn the indifference of all countries and in a crisis will be friendless.[56]

Moreover, the US and the West adopted a policy favouring Pakistan over India with regard to Kashmir at the UN Security Council, obliging the Soviet Union to exercise a veto to safeguard Indian interests in 1957 and 1962. The liberation of Goa in 1961 was severely criticized by the US and the West, no doubt welcoming a chance to debunk the moralistic exhortations and denunciations of Nehru and Krishna Menon. Although, despite its similar preoccupations to the Soviet Union, and India's equivocal stand on the Cuban missile crisis, the United States led the West in supporting India against China in 1962, the positive effect of the arms supplies after 1962 were negated by the West attempting to achieve a compromise between India and Pakistan on Kashmir, and the arms aid had ceased by the time of the 1965 Indo-Pakistan war.

In January 1962, to balance US assurances to India concerning a possible conflict with China, President Kennedy reconfirmed a previous American commitment to President Ayub Khan of Pakistan, writing that, 'as a firm ally, Pakistan is entitled to the reaffirmation you have requested of the prior assurances given by the USA to Pakistan on the subject of aggression against Pakistan. My government certainly stands by these assurances.'[57] These assurances related to a 1959 agreement that in case of aggression against Pakistan, the US would take 'appropriate action, including the use of armed forces as may be mutually agreed upon, to help Pakistan'.[58] In short, American actions in the subcontinent did not convince Indian policy makers that closer ties with the USA were worth the price of jeopardizing Russian friendship, and it was believed in New Delhi that 'for India to follow any other policy than the one which she was following – that of non-involvement in the Cold War – would be suicidal, because the course of the Cold War, whatever its origins, was being determined by the opportunist policies of the United States'.[59]

V.K. Krishna Menon

Krishna Menon was Nehru's leading adviser and practitioner of Indian foreign policy from Independence until 1962. The holder of numerous posts in the government until his resignation after the defeat by China, he was known to be especially energetic in the corridors of the Geneva Indo-China discussions and during the Suez negotiations, and as a invariably strident critic of the United States and Pakistan at the United Nations. For his policy of non-alignment to have any chance of success, Nehru needed the cooperation of the socialist bloc, and for that purpose, Krishna Menon served the cause well, though he found few admirers in the West, and American Assistant Secretary of State Joseph Sisco was to say many years later, 'when many Americans think of India they think of Krishna Menon, and that's not an inaccurate image'.[60] Krishna Menon also had no shortage of critics back at home in India, due to what was considered his unwholesome influence on Nehru. The interpretation of Nehru in some circles as being anti-West was due mainly to Krishna Menon. Krishna Menon's disdain, notwithstanding his anti-West bias, of the Afro-Asian group and his implacable hostility to Pakistan prevented any prospect of cooperation in South Asia and damaged India's reputation, particularly since Krishna Menon's preferences and prejudices and pathological aversion to Pakistan had 'nothing to do with the national interest but were based purely on personal factors'.[61] Non-alignment was conducted by Krishna Menon in an idiosyncratic hectoring style that brought upon India a widespread dislike. Dutt is frank in his dislike of Krishna Menon:

> Krishna Menon has never been objective, intensely anti-American and anti-West. He has influence with PM. Why should I be a silent spectator of what I think to be unfair assessment of facts? . . . Spoke to N.R. Pillai about my mental torture. He said he was passing through similar agony.[62] French Ambassador told N.R. Pillai that Krishna Menon's attitude towards French delegation [at the UN] definitely unfriendly. Krishna Menon's generally severe attitude towards some delegations severely criticized by others. This is no help.[63] Krishna Menon cannot open his mouth without irritating people.[64] Defence Minister Krishna Menon has an almost vested interest in our quarrel with Pakistan. This gives him a political platform and he is a hero in the public eye for his stand on Kashmir.[65]

India moralized against the Cold War, but had its own Cold War with Pakistan, and New Delhi opposed non-alignment by others when it came to its relations with China and Pakistan. Nehru showed an indulgence to communist states he did not show to the West, and this, and the free rein given to Krishna Menon, stoked Western alarms about India.

Nehru undoubtedly entertained an abiding concern about the fitness of Washington for world primacy, but also found communism's absolutist ways unacceptable. This distinction was blurred by the reliance he placed on the likes of Krishna Menon, whose indispensability and influence on Nehru were incomprehensible to most observers. In charge, in fact if not in official position, of India's ties with the communist bloc, Krishna Menon had regarded any attack on India by China as inconceivable. He held the view that China would not be so foolish as to lay itself open on two fronts; to an attack by the USA in the East over Taiwan and at the same time to antagonize India in the South. Such a delusory opinion, possibly promoted by Beijing itself as disinformation to a gullible Krishna Menon, proved catastrophic to India, to Nehru and Krishna Menon himself, and to the non-alignment policy pursued since Independence.

Nehru may have been a good judge of character in respect of Panikkar, but was certainly not so with regard to Krishna Menon. Krishna Menon had misled Nehru on Hungary. He resisted taking military aid from the West after India's defeat in the 1962 war with China, saying it was a dereliction of non-alignment. He persuaded Nehru that a non-aligned movement would strengthen India's voice in international affairs. He had opened discussions with the Soviet Union for defence supplies and joint production, which would only materialize after the 1962 crisis, and for all his disagreeable traits, had set the scene for the intimate links between India and the Soviet Union that would develop from the death of Nehru until the end of the Cold War, during which, as one observer put it, 'some Indians lean as far towards communism and the Soviet Union as their so-called neutralism permits'.[66]

Assessment

It could be justifiably claimed that the non-aligned policy up to 1962 and the conflict with China had enhanced India's image on the world stage, that it was the least costly form of promoting India's diplomatic presence as leader of the newly decolonized, that it was a sensible approach to power politics when India was weak and initially looked upon askance by both blocs, and the best means of encouraging economic assistance from every quarter. There was also the matter of group solidarity with other Third World countries, as Dutt explains:

> And once we approach an international problem with an attitude of giving the maximum support to one party in the Cold War, then we really cease to be non-aligned. Also that would reduce our basic strength. The question however remains; if increasingly we get iso-

lated from Afro-Asian countries, that itself would seriously affect our weight in international counsels.[67]

Non-alignment gave freedom to newly independent countries to develop relations with all states, including those in alliances. Some chose to be non-aligned because their geographical proximity to great powers made them uneasy. By the period 1960–2, and the colonial 'scuttle' from Africa, non-alignment had become accepted as part of the international political scene, and the newly formed Organization of African Unity in 1963 at one stroke pronounced all its member states to be non-aligned. The supporters of the non-aligned policy would say that it was more than a survival strategy in the Cold War; it was a response to the North-South divide, and a campaign for opposing imperialism and racism – though this was largely over by 1962 with the colonial exit of Britain and France from Africa, other than for white-minority rule south of the river Zambezi – and for keeping clear of the Vietnam War. Non-alignment provided a ray of hope for some foreign policy autonomy not only for India but for all weak countries of the Third World. It helped to the extent that every country had an opportunity to choose between joining either bloc or remaining non-aligned. It also helped the UN to remain an important actor on the global stage by creating a group of countries that were not identified with either Cold War bloc. Non-alignment was politically and economically profitable, at least in the short term, to countries that chose that policy, and however much it might have been criticized by the West, it was not strong enough as a national or moral force, or even as a movement, to cause any real harm to Western interests.

Non-aligned India was chairman of the Korean Neutral Nations Repatriation Commission that supervised exchange of prisoners in 1953, part of the UN Emergency Force after Suez in 1956, and a component of the UN peacekeeping force in Congo in 1960. But non-alignment did not prove an adequate policy for India in handling its own neighbourhood; nor did it lay down any strategic or pragmatic path for India in avoiding wars with Pakistan or China. In the 1950s, India clearly punched above its weight, but during and after the 1960s, the reverse was true. Non-alignment was not an end in itself, but a means; and the

India-China conflict in 1962 showed that non-alignment was not a safeguard or barrier for any non-aligned country against aggression. Non-alignment would have helped India in its participation in UN peacekeeping, its campaign against apartheid, and its appeals for decolonization and international disarmament, but Nehru's commitment to reduce the use of force in world politics came a cropper in his relations with China. India played an almost lone hand against colonialism and racism in the UN until many African countries achieved their independence from Britain and France after 1960. Independent Africa had appreciated India as the leader against colonialism and racism, but when it came to India's national interest, such as during its conflicts with China or Pakistan, then Africa tended to be hesitant and self-consciously neutral. Krishna Menon's catchy dictum that 'a non-aligned nation must be non-aligned with the non-aligned to be truly non-aligned'[68] sprang up to kick India in the teeth, with only two countries of the Non-Aligned Conference of 1961 supporting India against China; these were Cyprus and Ethiopia.

After 1962, non-alignment came under attack, not least in India, and following the war with China, Indian non-alignment of the much-admired Nehruvian vintage was effectively dead. As Nehru said on All India Radio in 1962, 'We were getting out of touch with reality in the modern world, and we were living in an artificial atmosphere of our own creation',[69] and in a television interview in New York in December 1962 that 'there was no non-alignment *vis-à-vis* China'.[70] Nehru's sense of self-confidence and superiority crumbled, and perhaps the only reason India did not move into the US camp at that time was that Washington was basically indifferent, and there was an unexpected change in presidents with the assassination of President Kennedy. Perhaps the truth was that India was too big to align itself comfortably with any country, and no superpower really sought to forge any formal alliance with India.

Nehru and his successors as prime ministers of India were fearful of the power and influence of Indian communists and of their connections with international communism and particularly, their ties with Moscow. From 1947 until Rajiv Gandhi, it was a constant factor in New Delhi's relations with the Soviet Union. Dutt remarks that when talking to Nehru about the enthusiastic reception given in India to Bulganin and Khruschev in 1955 and its effect on the Indian communists, Nehru declared, 'I think it will take the wind out of their sails'.[71] Dutt was present at discussions between Nehru and the Soviet leaders:

> Talks were brutally frank. PM referred to Communist Party of India – popular belief that it receives guidance from the Soviet Communist Party, that large funds come to it from Russia, that Indian communist leaders visit Russia to receive advice, etc. Khruschev replied that they as communists had sympathies with communists all over the world; not a fact that they helped parties in other countries . . . and even if the Russians wanted, they could not prevent activities of communist parties elsewhere.[72]

In 1948, Nehru had given aid to the Burmese government with the approval of the Commonwealth to fight the local communists. In India there had been no unanimous approval of non-alignment: in the 1950s and early 1960s, the Indian Left had denounced it as sitting on the fence, and stressed the primacy of decolonization as the sole agenda at the first Non-Aligned Conference at Belgrade in 1961 even as Nehru preferred to speak of world peace and disarmament. The non-alignment policy which was eventually accepted by the Soviet Union under Khrushchev, and by China after the Korean War, helped the Indian government under the Congress party since the communists in India were deprived of support in the foreign policy objectives of the communist bloc. In the post-Stalin period, Soviet foreign policy abandoned the earlier strategy of party-to-party ties, and adopted a policy of government-to-government relations. The assurances given by Khruschev to Nehru were therefore factually correct.

Nehru knew that communism was an ideology that could not be destroyed by force. Also that, after communist Yugoslavia's break with the Soviet Union, there was no such thing as 'global communism' without the presence of many local variants. But Nehru's blanket condemnation of pacts and alliances had irritated smaller but important developing countries like Turkey and Iran, and he was unable to unite the Third World under uncontested Indian leadership. Perhaps the Korean War had not been such a triumph for India's non-aligned policy as was made out in New Delhi; a leading contemporary Indian diplomat wrote in his memoirs that 'the Korean War left a legacy of misunderstanding on both sides',[73] and in a diplomatic *Rashomon* effect, Kissinger makes no mention of the Indian role or non-alignment in the chapter on Korea in his book *On China*.[74] If Nehru had taken an anti-Chinese position along with the US on North Korean aggression on South Korea or on the Chinese occupation of Tibet, it is hard to say what may have transpired. Suffice it to say that before the Non-Aligned Nations Conference in Belgrade in 1961, positions were certainly much more fluid. There is no mention of the term 'non-alignment' in K.M. Panikkar's book *An Autobiography* although the author deals with the Korean War, and he was later Ambassador in Egypt under Neguib and Nasser. Neither is the phrase 'non-alignment' mentioned as such in a second Panikkar book, *In Two Chinas*. This is as curious as Conan Doyle's dog that did not bark in the night. It would not be for the first time in history that a political term has gained greater currency in the decades when its hey-day was effectively over. In the case of non-alignment, its movement, represented by succeeding summit conferences, usurped the original intent and substance of the philosophy by showing favour unequivocally towards the Soviet Union.

India was dependent on food aid mainly from the USA (India had also received some food supplies from the Soviet Union and China), and for military and industrial technology and political support at the UN from the Soviet Union. In consequence, Nehru could not condemn Moscow on Hungary in 1956 or Washington in 1958 over its intervention in Lebanon. By 1957, the Indian planned economy had run into very serious difficulties, and the Aid India Consortium was established. This was to play a part in Indian non-recognition of the German Democratic Republic; the Federal Republic of Germany was too important a donor to be risked by a breach of the Hallstein Doctrine of 1955. In circumstances when China and the Soviet Union had split ideologically, the US would pay court to Mao Zedong, and de Gaulle snapped France's fingers at NATO, non-alignment 'as an emollient of the Cold War ceased to have any relevance'.[75] 'You could not be non-aligned towards a threat of war to your own country,' said Nehru.[76] But Indian non-alignment could exist only if the

West's military strength contained the East's and vice versa. After 1962, given its material weakness, India could play little meaningful role in world affairs for the next three decades.

Yugoslavia and Egypt became non-aligned by defying the great powers and were the prime movers to summon the first non-aligned conference. India, which held out for peace without confrontation, became a third co-sponsor. Any version of foreign policy allegedly based on morality is not adopted in a historical vacuum, and so could not mean the same thing for all nations. Thus, in theory, there could never have been a coalition of non-aligned nations in any movement. Nehru was fully aware of this contradiction and used his influence to resist a non-aligned secretariat and bureaucracy. At the first conference in 1961 at Belgrade, where there were 25 founder-member countries present, there was a clear division between those nations pressing for positive cooperation with both blocs which were led by Nehru, and those for intensified confrontation with old imperialism headed by Indonesia's President Sukarno. This internal confrontation gathered momentum after the revelation of the deepening Sino-Soviet rift. Rikhi Jaipal, a leading Indian apologist for, and participant in, many of the non-aligned conferences, refers to the first Belgrade conference[77] without any reference to the Soviet Union's nuclear testing from 1 September 1961 – in terms of yield, the largest in history up to that time. Nehru and Nkrumah of Ghana were dispatched by the conference to Moscow, and Sukarno and Keita of Mali to Washington to plead for urgent Kennedy-Khruschev negotiations for disarmament and to remove the danger of war. These two missions to Washington and Moscow basically achieved nothing. In 1961 there was no mention of any second non-aligned conference. By the mid-1960s, and after its war with China, India 'though still a profoundly committed member of the non-aligned movement . . . the foreign service came to realize that the movement itself should not be expected to be supportive of India . . . even if an Indian stand was legitimate and valid on objective considerations.'[78] The last years of Jawaharlal Nehru saw the atrophy of his non-alignment ideas based on idealism, and there were to be no more triumphs for Indian non-aligned policy after Korea, Indo-China, Austria and Suez.

II. THE AGE OF REALISM

The period from Jawaharlal Nehru's death in 1964 until the end of the Cold War and the break-up of the Soviet Union in 1991 was one in which India encountered severe difficulties. There was the breakdown and abandonment of the idealism of the Nehru years, and a strong tilt towards realism in foreign affairs and involvement in power politics, with non-alignment becoming little more than a fig-leaf to cover India's growing affiliation with the Soviet Union. The Five Principles of Peaceful Coexistence concluded with China in 1954, which were exemplary in conceptual terms, were no longer referred to by New Delhi except with some embarrassment, and were considered overtaken by events.

There was continuous tension with Pakistan and two wars in 1965 and 1971, fabricated crises like the Indian military operation codenamed 'Brasstacks' of 1986–7, tremendous upsurge of unrest in Kashmir from 1989, stoked both openly and surreptitiously by Pakistan, and the liberation of Bangladesh from West Pakistan in 1971 that soon produced an unfriendly country to India's eastern border after 1975. In addition, India experienced unease and periodic friction with China and the United States, droughts and natural disasters and a massive influx of aid. A Tamil secessionist movement in Sri Lanka from the 1970s onward found New Delhi wrong-footed and bungling its foreign policy options. Domestic turbulence occurred, with frequent changes of government, including the death in office of a prime minister, the first of several non-Congress governments in power, the assassination of one prime minister and one former prime minister, and the declaration of an emergency by Indira Gandhi with the suspension of civil liberties. The Soviet intervention in Afghanistan and the rise of Islamic extremism, especially centred in Pakistan, the arrival of Gorbachev, the end of the Cold War and the abrupt demise of a strategic ally in the USSR dramatically changed Indian perspectives of the entire international landscape. Until then, non-alignment continued to be the official Indian foreign policy lodestone, but New Delhi's alignment with Moscow during this period was consistent and predictable.

The Soviet Union

Nehru himself realized, before the Belgrade Non-Aligned Conference of 1961, that the classical age of colonialism was over, and that the new international priorities concerned the questions of peaceful coexistence between the two power blocs. Even when deprived of the malign influence of Krishna Menon, Nehru's default inclination was to lean towards the socialist countries. With the perceptibly growing links between Pakistan and China, and Johnson replacing Kennedy as president in Washington, the inclination to see the Soviet Union as an indispensible balancer against USA, China and Pakistan, individually or collectively, grew ever stronger in New Delhi. Moscow was responsive; as early as 1962, even before the India-China War, the Soviet Union had offered to India its modern MiG-21 fighter aircraft, a proposition which was leaked to the Indian press and 'caused some flutter among western circles'.[79] After Nehru's death, the intellectual underpinning for non-alignment was gone, to be replaced by continuous and at times egregious lip-service, but in reality, a version of balance of power evolved that was totally dependent, for India, on good relations with Moscow.

Would things have been different if India had not chosen so steadfast an alignment? Would India have reaped the benefits of friendly relations with the Soviet Union even if it had pursued a more even-handed approach towards the two blocs? The answer has to remain hypothetical, but non-alignment was of course pre-conditioned on an assumption that the Cold War would last indefinitely. Indian leaders never assessed correctly how much the people in Eastern Europe disliked communism and the Soviet yoke: in fact, after Nehru, they never even recognized the need to make any such evaluation. It could theoretically have been possible for New Delhi to conduct a more parallel relationship between the two blocs. The Soviet Union obviously held the view, especially in the context of the Sino-Soviet split, that close ties with India were of great value to it, but until Brezhnev's 1969 Asian Collective Security proposal, Moscow had made no effort to create any sort of binding understanding, and the impetus for the 1971 Friendship Treaty came from New Delhi. On the other hand, there was no basic conflict of national interest between India and the Soviet Union. But outside the parameters of the Cold War, the USSR was not only supremely cautious about risking any possible nuclear or conventional conflict with the USA, but remained objectively neutral – in the Soviet-sponsored Indo-Pakistan Tashkent Conference of 1965, on the Non-Proliferation Treaty of 1968, and Soviet arms sales to Pakistan in 1968. Khrushchev told Indian Ambassador T.N. Kaul in 1963: 'we do not want you to spoil your relations with America' . . . and . . . 'we would like you to normalize your relations with China'.[80] Moscow wanted India to settle matters with Pakistan after the 1965 War. It wanted India to sign the NPT and refused to sell enriched uranium to India after the 'peaceful' nuclear explosion of 1974. It urged India to complete its military operation in East Pakistan quickly since it could not prolong its support at the UN for the Indian action in opposition to Western pressure. There was an American – Soviet consensus after the Bangladesh War that India should be prevented from dismembering West Pakistan, and the Soviet leadership in Moscow routinely shrugged off repeated allegations by Indira Gandhi that the USA and its CIA were out to de-stabilize her government.

Such even-handed actions by the Soviet Union did not in any way discourage the many votaries in India for ever-more intimate ties with Moscow. Many in the Indian leadership, so attuned to vociferously supporting the Soviet position after nimbly abandoning their role as cheerleaders for the Chinese in the late 1950s, refused to discern that Moscow's support for India could never be functional outside the fundamental constraints and circumstances of the Cold War and US-Soviet-Chinese triangular rivalry. The idea that the Soviet Union would sell arms to Pakistan was considered heretical by people like Kaul in 1964, and they were as caustic to the dissenters and sceptics of this attitude as Nehru and Krishna Menon had been to those who had been suspicious about Chinese good intentions a decade earlier. The Indian foreign policy establishment's ability to manoeuvre was necessarily circumscribed, for it could not publicly criticize the only nation that it felt was sympathetic and could contain China. Accordingly, India did not condemn Soviet intervention in

Czechoslovakia in 1968 and abstained in the UN Security Council over the clauses condemning Moscow.

The Soviet Union had not sought to enter into any military alliances and obligations outside Europe, but its attitude changed after 1971 and Kissinger's and Nixon's visits to China. The Indo-Soviet Treaty of Friendship and Cooperation had been under negotiation for three years, but was brought swiftly to a conclusion in August 1971. The Treaty was not regarded as a deviation from non-alignment by the contracting parties, because the Soviet Union explicitly respected India's non-aligned policy in Article 1V, and each side undertook to abstain from providing any assistance to a third country that engaged in armed conflict with the other party. In the event of either side being subjected to an attack or a threat thereof, the parties were immediately to hold consultations in order to remove such a threat and to take appropriate effective measures to ensure peace and the security of their countries. According to its supporters, the treaty prevented conflicts between China and India, China and the Soviet Union and the Soviet Union and the USA during the Indo-Pakistan War for the liberation of Bangladesh, but the fact remained that the nature of such a treaty with one of the big powers was something of an anomaly for Indian non-alignment. In effect, at the UN Security Council during the debates on Bangladesh, India did not need to rely exclusively on the Soviet Union, since Britain and France normally abstained on any resolution critical of Indian involvement. Of even greater significance than the treaty was Soviet president Brezhnev's proposal in 1969 of an Asian Collective Security System under Soviet protection, which called for renunciation of use of force in international relations, respect for sovereignty and inviolability of borders, non-interference in the internal affairs of others, and cooperation with full equality and to mutual advantage. This was seen as a stratagem for the containment of China, and Beijing regarded it as encirclement by a Soviet-inspired strategic cordon. Pakistan, China's all-weather friend, played an important role in preventing that from happening. During his visit to India in 1973, Brezhnev made a final effort to enlist Indian support for this idea, but New Delhi rejected it because it would involve India in the Cold War, and was able to finesse Brezhnev by pointing out that it would run counter to Article 1V of the Indo-Soviet Treaty by which the Soviet Union had agreed to respect Indian non-alignment.

On Vietnam's Soviet-backed invasion of Cambodia to eject the Khmer Rouge in 1978, and the Soviet intervention in Afghanistan in 1979, India was studiously agnostic, and refrained scrupulously from any public condemnation. To its critics, the Indian government pleaded that friendly persuasion from amicable quarters would serve a better purpose to achieve a Soviet pull-out from Afghanistan than any condemnation by the international community, and there was no point in taking a stand that did not help to defuse a crisis. But such persuasion, even from friendly quarters, obviously led nowhere, as was entirely predictable. It is unlikely that Indira Gandhi herself believed that her muted counsel to Moscow would have any effect. In the end, it was to be the arrival of Gorbachev as General Secretary of the Communist Party that would lead to the Soviet withdrawal from 1989 onwards.

India did not need foreign bases or troops on its soil to maintain its territorial integrity and sovereignty, but it was in need of reliable partners for essential strategic imports and weapons. It was not entirely dependent on the Soviet Union, but Prime Minister Indira Gandhi could scarcely alienate a country like the Soviet Union that gave India defence supplies and technology at a time when the West, led by the USA, was heavily arming Pakistan, and in the process of undermining the Soviet Union in Afghanistan, was creating the monster that was to become Islamist terrorism. 'It's not that the Soviet Union loves us,' claimed Indira Gandhi candidly, 'but it's the weaker of the two superpowers and needs us more than we need them.'[81] Any reservations about Moscow's actions beyond USSR's borders could not be allowed to endanger the valuable asset of Indo-Soviet friendship. How this, and the 1971 Indo-Soviet Treaty of Friendship and Co-operation squared with non-alignment and the principle of judging each international issue on its merits was never explained; the only answer could have been the rationale of realpolitik. Over the Soviet intervention in Afghanistan, India fell out of step with world Islamic *ummah*, the international community as represented by the UN General Assembly, and the rest of South Asia. The plain fact was that India could not afford to displease the Soviet Union, and so compromised on its non-alignment policy, which was dispensable and had diminished in importance as the corner stone of Indian foreign policy. Soviet actions in Afghanistan were nothing less than a superpower invasion of a small non-aligned country that had been one of the founder members of the Non-Aligned Movement. Hypothetically, if India had joined the majority view of the non-aligned, it might have mitigated US alarm, kept the big powers out of South Asia, and even helped to extricate the USSR from the Afghan quagmire. More practically, it was the very first time Pakistan had been faced with a non-Indian threat, but India derived no advantage from that unique situation.

The United States

It rankled with India that the West did not provide support in the form of sufficient or consistent arms supplies after 1962, and tried to pressurize New Delhi to settle with Pakistan – though the Soviet Union did the same, with perhaps greater subtlety, after the Indo-Pakistan War of 1965. It was an article of faith in New Delhi that assistance from the socialist bloc was without strings, whereas Western help was not forthcoming, at least in the measure and on terms acceptable to India. For monetary aid and food supplies that were abundantly furnished from the West, from 'ship to mouth' as the saying went in the leanest years, Indian leaders claimed to be grateful though they rarely gave any public expression to that sentiment, and they were not prepared to modify their policies, which was interpreted by the West as a lack of proper appreciation and acknowledgement that rankled equally badly.

Therefore the relationship between India and the leader of the West, the USA, was at best lukewarm, and subject to periodic downturns approaching outright hostility, especially during the Nixon/Kissinger period of office in the early 1970s, and even with President Carter in the late 1970s . There were major Indo-US disagreements on Vietnam, Bangladesh, Cambodia and Afghanistan. New Delhi was happy to cite lists of complaints against USA – weapons to Pakistan, lack of support over the status of Kashmir, the cut-off of nuclear fuel for the Tarapore Power Plant in 1978, non-respect for the sovereignty and independence of other states, pressure on international and external policies, and dealings with states that were non-aligned, but not unfriendly, with the superiority complex of a sole superpower.

The USA also had its litany of complaints; Indian refusal to sign the Non-Proliferation Treaty, failure to criticize the Soviet Union over its interventions in Czechoslovakia and Afghanistan, and the removal of civil liberties during the emergency. The imagined existential threat from the Soviet Union was always good politics in Washington, and any country seen as proximate to Moscow was considered suspicious and unsympathetic, if not downright hostile. Nixon, in a reprise of Dulles' anger, was opposed to India's South Asian policies and wanted the US-Iran-Pakistan-China combine in 1971 to catch India in a security crunch. He cut economic and military aid to India in November 1971, and persistently urged China to indulge in troop movements on the border to bring pressure to bear on India to stop supporting the Bangladeshi liberation struggle against Pakistan. The USA may have been agnostic towards non-alignment after Dulles, but while the military aspects of the Cold War grew less with Moscow calling for détente and peaceful coexistence, political, economic and ideological rivalries were still sharp and affected Indo-US relations.

Nonetheless, there were also brighter moments in bilateral ties during the period; there was invaluable American assistance to India in the Green Revolution, and help to set-up Indian Institutes of Technology in the 1950s and India's first nuclear power station at Tarapur in the 1960s. In 1971 Kissinger told the Indian ambassador in Washington that the US understood and appreciated the non-alignment of India, and did not think that the Indo-Soviet Treaty of 1971 specifically violated non-alignment, though the American may have been dissembling for his own purposes. In 1980, the US agreed to resume fuel to Tarapur via France. Throughout these years, the United States remained India's leading trade partner. The arrival into power of modernizers like

Gorbachev in Moscow and Rajiv Gandhi in New Delhi changed the climate considerably with *perestroika* and *glasnost* in the Soviet Union, and the initial steps towards liberalization and globalization in India. This made India look more to the West for science and technology to drive forward the economic changes, while America agreed to supply a super computer (India was the first recipient after Japan) and some sensitive defence technology, and supported the Indian role, including forceful interventions, in Sri Lanka and Maldives. This implied that Washington was ready to recognize the primacy of India in its sub-region, and was willing to de-couple its ties with India from those with Pakistan.

Non-alignment as Indian Policy after Nehru

Nehru's death in 1964 did not create any ripples or misgivings in the Non-Aligned Movement, which held its second conference shortly after his death. Belgrade had not determined on any subsequent conference, and the summit in 1964 took place because Indonesia, supported by China, wanted to stage the tenth anniversary of Bandung in 1965, but excluding Yugoslavia. Sri Lanka and Egypt then set to work to preempt this with a second non-aligned conference at Cairo, and India essentially went along with the proposed summit. By this time, the Group of 77 had originated in 1962 at Cairo and the first UNCTAD had taken place in Geneva in 1964, both dominated by countries from the Third World. Many countries had become independent in the period from 1960 to 1964 during the emancipation of Africa by France and Britain, and now had a majority in the UN General Assembly, where something like a developing country bloc had emerged. It was due to this Third World majority at the UN that two special sessions of the UNGA were held on disarmament, and proposals like the unimplemented and unimplementable New International Economic Order and the New International Information Order came into discussion.

After Nehru, who was never enthusiastic about the creation of any third bloc, the Non-Aligned Movement for India became a mascot or ritual to be invoked by rote. The sophistication of

Nehru degenerated into meaningless formulae that acquired moralistic and pseudo-idealistic overtones. Nehru had wanted to engage the West and confine non-alignment to a few big issues like co-existence, peace and disarmament, and he would have been uneasy with the Non-Aligned Movement's subsequent anti-Western radicalism and neo-Marxist ideology. Radicalism in the movement was propelled by the assumption that the 'western democratic system is failing in every Asian and African country',[82] socialism was triumphing, and that the dependence of the West on oil when prices went up would give the whip-hand to producers of primary products. But a distortion was caused by the admiration for central planning as practiced in the Soviet Union, when state-controlled socialism came to be looked upon as a second emancipation. With policies driven by doctrinaire ideologies and their known sympathizers, planning was regarded as synonymous with controls, and the Indian economy became the most regulated one outside the communist bloc.

Other newly independent countries, being enthusiastic votaries the corporate ideology of the Non-Aligned Movement, were equally locked into rigid economic dogma and stifling statist systems, with controls over resources, suppression of private enterprise, corruption by politicians and bureaucrats, and a mindset that would not leave the Third World for decades. This slowed down their development and made it harder for them to adjust to an increasingly interdependent and globalized world. The leadership of the non-aligned countries was meanwhile taken up enthusiastically by Yugoslavia, which set itself up as the custodian and chief articulator of the imperishable principles of non-alignment's ideology.

After the Cairo Conference of 1964, which again left unspoken the need of any third such meeting, there was a pause of six years. During this interlude, India's bitter experience of 1962 was repeated by the complete lack of non-aligned support during its war with Pakistan in 1965. But unchastened, India continued to attend all the subsequent conferences, the third one taking place at Lusaka in 1970. Yugoslavia actively promoted this third conference, because it was fearful of isolation and any repetition of the Soviet Union's intervention in Czechoslovakia of 1968.

At Lusaka, the whole paraphernalia of hierarchy and bureaucracy was unleashed, including standing committees, ministerial consultations, ministerial conferences, regional item-specific cooperation groups and preparatory meetings, together with a cascade of ever-mounting paper work, that would forever dog the Non-Aligned Movement in the future. It was also determined at Lusaka that subsequent conferences would be convened at three-yearly intervals.

Accordingly, the Non-Aligned Movement assembled for its fourth conference in 1973 at Algiers. Algiers meant further radicalization. This summit, very pro-Soviet in character thanks to its host's ideological preferences and the presence of a strong socialist bloc at the meeting, claimed to reveal a consensus that was at variance with the internal and external policies of a considerable number of participating countries. OPEC had by then expanded into a powerful economic force, and the conference upheld the right of members to use raw materials and primary products as a weapon against the developed world. Non-alignment after Algiers would lay stress on condemnation of vested interests opposed to the progress of developing countries and the struggle for economic emancipation. The movement gave unqualified support to the principle of nationalization, but with the steep oil price rise, non-aligned OPEC countries callously let down the rest of the membership whereas the developed countries were able to cope much better with the inflated prices. A non-aligned coordinating bureau was set up, and it announced that 'any aggression against a nonaligned country would constitute aggression against all nonaligned countries',[83] a completely empty but typically hyperbolic declamation.

The fifth Non-Aligned Conference was held at Colombo in 1976, the first in Asia. The number of 'reservations' or registered formal disagreements with the agreed text, which had been in single figures at the past two summits, reached the level of 38. This reflected the mounting impatience and frustration among the conscientious objectors in the membership. Even on superpower détente, there was division in the ranks as to whether détente or its absence was the more dangerous. Some countries, moreover, even opposed the Helsinki process of security and cooperation in Europe. The sixth summit was at Havana in 1979. This was a most unhappy choice of venue for the Janata government in New Delhi trying to strive for greater even-handedness in its execution of a non-aligned policy. Members agreed that the co-ordinating bureau played a useful role at the UN to provide information and guidance to non-aligned countries, but basic differences on the definition and role of non-alignment emerged, and to paper over the cracks, resort was made to 'more a drafting exercise than a deliberative process',[84] with much repetition and reaffirming of all previous statements. The fundamental contradiction in non-alignment was that it was rapidly becoming a mere imitation of the two military blocs, an outcome that Nehru had correctly predicted. This came to a head at Havana where the movement's identification with the socialist Eastern bloc was finally affirmed, though a proposal by Cuba to declare socialist countries as the 'natural ally' of the Non-Aligned Movement was unsuccessful. Differences emerged even on what consensus meant, and the number of reservations mounted. Pakistan had made a bid for membership of the movement from 1962 onwards, and after the dissolution of SEATO and CENTO, appeared in the gathering at Havana as a full member for the first time.

Among those expressing disgust with the direction the movement was taking in Havana was Singapore's Prime Minister Lee Kwan Yew, who felt that subversion of non-aligned values had been going on unchecked for the past several years. He shared a general view that the movement had been brought to the brink of collapse by Soviet Trojan horses, and was unsure if the movement was worth preserving. In a booklet sponsored by the Singapore Foreign Ministry, the Havana summit was described as the lowest point of degradation, and India was asked to rescue the Non-Aligned Movement from the 'brothel area into which it had wandered'.[85] Nevertheless, Singapore may have downgraded the movement in its priorities but it did not, like all the other like-minded countries who shared the same belief to a greater or lesser extent, bother formally to withdraw. After the Soviet intervention in Afghanistan, the next few years saw the Non-Aligned Movement polarized with Cuba as its chairman, whose position was at variance with the non-aligned majority.

At home in India, the champions of the Soviet Union reigned

supreme and unchallenged during this period. Even the far Left, which had still only equated non-alignment with anti-imperialism and anti-racism, became more positive towards the country's non-aligned policy by the 1970s because India had drawn ever closer to the Soviet Union and the socialist bloc, and rejected the expeditionary impulses of the Western agenda. It was important for politicians and senior civil servants to display their open enthusiasm for the Soviet Union in order to progress in their careers. 'Even Indian Ambassador Kewal Singh,' records a bemused Indian journalist in Moscow at that time, 'began his official meetings in the Foreign Office with a 10-minute prelude to friendship each time he met a high official.'[86] In 1979, Jagat Mehta was dismissed as foreign secretary for being considered insufficiently committed to the Soviet Union and too pro-American by Prime Minister Charan Singh because the premier felt it was not good for the government's public image to have a putative American sympathizer as the foreign secretary before a general election. This was yet another Cold War fallacy, and it did not further Charan Singh's cause. Indira Gandhi won the election handsomely, and to no one's surprise, a two-year extension in an ambassadorial capacity that had been promised to Mehta by Charan Singh was promptly annulled by her. It was small wonder that diplomats and other civil servants and politicians who sought Indira Gandhi's favour either meekly followed a pro-Soviet line or chose to be the cheerleaders of it. 'Non-alignment accustomed us to a kind of blackmail leverage,' wrote Mehta, 'presuming on the West and tilting towards the East.'[87]

Pro-Soviet non-alignment, as it had been practiced by Indira Gandhi, was criticized as being lop-sided by the Bharatiya Jana Sangh, which was a constituent in the 1977 Janata government under Prime Minister Morarji Desai. Desai felt such a policy of non-alignment was only a sham if India was over-dependent on the Soviet Union for its economic and defence requirements, and set out promising a 'genuine' or 'equi-distant' non-alignment policy that would entertain more balanced relations with the two superpowers. He was supported in this endeavour by Foreign Minister Atal Behari Vajpayee and Foreign Secretary Jagat Mehta. The interjection of 'genuine' before non-alignment by the Morarji Desai government provoked speculation that this would mean India turning away from the Soviet Union and towards a pro-West stance, and reflected the common perception among its critics that non-alignment did not mean any independence of policy decision-making, but just the leveraging of blackmail. To New Delhi's chagrin, close neighbours like Nepal were looked upon as exponents of such cynical non-aligned opportunism in balancing the demands of India and China. Dutt had, a decade earlier, commented on this same trend:

> The King's policy is obviously to have some other friends on whom he could rely in case of serious difficulties with India. He is therefore seeking an outlet through Chinese territory by a new road to Lhasa and by establishing air service between Dacca and Kathmandu. His object is also to show India incidentally that he is an independent country and India's enemies are not his enemies. And both China and Pakistan are encouraging him in this direction.[88]

As it turned out, the 1977 election was only a small and temporary set-back for the pro-Soviet lobby. The Janata government of Desai's, once it took power, soon realized the imperative strategic requirement of close ties with Moscow. While Desai was able to avoid openly endorsing the Hafizullah Amin regime in Kabul, this was well understood by the Soviet leaders in Moscow who were themselves not very happy about the developments and policies pursued by the Amin communists in Afghanistan. And on the other hand, the fierce nationalism of Morarji Desai did not allow him to accede to the USA's pressure, exerted personally by President Carter that India sign up to the Non-Proliferation Treaty.

India had showed no interest in hosting a non-aligned conference until New Delhi was brought in as a stop-gap. The seventh summit was to be in Baghdad, but the Iran-Iraq war made that venue an impossibility. While lamenting the irony that two non-aligned countries were fighting each other, the movement gratefully accepted New Delhi's offer to step into the breach. Like its earlier manifestations, the conference proved to be 'no more than an exercise in consensus drafting'.[89] India did its utmost to prevent any criticism of the Soviet Union in Afghanistan or of Vietnam in Cambodia, even obfuscating the topics under the headings of South-West Asia and South-East Asia, in contrast to headline prominence given to Mayotte and Malagasy Islands; and the final document resorted to calling vaguely for withdrawal, non-interference and non-intervention in the internal and external affairs of states. The Non-Aligned Movement by 1983 was in evident and considerable disarray, and Jaipal concluded that 'the capacity of the non-aligned to serve . . . as a bridge between the two military blocs has diminished to the point of no return'.[90] For India after the 1962 War, when all its problems could not be attributed to the West's imperialist machinations, foreign policy expended considerable time and effort in search of an elusive non-aligned consensus. There were no more exclusive Indian victories to be claimed for its non-alignment policy as there had been before the movement came into existence, since those had been due primarily to Jawaharlal Nehru's personal efforts, charisma and mediation.

The policy of military alliances such as SEATO and CENTO had arguably proved a failure in the containment of communism, but the Non-Aligned Movement was equally to have no success in breaking the mould of the two power blocs, and played no role in the eventual disbanding of SEATO in 1977 or CENTO two years later. Those developments had more to do with Turkish Cyprus and the Ayatollah revolution in Iran. The Non-Aligned Movement was reduced to being only a bystander or pressure group; decolonization was almost over, but the arms race continued, even among the non-aligned. There were conflicts between the non-aligned themselves, and superpower attacks against the non-aligned as in Afghanistan, Grenada and Lebanon. As a self-appointed guardian of peace, the movement stood exposed, while slogans of anti-colonialism and anti-imperialism became a pretext for anti-Western attitudes. Yet, there was no point in flogging a dead horse, as Nehru had foreseen as far back as 1961. 'A kind of intellectual vested interest had taken root in the presumed permanence of the Cold War',[91] and the movement failed to grasp the implications of superpower détente which was its own declared goal. The Non-Aligned Movement did not introspect on the implications of the militarization of the Third

World and its external dependence, and verbal solidarity and drafting gamesmanship became the all-important preoccupation. The movement professed to be based on principles, but carried no moral authority, and it had become ineffective and ritualistic.

The receipt of foreign aid had softened the determination for self-sufficiency and efforts for economic development, improved infrastructure and food security, while dependence on the old metropolitan centres intensified. Third World-designed institutions for cooperation like the East African Community disintegrated, as did the once-respected Yugoslavia–UAR–India non-aligned troika. The economic interests of the non-aligned were vastly diverse; there was little scope for tri-continental South-South cooperation, no discussion on a separate energy affiliate, and OPEC countries in fact became the main conduit of resources from the poor developing world flowing into the coffers of the rich developed world. The Non-Aligned Movement was ideologically amorphous and suffered contradictions and even internal wars. Its ability to heal international conflict issues was shown to be zero. It had no effect in inter-non-aligned quarrels, let alone in Cold War conflicts in Vietnam, Afghanistan, South-West Africa or Central America. These issues could not be dealt with selectively, so they were not addressed at all. Communism could not be denounced by democracies playing the China card, or capitalism by countries in hock to the IMF or IBRD. The non-aligned wagon was hitched to the Cold War which proved to be only a temporary aberration. Within the movement, unlike at the UN, there was no way of expressing dissent, no negative vote and no abstention: there were only the multitude of reservations that no one bothered with or remembered, and were never circulated along with other non-aligned summit documents at the United Nations. This gave an opportunity for non-aligned nations to adopt one view in the movement and quite another in diplomatic practice.

Even the assertion that the Non-Aligned Movement speeded up decolonization was open to some question, because the greatest help to liberation movements came from outside the movement. It may have assisted in the isolation of white minority rule in Rhodesia, South West Africa and South Africa, but the apartheid regimes were brought to an end by the fall of the Portuguese Empire and the end of the Cold War. The movement did not lead to the weakening of military blocs or removal of bases – indeed, members of blocs and hosts of bases were permitted to join the movement – and the dependency of Third World countries on one or other of the superpower blocs continued and even increased. The non-aligned countries could not expect respect from others if they showed no respect for non-alignment themselves. Despite the rhetoric, there was never any collective self-defence. Non-aligned countries had long suffered from a crisis of identity: while the movement's objectives were universalistic, the movement's summit declarations showed that regionalism superseded universalism with narrow agendas. 'It is a tired movement badly in need of rejuvenation', lamented one of its leading Indian participants, Rikhi Jaipal, as early as 1983.[92]

He was not the only one; other voices added to the chorus of lamentation. From the mid 1980s onwards, 'the non aligned movement was fading';[93] 'multilateral organizations and arrangements among the developing countries were losing their utility and sense of purpose such as . . . the non aligned movement';[94] 'the cohesion and political relevance of the movement as it existed was in the process of disintegration';[95] the 'unity of NAM was getting eroded';[96] and the movement 'diminished in influence'.[97] After the demolition of the Berlin Wall, the Non-Aligned Movement also came down to earth at Belgrade in 1989 with a 10-page declaration of basic principles and final documents circulated at the UN of 153 pages, as opposed to the 332 pages produced by the previous summit at Harare in 1986.

As for India, it gamely continued to mouth the same slogans as before, despite repeated painful experiences in the conferences. During the Janata period, India's credibility, image and influence in the movement may have diminished, but there was no tangible balancing benefit in response from the USA and the West, who no longer took the movement seriously. When an Indian participant in the Indo-US dialogue of 1982–4 claimed that 'genuine non-alignment' was tautologous, like 'honest truth',[98] because it did not mean equidistance from the two superpowers, this was considered as nothing other than a feeble justification for an unspoken alliance with the Soviet Union. Moscow felt comfortable with the movement since it gave the USSR unstinting support at little cost or effort, and it was more credible than other Soviet-sponsored front organizations such as the Afro-Asian Peoples Solidarity Organization. Repeated neighbourhood problems for India had showed that non-alignment was not a safeguard or barrier against aggression, and in the movement there was no support for Indian nuclear weapon status and some strong resistance to it. Despite the obvious diminishing returns, lip-service and obeisance had to be paid to non-alignment in India as a legacy of the great leader Nehru, and critics and sceptics were not to be countenanced; after the New Delhi summit, a critical assessment of the non-alignment policy by Jagat Mehta was rejected by the editors of the journal of the India International Centre in New Delhi, who did not wish to risk the displeasure of the authorities.

III. THE AGE OF OPPORTUNISM

In November 1989, the Berlin Wall was pulled down, and the border separating East from West Germany was effectively opened. Nationalist movements strengthened in Eastern Europe, and emerged in Georgia, Ukraine, Moldova, Belorussia, and the Central Asian republics. The power of the Soviet central government was considerably weakened by these movements because it could no longer rely on the cooperation of communist leaders in the Union's republics. The situation came to a head in August 1991. In a last-ditch effort to save the Soviet Union, which was floundering under the impact of the political movements that had emerged since Gorbachev's *glasnost*, a group of hard-line communists staged a *coup d'état* by kidnapping Gorbachev, and announcing he was ill and would no longer be able to govern. The country went into an uproar; massive protests were staged in Moscow, Leningrad, and many of the other major cities of the Soviet Union. When the coup organizers tried to bring in the military to quell the protestors, the soldiers themselves rebelled and would not fire on their fellow countrymen. After three days of protests, the coup leaders surrendered, realizing that without the cooperation of the military, they did not have the power to control the country. After the failed coup attempt, the Soviet Union collapsed. The population would accept nothing less than democracy; Gorbachev conceded power and resigned. In December 1991, the Union of Soviet Socialist Republics disintegrated into fifteen separate countries and in its place, a new entity called the Commonwealth of Independent States, composed of most of the independent countries of the former Soviet Union, was formed.

The Cold War had come to an end with a whimper after forty years and the entire rationale of the Non-Aligned Movement needed to be re-examined. India had lost the leverage of having a superpower constantly positioned on its side in moments of crisis, and was obliged at the same time to adjust itself to globalization and free market economies, and to new Western-dominated norms for environment and human rights. A new international order had been brought about, not through international consensus, nor external mediation by a group not affiliated to either bloc, but by powerful countries in the West led by the United States. For India, there was equally no wide consensus at home on how to react to this dramatic change in the world landscape. Ideological rigidity on the part of elements in the Indian political leadership, parliament, policy think tanks and the media also seriously and adversely affected the ability of New Delhi to assess the implications of these developments for the policy of non-alignment.

During and after the attempted coup against Gorbachev in 1991 by his erstwhile colleagues Defence Minister Yazov, Vice-President Yanayev, the KGB's Kruschkov and five others, derisively called the 'Gang of Eight', the Indian apologists for the Soviet Union were greatly disoriented and totally unable to suggest any new moorings for Indian foreign policy. Non-alignment 'will have to be adapted to the changing world situation from time to time . . . India is somewhat concerned,' wrote T.N. Kaul in a masterpiece of under-statement in 1992, 'but unable to exert much influence through the non-aligned movement.'[99] During Gorbachev's brief ouster in the communist coup, the

Indian ambassador in Moscow, A.S. Gonsalves, ludicrously protested that 'India cannot be party to the break-up of the Soviet Union', – but India could in fact do nothing about it, and still less could the Non-Aligned Movement. Rejection of the West had become second nature among Indian politicians and policy makers, both of the Left and the Right, and also among the circles of the traditional Hindu moralists. The old independent spirit of decolonization and the freedom struggle had by then degenerated into knee-jerk anti-Western attitudes, stoked by laughable allegations such as Indira Gandhi's paranoia and repeated warnings of a 'foreign hand'. Although as the successor state of the Soviet Union, the Russian Federation was gravely weakened, its former ally India was both unwilling and unable to let its former engagement with the Soviet Union wither away completely, though the previous lofty rhetoric and ideological commitment were now clearly passé.

Post-1991, Russia inherited the Indian debt, and Indian links were focused on Moscow because other states in the CIS were relatively unknown to Indian technicians and businessmen. The dismal Russian story was one of dislocation, fall in production, inflation, capital flight, underemployment, corruption, privatization, shock therapy, currency depreciation, social decay, mafia, organized crime, Chechen unrest, the financial wrench of 1998, revaluation of the rouble, the recovery before the global downturn of 2007–8, and the depredations of grasping oligarchs. The wonder is that the social decay and the pervasive sense of futility did not lead to a revival of Soviet-style communism, which would certainly have been met with profound relief and satisfaction among the political leadership and intellectual circles in New Delhi.

Despite these uncertainties, the pronounced new pro-Western tilt in Moscow and the initial lack of any coherent strategy by the Indian authorities, and despite the prevailing chaos, there remained one stable factor; the persistent role of the Russian state. This gave India an opportunity for innovation, and previous associations with Soviet technology helped India laboriously to pick up the threads. Military cooperation post-1991 proved essential to the future relationship, and trade and economic ties continued, though diminished in scale. The agreement to settle Indian debts to Russia as the successor state of the USSR over the period of 1993–2005 was important to the recovery of ties, and the export of Russian armaments to India gained momentum to exceed considerably what had existed before the demise of the Soviet Union.

India had clearly been caught on the wrong foot by the events in the USSR from 1989 to 1991; it had been wilfully ignorant of the domestic resistance to the Soviet Communist Party. Both the Moscow and New Delhi governments were unadventurous, and the new Russians took pains to prevent any return to past patterns, but Indian middlemen, non-resident in Russia and India, were essential in the rebuilding process: they had access to offshore funds and were not tied down by restrictive Indian regulation. Indian investment in Russian oil and gas exploration also played some part in creating new links. Although trade figures did not much change and remained unimpressive, the previous Indian public sector contacts, and the demand for spare parts by the armed forces provided some stability and a basic framework, while servicing the Indian debt extended a substantial subsidy for exports. The Indian customer was an important factor that enabled some Russian industries to survive, and as far as the arms production units in Russia were concerned, Indian orders threw them a life-line, since they were not obliged to adjust to the market economy as did other parts of the Russian economy – the state still controlled 80 per cent of the armaments industry. India helped Russia to emerge as a major player in the arms marketplace, some new bi-national projects were undertaken, and supplies and spares could be sourced from third parties like Israel. After 2000, Russian economic recovery was led by the oil and gas sector, and the state gradually increased its capacity to direct the economy, at the same time dealing firmly with those who challenged its authority.

During the Yeltsin years, Foreign Minister Kozyrev was as profoundly indifferent to ties with India as had been his predecessor Shevardnadze, and the Russian veto in the UN Security Council to protect Indian interests became highly problematic and too dependent on the personal whims of the Russian permanent representative to the United Nations. Various other fundamental Indian assumptions had also collapsed by middle of the 1990s. There was the flowering of an US-China friendship. The Chinese economy was growing fast and eclipsing even the GDP growth of the developed countries. Developing countries were often pitted against each other in conflicts in the Third World. The state socialist model came under severe stress, and the South-East Asian economic prototype became the new paradigm. The UN, with its pronounced developing country majority, came to be a hate-figure among the US conservative lobby although paradoxically the collapse of the Soviet Union led to US dominance in the world body, leading to humanitarian interventions and the installation of neo-protectorates and blatant abuses of state sovereignty. There was no effective collective bargaining by the G-77 in GATT/WTO because there were too many divisive regional or sector-specific interests. India's previous activism in the Non-Aligned Movement was a thing of the past; it may have once generated some political goodwill for India in the Third World, but it was intangible and could not be translated into any practical benefits.

In the late 1980s, Prime Minister Rajiv Gandhi, claiming the inheritance of Jawaharlal Nehru and Indira Gandhi, had tried to forge a new role for India. His ideas were not innovative and were wrapped in the vestments of the past on the environment, disarmament, and South-South cooperation, and this was basically a tinkering around the edges of a presumed new assertiveness. Non-alignment as a sensible power play, the best route for promoting a diplomatic presence from a weak position, conferring an international profile on India as leader of the newly decolonized, and as an enabling mechanism for economic assistance from both camps, were credible theses during Nehru's time and even, in a greatly diminished manner, in the age of realism, but after the end of the Cold War, such arguments could hardly be sustained or make sense. The Third World was itself a construct of the Cold War, but the Second World had collapsed in ruins, and these new circumstances had to force a change from collective identification with the Third World to an opportunist promotion of India's own interests. Standing up to the West in the name of the Third World was now old hat; there was no traction in Third World trade unionism and none at all in non-alignment. Unless it shed its old ideological baggage, India faced a long slide in both economic and diplomatic terms.

India's initial reaction to the dramas following 1989 was that non-alignment was still valid, but the Congress party leadership tried to come up with some face-saving alternatives in the event that the movement fell apart through massive defections, since any overt break-away from Nehru's foreign policy ideas, even without formally rejecting them, would have caused uproar domestically. Prime Minister Narasimha Rao summoned a meeting of senior serving and retired foreign service officers and assorted 'intellectuals' to opine on the subject to enable him to chart a way forward, but the exercise was not productive. All those present proved inflexibly wedded to the past clichés and strongly pressed for the continuation of an active role by India in the Non-Aligned Movement. The lone exception was Brajesh Mishra, a former ambassador and then a member of the BJP, who was later to be the National Security Adviser, but even in that subsequent policy-making position, he was unwilling or unable to translate his thoughts into action.

The Indian analysts in decisive government positions said that even if there were no longer two blocs, non-alignment would still be relevant because it had concerns other than just bloc politics; namely socio-economic development and peace and equity in inter-state relations. 'From 1989 onwards the unity, cohesion and influence of the Non-Aligned Movement declined substantially', but 'we should lead the way to reorient the focus of . . . the non-aligned to form a network of like-minded countries'.[100] All that was necessary, apparently, was to refocus the non-aligned movement and carry on as before. There should be a new stress on economics in the making of foreign policy, taking the cue from China. India, it was claimed, could not disown the foreign policy of the past in the same way that it could not disown its previous socialistic economic policies. Therefore, there was no formal distancing from the Non-Aligned Movement, and the crucial moment to take a hard decision to make a clean break with the past was lost. But there was a shift in emphasis nevertheless; in some election manifestos during and after the 1990s, neither the BJP nor the Congress parties made any mention of non-alignment as a principal feature of foreign policy. A former senior civil servant wrote sadly that 'the former non-alignment is heard but no longer a major force',[101] and another, that 'we have hardly taken any initiative within the non-aligned movement, have taken a back seat in Cambodian negotiations, and have been unable to become a member of the three-nation steering group at the G-15 meeting at Kuala Lumpur'.[102]

The 1989 ninth non-aligned summit at Belgrade noted that: 'the world is at the cross-roads; tension is no longer at breaking point, but neither is peace stable; stagnation is not general but neither is development. While there may be reason for hope, there is no cause for undue optimism.' The fruits of science and technology had not served the cause of 'freedom, independence and national identity', and non-aligned countries' 'basic interests . . . demand that we play an active and direct role in the management of world affairs'.[103] This seemed to be an appeal for continued solidarity in the Non-Aligned Movement, and friendless Burma even rejoined the movement in 1992, but obviously belittled rather than added value to the organization. The tenth summit at Djakarta in 1992 was the first Non-Aligned Conference after the Soviet Union's break up, and by then, most countries' participation in the Non-Aligned Movement was *pro forma*. The truth was that multilateralism in the shape of such forums like the Non-Aligned Movement had become progressively irrelevant by the turn of the century.

At Djakarta, India, still looking for a role, suggested an amended agenda of nuclear disarmament and weapons of mass destruction, an equitable trading regime, and uniting against terrorism, violence and extremism to contest a new world order that was unequal and discriminating. The disintegration of Yugoslavia into several independent republics, and scant interest from Latin America vitiated the atmosphere, leaving the form but no substance. Narasimha Rao's statement at the summit that 'the movement has a strength derived from solidarity' was comically absurd. Nothing could have been further from the truth. India had been in the forefront for global disarmament and pressure on the two superpowers to end the arms race, but now it was involved in an arms race in South Asia with Pakistan, which soon was to include the possession of nuclear weapons. At the twelfth summit at Durban in 1998, most member countries were displeased with Indian nuclear weapon testing, and New Delhi had its work cut out to water down a draft text prepared by the host South Africa that specifically denounced the tests.

Non-alignment for New Delhi had become prosaic; it was no longer the reason for bombast or self-congratulation. It is difficult to see why India strove so hard to keep the Non-Aligned Movement alive other than because of the customary governmental inertia. Continued participation in the movement served no national purpose when the body's main exhortations were to counter the strains imposed by globalization – from which India had benefited more than most other countries despite its halting and incomplete economic reforms. Only the customary obfuscation and drafting legerdemain saved the movement from a large split, defections and collapse. The consensus decisions of non-alignment were weaker even than the majority resolutions adopted by the UN General Assembly on same issues, and there was nothing India could accomplish through the movement's periodic conferences that it could not achieve through any other international institution. And there were a decreasing number of volunteers to host the summits, illustrated by the fact that Iran is to be the host in 2012, a venue likely to inspire a poor attendance at the summit. Belgrade, the capital of Yugoslavia, now sadly reduced to the rump of Serbia, hosted a low-profile ministerial-level gathering in 2011 to mark the fiftieth anniversary of the first Non-Aligned Conference in 1961, though ironically, Serbia was excluded from the movement in 1995, and is no longer a full member but only an observer. This decision by Belgrade has incurred the wrath of even top officials of the ruling political party in that country. The head of the Serbian parliament's foreign affairs committee said the decision to host the meeting should be reviewed since Serbia no longer needed to identify with Third World countries as its ties were being strengthened with Europe and the movement had little to contribute to Serbia's quest for integration with the European Union. So even the anniversary of the birth of the Non-Aligned Movement at its original venue became intensely controversial.

After the triumph of the Muslim *jihadists* over the Soviet Union in Afghanistan in 1989, Pakistan became much more aggressive towards India. And when Islam's troubles with the West and Islamist terror against India reached centre-stage, there was the rise of Hindutva in India which affected domestic politics, and resulted in BJP governments in the federal centre and in many states. China had now become the second most important world power, economically and politically, and remained always doubtful about India, especially since New Delhi voiced opposition to a G-2 comprising USA and China. In this unpromising international climate, India had to move 'from its past emphasis on the power of the argument to a new stress on the argument of power'.[104] In the immediate aftermath of the Cold War, India had to reckon with a sole superpower dominating international politics, but its relations with the USA were weak. It was natural that the dominance of the USA created a sense of unease in India, and the pursuit of a multi-polar world was the only alternative to alliance with, or opposition to, Washington. To counter the leadership of the West in global affairs, closer ties between Moscow, Beijing and New Delhi were sponsored by the now orphaned pro-Soviet lobby in India, people who thought India's interests were impossible to reconcile with the USA. The attempt was to obviate or constrain a uni-polar political world – but foreign policy experts knew that each of the three capitals really wanted to forge a special relationship bilaterally with the USA, and the triangle was only to leverage a better claim with Washington. All three countries realized that they could not make material progress in opposition to the USA, and were careful not to make the triangle look anti-American.

The various later aggregations like the Brazil-Russia-India-China, Brazil-South Africa-India-China, India-Brazil-South Africa groupings, and others in Asia like the Mekong-Ganga Cooperation and the Bay of Bengal Initiative did not serve the purpose of creating any new pole around which elements disgruntled with the United States could find any comfort; at best these were issue-based alliances. The G-15 was only an enabling mechanism to interact with the G-7 and for North-South cooperation, and did not even serve these objectives. Abstract battles over ideologies gave way to strategic partnerships over issues like terrorism. In the end, building a new relationship with the USA was the only answer, together with closer ties with the second tier of countries like France. To safeguard and promote Indian interests, it was essential for India to create new commonalities of interests with Washington, and while some Indian representatives to international organizations still chose to indulge in the archaic language of the world prior to 1989, especially on human rights and state sovereignty, these commonalties were found in the development of peaceful uses of nuclear energy, access to new technologies, the growth of the Indian software industry and the Western fears of the rise of an unpredictable China. Many of the leading champions and beneficiaries of the erstwhile Indo-Soviet connection made haste to cast off their worn-out ideological clothing and suddenly discovered exceptional virtues in cultivating Washington.

To what extent was Indian non-alignment ever even-handed? The policy was termed 'bridgemanship' by writers Murthy and Shrivastava,[105] but in truth it had little to do with building any bridges between the blocs, and its strongest advocates could not make any sustainable claims to even-handedness. In practice, although Indira Gandhi described the non-alignment grouping as the world's biggest peace movement, it was never that, and it was not 'bridgemanship' either. There was never any attempt at a policy of equidistance between the two blocs, no attempt at establishing credibility as an interlocutor both with Moscow and Washington, and the Non-Aligned Movement generated overwhelming anti-Western rhetoric in its successive meetings. It was always claimed by Indian spokesmen that the reason for the criticism of the West and not the Soviet bloc was the latter's support against colonialism and racism, its assistance to developing countries, support for the Palestinians and a new economic order. The movement's close identity with the Soviet Union allowed Kabul to retain its seat in the movement during the Soviet invasion, but not Kampuchea, a founder member, during the Vietnam occupation.

New Delhi accepted the Hallstein doctrine of 1955 for a long time before it recognized the East German Democratic Republic in 1972, despite mutual irritation and occasional distrust between New Delhi and Bonn between 1954 and 1966, on the pretext that recognition would jeopardize the prospects of German re-unification though the real cause was to protect the economic relationship with the Federal Republic of Germany. There are few other instances of any sympathy towards the Western position in matters relating to the Cold War. There were certainly some high officials in the Foreign Office who were uncomfortable with the pro-Soviet inclination; among them are variously cited Girija Shankar Bajpai, Subimal Dutt, Rajeshwar Dayal, Badruddin Tyabji and Jagat Mehta, but their remonstrance had finite limits within the constraints of their careers, and their objections were easily over-ruled by the cohorts of genuine and counterfeit admirers of the Soviet Union among the ranks of ministers and officials. Assertions of any independence of opinion in New Delhi departing openly from the Soviet line are infrequent; among these were Nehru's remaining in the Commonwealth of Nations which was dominated by Britain until the early 1960s; Nehru's opposition to Khrushchev's plan in 1958 to declare Berlin as a free and demilitarized city; his support for Hammarskjold against Khrushchev's fulminations and the Soviet proposal to replace the UN secretary-general with a troika – one representative from each bloc and one from the neutral countries; his departure from the Soviet line in newly-independent Congo; his opposition to the 1961 Soviet nuclear testing; India's opening diplomatic relations with Malaysia in 1963 despite Soviet opposition to the formation of Malaysia; and, in the post-Nehru period under Indira Gandhi, the final negative reaction in 1973 to Brezhnev's 1969 plan for Asian collective security under the Soviet umbrella.

The Soviet Union's concerns and reservations about Indian policies have been cited earlier. Its open criticism of non-alignment and Indian positions are even fewer. Dutt records two instances when Moscow was less than happy with India. The first was in 1961, when the Soviet Union was disappointed with the outcomes of the Belgrade Non-Aligned Conference. The Soviet

Union was cold towards the non-aligned summit's appeal, carried personally by Nehru and Nkrumah, that Khruschev and Kennedy should meet, rejecting the utility of bilateral talks and any restraint on nuclear testing while asserting that the latter was a matter of Soviet self-defence. Dutt, who was present at the talks Khruschev held with Nehru and Nkrumah, recorded Khruschev as saying, 'non-aligned nations have not expressed themselves sufficiently strongly, always trying to hold the balance', because 'US and West Germany tempting with offers of aid'.[106] And the second incident was later in the same year. Dutt's diary entry reads:

> Saw Firyubin [Soviet deputy foreign minister] at his request. He read out a note referring to PM's [Nehru] television speech at New York and called it unfriendly and not in accordance with facts. PM in a television discussion with Adlai Stevenson said that in Eastern European countries parties had taken over power aided by outside elements. There was strong pressure on the people, but it was not colonialism. This was the first time within my knowledge when Soviet government has lodged a protest.[107]

There was no need of any definition of non-alignment during Jawaharlal Nehru's lifetime, since the author of the concept embodied and personified the policy with his every action in international affairs. After Nehru's death, the Congress government until 1977 hallowed Nehru's name and imposed on the policy a doctrine, a theology and even ascribed divine origins to what was essentially an instrument of international manoeuvring, even as Indian policies and the Non-Aligned Movement tilted strongly to the Soviet Union as a 'natural ally'. Whether Nehru would have concurred with this description of one of the two superpowers is a moot point.

In the final analysis, the Indian non-aligned policy was nothing more or less than the practice of an old-fashioned balance of power. Pakistan was always a factor for India from the earliest days of independence, and working with Pakistan would have been problematic were India to have showed inclinations of cooperating closely with the Western camp. Western support for

Pakistan on the status of Kashmir inclined India psychologically towards any non-Western pole. One was available with the Soviet Union after the death of Stalin. Nehru would dearly have liked China to have been in the same camp, but the Sino-Soviet and Sino-Indian problems which surfaced in the 1950s made that prospect unthinkable. After the Cold War, there were feeble attempts by non-aligned loyalists in the government and academia to redefine a policy that was anachronistic and irrelevant, meaningless and at times farcical. The changing world had moved on, and the new times called for non-ideological opportunism by New Delhi.

In practice, India was probably too big, and with too long a history of being invaded and colonized, to risk its new-found independence by any formal attachment to another state. But the high priesthood of non-alignment was anxious to imbue it with more lofty philosophical attributes. A former Indian diplomat wrote, 'it seems to bear the imprint of the cultural tradition which tends to express many positive values and actions in negative terminology'.[108] Nehru was himself not guiltless in this endeavour to establish a canon; he said, 'I have not originated non-alignment; it is a policy inherent in . . . India, in the conditioning of the Indian mind,'[109] adding, 'there was no Cold War in Ashoka's heart.'[110] It was claimed, with no historical evidence in support, that India had always stood for morality and principles, together with completely irrelevant references to idealism, non-violence, Buddha, Ashoka, Gandhi and even Islam. One of many purveyors of such nonsense was Rikhi Jaipal who in his book on non-alignment cites far-fetched and ancient analogies like Indian cultural roots, Buddhism, the caste system, and even non-aligned 'sources' from the third century BC. It is improbable that such assertions were found convincing by any but the most credulous.

Nevertheless, ancient India doubtless did have a larger atheistic and agnostic literature than any other classical civilization, and an Indian tradition of ambiguity in the face of eternity can be traced back as far as the *Rigveda*, which enshrines at its centre the idea of uncertainty about the divine. 'Who really knows?' it asks, 'Who will here proclaim it? Whence was it produced? Whence is this creation? Perhaps it formed itself, perhaps it did not. The one who looks down on it from the highest heaven, only he knows – or perhaps he does not know.'[111] The strange mix of spirituality and skepticism is thus rooted in a very ancient strand of Hindu agnostic thought.

Loyalists seized on this agnosticism to buttress their argument; thus, non-alignment was not negative, not neutrality, not isolationism, not passive, not indifference, not impartial, not plague on both your houses, not moral or virtuous, not idealistic, not exclusive, not ideological. The negative in the term 'non-alignment' was itself unusual and even unique in the international epistemology. Rajiv Gandhi decreed the use of the word 'nonalignment' without any hyphen, apparently to mitigate the negativity, but he was unable to circumvent the rules of grammar.

Nehru had said that India's foreign policy was so simple that even a *ekkawala* [driver of a one-horse-drawn cart] in Lucknow could claim to understand it, but Gundevia, who quotes Nehru's dictum,[112] then spends a full chapter in an attempt to explain and defend it. Non-alignment meant the rise of a new political factor in the world, 'an unusual phenomenon in world politics that cannot be understood within the confines of the traditional approaches in international politics',[113] and its very ambiguity gave it traction and academic respectability.

Morality was considered to be an essential part of Indian nonalignment; this was obligatory for a nation of Gandhi's putative followers. The pre-Independence thinking of Congress leaders who fought for Indian Independence was held to be idealistic and moralistic. It was Nehru's view, said such theorists, that the USA did not have the moral standing to lead the world. This naturally leads to the question whether he found the Soviet Union, of Stalin's brutal purges and forceful foreign interventions in what it considered to be its sphere of interest, endowed with moral qualities. A moral compass does not make for good foreign policy nor serve a national purpose, and whether in Nehru's time or thereafter, the high-flown exhortations from New Delhi served to infuriate India's critics but did not actually determine the nature of Indian priorities.

Nehru himself rarely used the term 'non-alignment', regarding it as having passive and negative connotations. He did not favour the term 'positive neutrality' either, but preferred 'keeping aloof from blocs' or following an 'independent policy'. Non-alignment was not pacifism, and not even non-interference in the internal affairs of others, and therefore it was hard to define in spite of the chorus of words used in the effort by experts and non-experts. It was equally hard, of course, to identify the breaches of non-alignment. Once again, Nehru did not assist matters. 'We mean,' he said in 1958, 'non-alignment with military blocs,'[114] but he went on to claim, 'we are free to join an alliance'[115] . . . 'an alliance . . . need not stand in the way of independence of the country,'[116] and he further said in Parliament on 9 December 1958, that his policy could be described as 'acting according to our best judgement'. This seemed to suggest that no objective or impartial assessment of a country's non-alignment was ever possible, and it could only be a subjective consideration. Even the Janata Party in 1977 could not produce a more 'genuine' version of the policy; nor even an alternative or accurate definition.

What Nehru did not, or could not, do, the Non-Aligned Movement could hardly have done any better. Basically, non-alignment was to introduce an independent, open-ended and democratic approach to international affairs, though the movement vitiated these very principles. Perhaps, driven by the legitimate fear of divisions in its ranks, it never cared to define itself. The Belgrade conference in 1961 stated that non-aligned nations did 'not wish to form a new bloc and cannot be a bloc'. So non-alignment was left to mean non-conformity and all things to all men, and the qualifications for granting admissions to new members did not convey any clear guidance either. And people like Kaul, the senior Indian diplomat, further muddied the waters by claiming that non-alignment was not itself a policy, only part of a policy, posture or attitude, rather than a policy attributed to Nehru.[117]

Outlandish claims made for the policy of non-alignment led to some interpretations that belonged to the theatre of the absurd rather than the sphere of inter-governmental relations. In a book edited by former Foreign Secretary M. Rasgotra it is suggested that the Cold War and bloc politics were not the sole reference points for non-alignment since the policy pre-dated 1940, at which date, it is claimed, the Cold War came into force.[118] It goes on to say that China opted for a policy of its own form of non-alignment after 1982.[119] Jaipal, who never shrinks from the most extreme and untenable of contradictions, states that 'the fact that different practitioners of non-alignment are in actual practice beholden to one or the other superpower . . . is a reflection of the . . . respect displayed for their non-aligned status.'[120]

In the practice of his foreign policy Nehru was a realist, though he publicly articulated his ideas in the vocabulary of idealism. Moralism and idealism became internalized in his own country, and contributed hugely in obfuscating the reality. Brajesh Mishra asserted that 'in the post-Nehru period, non-alignment became a mantra just as Gandhiji's non-violent struggle became the "moral path"; the fact that these policies were grounded in strict rationality and realpolitik was lost sight of'.[121] Jaipal concurred; his book on non-alignment is full of pseudo-philosophical cant and religious allusions, but he is forced to conclude that 'to be non-aligned is to be no more virtuous or meritorious than to be aligned'.[122]

The non-aligned policy as practiced by Jawaharlal Nehru was within a short space of time superseded by, and subsumed in, the Non-Aligned Movement. The development of the movement was intended to prevent the threatened division of the world into two or more antagonistic blocs and spheres of influence, and to create an environment for the reduction of international tensions. But non-alignment thereafter lost its individuality as a nation's specific option of decision and action, which disappeared in a miasma of group declarations and rhetoric without consequence or result. As the architect and embodiment of non-alignment, Nehru was never enthusiastic about its transformation into any formal Non-Aligned Movement, and he was opposed to a secretariat and institutionalization because that would convey the impression of a third bloc. The 1961 conference, the only one attended by Nehru himself, was supposedly an *ad hoc* exceptional gathering. Nehru envisaged a non-aligned policy that was not rigid, doctrinaire or dogmatic, and his fears about the future rationale of any movement proved to be more than fully justified. As the numbers of the non-aligned countries grew (and the Organization of African Unity declared in 1963 that all its members were *de facto* non-aligned) and the Non-Aligned Movement, complete with capital letters, became an institutional reality in the 1970s, the movement became ideological and identified closely with the Soviet Union in the Cold War.

Nehru's ideas in principle were robust – to take aid from the West and multilateral sources, and engage in healthy economic, trade, investment and technology relationships with both camps. With no charter or constitution, no rules of business, no majority vote, no headquarters, no secretariat and no organizational structure, the grouping of non-aligned nations was in theory well-placed to serve that purpose, but there was no unity in diversity and the contrived consensus in the Non-Aligned Movement was not reflected at the UN or at other international forums. While there was a papered-over semblance of the Non-Aligned Movement's unity at the declaratory level, there were obvious differences at the regional and national level. Sixty pages of reservations at the New Delhi summit in 1983, 5 pages being from Peru alone, only reflected the movement's error in trying to cover the global landscape with national, regional and sub-regional issues, and not restricting itself to those few areas where there could have been some genuine common agreement. There was no unity of purpose and therefore no strength of purpose. Instead it was an exemplar of minimal coalition politics and paper compromises.

The non-aligned criteria devised by a steering committee before the Belgrade conference in 1961 were: (1) An independent policy based on peaceful coexistence and not aligned with the power blocs, (2) Support for movements of national independence, (3) Not being a member of multilateral military alliances concluded in the context of great power conflicts, (4) Avoidance of bilateral military arrangements or regional defence pacts in the context of great power conflicts, and (5) In cases of hosting bases, these should not be in the context of great power conflict. These criteria were always subjective, and they served to blur and falsify the distinction between aligned and non-aligned, whether in Cuba, Vietnam, Saudi Arabia, Pakistan, or Egypt. The Non-Aligned Conference at Colombo had urged its members to 'exercise unceasing vigilance to preserve intact the essential character of non-alignment, maintain unswerving fidelity to its principles and policies'. However, it was assumed that wide expansion of membership added to strength, akin to the identical fallacy in most other international organizations. Even violations of basic precepts like the stationing of foreign military bases and foreign troops in some member states were ignored, and, not surprisingly, the criteria quickly lapsed into oblivion. American strategic consensus partners like Pakistan, those with treaties on security such as Sri Lanka and Malaysia, and countries with bases and military facilities like Maldives, were all welcomed into the movement without particular scrutiny. Article 1V of the Indo-Soviet 1971 Treaty declared that the Soviet Union 'respects India's policy of non-alignment'; and that was considered sufficient as a disclaimer. Since there were no norms for non-alignment, no benchmarks could apply in attitudes to the two superpowers. No practical political line of conduct had been laid down. This lack of definition caused a credibility gap between theory and practice; if there were no norms, then how could one challenge departures from the norms?

Nehru's life-long and sincere commitment had been to reduce the use of force in international politics, though his policy came to grief over China. His non-alignment provided no security to India in 1962 when no non-aligned country came to India's aid against China, and not even in 1965 against the indubitably allied Pakistan. After 1962, given its material weaknesses, India could play no meaningful role in world affairs for decades, and the two wars with Pakistan in 1965 and 1971 and periodic limited conflicts with its Western neighbour thereafter put paid to any pretensions at a wholly pacific foreign policy. India's ties with the Soviet Union which grew apace, and beneficially for India as the Sino–Soviet split deepened, made the multilateral projection of its foreign policy through the Non-Aligned Movement singularly and blatantly contriving.

On disarmament and South-South cooperation, however ineffectual it may have been in terms of practical results, the Non-Aligned Movement was the only organization that kept these in the forefront of the agenda, but objectives could not be treated as achievements, and they did not create opportunities for the non-aligned to have a meaningful say in world affairs. The movement would no doubt lay claim to achievements concerning decolonization, anti-racism, creating a platform for weak and small states, and pointing out the inequity of the existing information order. But it is hard to avoid the conclusion that the most important single achievement to record is that the Non-Aligned Movement has somehow survived into the twenty-first century. Like the British Commonwealth and a host of other international organizations that have outlived their sell-by dates, the member states cannot bring themselves, due to built-in inertia, to apply the *coup de grâce*. The best compliment that J.N. Dixit, the Indian foreign secretary who attended the Djakarta summit, could pay the conference was that it provided a forum for the Indian prime minister to meet several of his counterparts – an eloquent commentary on the movement's diminishing returns for India. It is salutary to remember that even moribund multilateral organizations are rarely formally disbanded as was the League of Nations in 1946 – in the case of the League, after it had been completely inactive for seven years.

Among the Non-Aligned Movement's many weaknesses were that among its various members, there was in reality a plenitude of different alignments. The disarray was inherent in the basic contradiction between the right of dissent of sovereign states and the organizational need for conformity – a 'conflict between the faith and the church'.[123] The outcome of this dichotomy was the repetition *ad nauseam* of the continuing validity of the criteria of non-alignment without any effort in defining their purpose or seeing to their observance. Non-alignment had self-imposed restraints – the use of persuasion, moral pressure and consensus among them. It added to these limitations by not internalizing its own precepts like human rights, equality of economic opportunities and peaceful settlement of disputes, on the grounds of not wishing to violate the sanctity of domestic sovereign jurisdiction. Non-alignment was unable to translate itself into any kind of civil society movement. It could not stimulate South-South cooperation, and OPEC raising the oil prices in 1973 created enormous problems for the vast majority of non-aligned nations. A Research and Information System, fully funded by India, that was established to assist non-aligned countries after the New Delhi summit, remained neglected and under-utilized by ungrateful member states. Rajiv Gandhi's efforts to give non-alignment a new dimension with the Group of Fifteen came to nothing. In essence, the movement was long on the declaratory aspect but short on concrete steps for implementation. 'At most, it unsuccessfully flailed away at the inequities of the global economic and trading order'.[124]

The Non-Aligned Movement's failures were in the lack of collective action and collective self-reliance, absence of any mechanism for the peaceful settlement of disputes, and the non-establishment of any new international information order or new international economic order. No collective action was ever taken against external security threats or aggression against non-aligned nations, and the movement's record even in intra-non-aligned disputes, such as Iran-Iraq, Pakistan-Afghanistan, Libya-Chad, Ethiopia-Somalia, Indonesia-Malaysia, Uganda-Tanzania, Cambodia-Thailand or Guyana-Venezuela, was uniformly lamentable. The movement failed to condemn the human rights violations rife among its non-democratic membership. It never adopted critical stands against the Soviet Union and it acquiesced in the ten year Soviet invasion of Afghanistan, a helpless, small, founder member of the non-aligned movement, which put paid both to the validity of non-alignment being universally accepted and the description of the Soviet Union as a 'natural ally' of the non-aligned nations. When the US invaded Grenada, another small and weak non-aligned country in 1983, the New Delhi summit thankfully grabbed the heaven-sent opportunity to deflect attention from Afghanistan and launch its broadside against the usual suspect. The Non-Aligned Movement was never able to break or even dent the pattern of the prevailing world situation. It only reflected the failures of the UN and the international community as a whole, and the marginalization of the influence and efficacy of multilateralism during and after the Cold War. It did not make any effective or tangible impact on international politics, which only went to prove once again that 'political influence not rooted in tangible ingredients of power has only limited effectiveness'.[125]

In February 1981, the first day of September was declared the international 'Day of Non-alignment'. This symbolic anniversary is neither generally known about nor cared about today. The occasion is only remembered and commemorated by a scant number of forlorn Indian leftists still dreaming of the heyday of India's ties with the Soviet Union that vanished over twenty years ago.

NOTES

1. A.W. Singham and S. Hume, *Non-Alignment in an Age of Alignments*, p. 394.
2. Henry Kissinger, *On China*, p. xvi.
3. Swapan Dasgupta, 'Insular Bharat', *Times of India*, 3 July 2011.
4. *Dutt Diaries*, 14 November 1952.
5. Ibid., 23 April 1957.
6. M.M. Rahman, *The Politics of Non-Alignment*, p. 359.
7. K.P.S. Menon, *Yesterday and Today*, p. 116.
8. Claude Arpi, *Fifty Years Ago*.
9. Ibid.
10. M.M. Rahman, *The Politics of Non Alignment*, p. 5.
11. *Dutt Diaries*, 7 March 1956.
12. C. Raja Mohan, *Crossing the Rubicon*, p. 52.
13. W.R. Crocker, *Nehru*, p. 137.
14. *Dutt Diaries*, 8 December 1956.
15. W.R. Crocker, *Nehru*, p. 117.
16. Rikhi Jaipal, *Non-Alignment*, p. 10.
17. M.M. Rahman, *The Politics of Non-Alignment*, p. 2.
18. Y. Gundevia, *Outside the Archives*, p. 346.
19. UNMOGIP, the UN Military Observer Group for India and Pakistan in Kashmir of 1949 was probably the first peacekeeping operation, but was never termed as such.
20. K. Natwar Singh, *My China Diary*, p. 38.
21. M.M. Rahman, *The Politics of Non-Alignment*, p. 169.
22. *Dutt Diaries*, 4, 5, 8, and 9 to 11 November 1956.
23. Ibid., 15 November 1956.

24. Ibid., 19 November 1956.
25. Ibid., 10 December 1956.
26. *World Culture*, Shanghai, 1949.
27. M.S. Rajan, *Non-Alignment and the Non-Aligned Movement*, p. 16.
28. J.S. Mehta, *Negotiating for India*, p. 55.
29. K.P.S. Menon, *Journey Round the World*, p. 5.
30. K. Natwar Singh, *My China Diary*, p. 118.
31. *Dutt Diaries*, 19 September 1955.
32. K.P.S. Menon, *Many Worlds*, p. 270.
33. Vallabhbhai Patel's letter to Nehru, 7 November 1950.
34. W.R. Crocker, *Nehru*, p. 103.
35. A.G. Noorani, *India-China Boundary Problem*, p. 15.
36. Ibid., p. 223.
37. *Dutt Diaries*, 7 March 1960.
38. Ibid., 27 April 1960.
39. Inder Malhotra, *Indian Express*, 'JN to JFK', 15 November 2010, and 'Letters from the Darkest Hour', 17 November 2010.
40. K.P.S. Menon, *Indo-Soviet Treaty*, p. 142.
41. R.S. Melkote and A. Narasimha Rao, *International Relations*, p. 358.
42. M.S. Rajan, *Non-Alignment and the Non-Aligned Movement*, p. 16.
43. K. Natwar Singh, *My China Diary*, p. 118.
44. *Dutt Diaries*, 18 November 1955.
45. Ibid., 11 January 1958.
46. Ibid., 3 June 1957.
47. Ibid., 20 November 1961.
48. Ibid., 14 December 1956.
49. Ibid., 16 December 1956.
50. Ibid., 1 October 1955.
51. Ibid., 15 November 1955.
52. Ibid., 23 April 1957.
53. T.N. Kaul, quoted by J.K. Ray, *India's Foreign Relations*, p. 24.
54. C.S. Jha, *From Bandung to Tashkent*, p. 358.
55. *Dutt Diaries*, 30 November 1961.
56. Ibid., 18 May 1957.
57. B.Z. Khasru, *Myths and Facts*, p. 371.
58. Ibid., p. 371.
59. K.M. Panikkar, *In Two Chinas*, p. 168.
60. J. Sisco, US Assistant Secretary of State, quoted in B.Z. Khasru, *Myths and Facts*, p. 228.

61. R. Dayal, *A Life of our Times*, p. 552.
62. *Dutt Diaries*, 16–17 November 1956.
63. Ibid., 5 December 1956.
64. Ibid., 23 April 1957.
65. Ibid., 7 March 1960.
66. N.D. Palmer, quoted in J.S. Bains (ed.), *Studies in Political Science*, Asia, Bombay, 1961, pp. 43–6.
67. *Dutt Diaries*, 6 August 1961.
68. R. Jaipal, *Non-Alignment*, p. 11.
69. Nehru quoted in R. Chatterji, *India's Foreign Policy*.
70. Ram Pradhan, posted online 27 November 2010.
71. *Dutt Diaries*, 19 November 1955.
72. Ibid., 12 November 1955.
73. S. Dutt, *With Nehru in the Foreign Office*, p. 221.
74. Henry Kissinger, *On China*, chapter five.
75. K.P.S. Menon, *Indo-Soviet Treaty*, p. 152.
76. Nehru, quoted in J.K. Ray, *India's Foreign Relations*, p. 29.
77. R. Jaipal, *Non-alignment*.
78. J.N. Dixit, *Indian Foreign Service*, p. 145.
79. *Dutt Diaries*, 10 May 1962.
80. T.N. Kaul, *The Future of the CIS*, p. 76.
81. S. Dutta Ray, *Looking East to Look West*, p. 235.
82. *Dutt Diaries*, 22 March 1962.
83. R. Jaipal, *Non-alignment*, p. 108.
84. Ibid., p. 130.
85. S. Dutta Ray, *Looking East to Look West*, p. 213.
86. S. Nihal Singh, *Ink in my Veins*, p. 149.
87. J.S. Mehta, *The Tryst Betrayed*, p. 299.
88. *Dutt Diaries*, 12 May 1962.
89. R. Jaipal, *Non-alignment*, p. 188.
90. Ibid., p. 3.
91. J.S. Mehta, *Rescuing the Future*, p. 365.
92. R. Jaipal, *Non-alignment*, p. 180.
93. J.N. Dixit, *Indian Foreign Service*, p. 192.
94. Ibid., p. 196.
95. J.N. Dixit, *Makers of Indian Foreign Policy*, p. 235.
96. Ibid., p. 201.
97. Ibid., p. 238.
98. S. Ganguly, *India-Russia Relations*, p. 43.
99. T.N. Kaul, *The Future of the CIS*, pp. 10 and 65.
100. J.N. Dixit, *Indian Foreign Service*, pp. 231 and 279.
101. N. Vohra and J.N. Dixit, *Religion, Politics and Society*, p. 17.

102. M. Rasgotra et al., *India's Foreign Policy*, p. x.
103. United Nations document A/44/551, 29 September 1989.
104. C. Raja Mohan, *Crossing the Rubicon*, p. xxii.
105. P.A.N. Murthy and B.K. Shrivastava, *Neutrality and Non-Alignment*, p. xviii.
106. *Dutt Diaries*, 6 September 1961.
107. Ibid., 6 December 1961.
108. J. Bandyopadhyaya, *North Over South*, p. 198.
109. R. Jaipal, *Non-Alignment*, p. 8.
110. K.P.S. Menon, *Yesterday and Today*, p. 118.
111. W. Dalrymple, *Nine Lives*, pp. 235–6.
112. Y. Gundevia, *Outside the Archives*, p. vi.
113. A.W. Singham and S. Hume, *Non-Alignment in an Age of Alignments*, p. 3.
114. M.M. Rahman, *The Politics of Non-alignment*, p. 7.
115. Ibid., p. 12.
116. Ibid., p. 35.
117. T.N. Kaul, *Ambassadors Need not Lie*, p. 49.
118. M. Rasgotra et al., *India's Foreign Policy in the 1990s*, p. 39.
119. Ibid., p. 109.
120. R. Jaipal, *Non-Alignment*, p. 3.
121. C. Raja Mohan, *Crossing the Rubicon*, p. 36.
122. R. Jaipal, *Non-Alignment*, p. 171.
123. J.S. Mehta, *Rescuing the Future*, p. 349.
124. S. Ganguly, *India's Foreign Policy*, p. 3.
125. J.N. Dxit, *India and Regional Developments*, p. 127.

REFERENCES

Aiyar, M.S., *A Time of Transition*, Penguin Viking, New Delhi, 2009.

Azar, Edward E. and John W. Burton, *International Conflict Resolution: Theory and Practice*, Wheatsheaf, Sussex; Lynne Rienner, Boulder Co., 1986.

Bandyopadhyaya, J., *North Over South*, Harvester Press, Brighton, 1982.

Banerji, S.K., *From Dependence to Non-Alignment*, Enkay, New Delhi, 1987.

Bhandari, R., *As I Saw it*, Har Anand, New Delhi, 1998.

Chari, P.R. et al., *Four Crises and a Peace Process*, HarperCollins, New Delhi, 2007.

Crocker, W.R., *Nehru*, Allen and Unwin, London, 1966.

Dalrymple, William, *Nine Lives*, Bloomsbury, London, 2009.

Dayal, Rajeshwar, *A Life of Our Times*, Orient Longman, New Delhi, 1998.

Dixit J.N., *Indian Foreign Service*, Konark, New Delhi, 2005.

———, *India and Regional Developments*, Gyan, New Delhi, 2004.

———, *Makers of India's Foreign Policy*, HarperCollins, New Delhi, 2004.

———, *External Affairs, Cross Border Relations*, Roli, New Delhi, 2003.

———, *India's Foreign Policy, The Challenge of Terrorism*, Gyan, New Delhi, 2002.

———, *India-Pakistan in War and Peace*, Books Today, New Delhi, 2002.

———, *Liberation and Beyond*, Konark, New Delhi, 1999.

———, *Across Borders*, Picus, 1998.

———, *Assignment Colombo*, Konark, 1998.

———, *My South Bloc Years*, UBS, New Delhi, 1996.

Dutt, Subimal, *With Nehru in the Foreign Office*, Minerva, New Delhi, 1977.

Dutta Ray, S., *Looking East to Look West*, Penguin/Viking, New Delhi, 2009.

Ganguly, Sreemati, *Indo-Russian Relations*, Shipra, New Delhi, 2009.

Ganguly, Sumit (ed), *India's Foreign Policy: Retrospect and Prospect*, Oxford University Press, New Delhi, 2010.

Graubard, Stephen, *The Presidents*, Penguin, New York, 2004.

Gundevia, Y.D., *Outside the Archives*, Sangam, New Delhi, 1984.

Jaipal, Rikhi, *Non-Alignment*, Allied, New Delhi, 1983.

Jha, C.S., *From Bandung to Tashkent*, Sangam, New Delhi, 1983.
Kaul, T.N., *A Diplomat's Diary*, Macmillan, New Delhi, 2000.
———, *The Future of the CIS*, Vikas, New Delhi, 1992.
———, *Ambassadors Need Not Lie*, Lancer, New Delhi, 1988.
———, *India and Indo-China*, Patriot, 1987.
———, *Reflections of a Non-conformist*, Lancer, New Delhi, 1986.
———, *The Kissinger Years,* New Delhi, Arnold Heinemann, 1980.
Khasru B.Z., *Myths and Facts: Bangladesh Liberation War*, Rupa, New Delhi, 2010.
Kissinger, Henry, *On China*, Penguin, New Delhi, 2011.
Landers, Brian, *Empires Apart: America and Russia from the Vikings to Iraq*, Penguin, London, 2009.
Mayall, James B.L. et al., *The Contemporary Commonwealth*, Routledge, London, 2009. Introduction by the editor.
Mehta, J.S., *The Tryst Betrayed: Reflections on Diplomacy and Development*, Penguin/Viking, New Delhi, 2010.
———, *Rescuing the Future*, Manohar, New Delhi, 2008.
———, *Negotiating for India*, Manohar, New Delhi, 2006.
———, *The March of Folly in Afghanistan*, Manohar, New Delhi, 2002.
Melkote, R.S. and A. Narasimha Rao, *International Relations*, Sterling, New Delhi, 1992.
Menon, K.P.S., *Yesterday and Today*, Allied, New Delhi, 1976.
———, *A Diplomat Speaks*, Allied Publishers, New Delhi, 1974.
———, *Indo-Soviet Treaty*, Vikas, New Delhi, 1971.
———, *Journey Round the World*, Bharatiya Vidya Bhavan, Bombay, 1966.
———, *Many Worlds: An Autobiography*, Oxford Univesity Press, Bombay, 1965.
Murthy, P.A.N. and B.K. Shrivastava (eds), *Neutrality and Non-Alignment in the 1990s*, Radiant Publishers, New Delhi, 1991.
Natwar Singh, K., *My China Diary, 1956–88*, Rupa, New Delhi, 2009.
Nihal Singh, S., *Ink in My Veins*, Hay House, New Delhi, 2011.
Noorani, A.G., *India-China Boundary Problem, 1846–1947*, Oxford University Press, New Delhi, 2011.
Panikkar, K.M., *An Autobiography*, Oxford University Press, New Delhi, 1977.
———, *In Two Chinas*, George Allen and Unwin, London, 1955.
Rahman, M.M., *The Politics of Non-Alignment*, Associated Publishing House, New Delhi, 1969.

Raja Mohan, C., *Crossing the Rubicon: The Shaping of India's New Foreign Policy*, Vikas-Penguin India, New Delhi, 2003.

Rajan, M.S., *Non-Alignment and Non-aligned Movement: Retrospect and Prospect*, Vikas, New Delhi, 1990.

Rasgotra, M. et al., *The New Asian Power Dynamic*, Sage, New Delhi, 2007.

———, *Genesis of Regional Conflicts*, Gyan, New Delhi, 1995.

———, *India's Foreign Policy in the 1990s*, Patriot, 1990.

———, *Southern Asia-Pacific*, Continental, 1988.

Ray, J.K., *India's Foreign Relations, 1947–2007*, Routledge, New Delhi, 2011.

Seventh Non-Aligned Summit, New Delhi, 1983, Institute of Non-Aligned Studies, New Delhi, 1983.

Singham, A.W. and Shirley Hume, *Non-Alignment in an Age of Alignments,* Lawrence Hill, Conn USA and Zed Books, UK, 1986.

Vasudevan, H.S., *Indo-Russian Trade and Military Cooperation since 1991*, Manohar, New Delhi, 2011.

Vohra, N.N. and J.N. Dixit, *Religion, Politics and Society in South and South East Asia*, Konark, 1998.

Articles and Other Manuscripts

Akbar, M.J., 'Indira: Great Heroes Make Great Mistakes', *Times of India*, 1 November 2009.

Aleksanyan, Tigran, 'Will the Non Aligned Movement Succeed in Multipolarisation?' 2008, *Despite Borders*, Central Eastern European Watch.

Arpi, Claude, 'Fifty Years Ago, the Asian Relations Conference', *Phayul.com*, 30 April 2007.

Bhadrakumar, M.K., 'Exaggerating the Threat Perceptions', 12 September 2009, US National Security Archive Update, 11 September 2009.

———, 'Fifty Years since Nikita Khrushchev's First Visit to the United States', 15 September 2009, Ria Novosti, 14 Septembar 2009.

Chatterji, Rakhahari, 'India's Foreign Policy: Some Open Questions', Jadavpur Association of International Relations, Kolkata, 2010.

Dasgupta, Amit, 'Divided Nations: India and Germany', unpublished.

Dasgupta, Swapan, 'Insular Bharat', *Times of India*, 3 July 2011.

Duffy, Gary, 'Brazil's Lula Raps "White" Crisis', 16 September 2009, www.news.bbc.co.uk

Dutt, Subimal, *The Dutt Diaries, 1938–62*, Private Collection, unedited and unpublished.

Evans, Martin, 'Whatever Happened to the Non Aligned Movement?' 2007, The Questia Online Library, Questia.com.reader.

Gupta, Ranjit, 'Prospects of a China-India Partnership', 2009, unpublished.

Hilger, Andreas, 'The Soviet Union and India: The Years of Late Stalinism', Parallel History Project on Cooperative Security, PHP website, 10 December 2009.

Jain, Devaki, 'Is the Non-Aligned Movement Relevant Today?', July 2009 (?).

Kapila, Subhash, 'India's Non Alignment Doctrine: A Policy Failure', www.boloji.com/plainspeak/009.htm 18 December 2005.

Makwana, Rajesh, 'The Non Aligned Movement: Renewed Relevance in a Time of Crisis', 25 August 2009, Share the World's Resources, www.stwr.org/index2

Mansingh, Surjit, 'Indo-Soviet Relations in the Nehru Years: The View from New Delhi', Parallel History Project on Cooperative Security, PHP website, 10 December 2009.

Mehta, Jagat S., 'In Conversation with the Author', Private Collection, unpublished.

Mehta, Pratap Bhanu, 'Five Balancing Acts', 2006, www.india-seminar.com/2006/560.

Mehta, Subrata K. and Jivanta Schottli, 'The New Dynamics of Indian Foreign Policy and its Ambiguities', *Irish Studies in International Affairs*, vol. 18 (2007), pp. 19–34.

Mohanty, Arun, 'Fifty-five Years to Indo-Russian Diplomatic Relations', *Business Messenger* (?).

Morle, Jefferson, 'World Opinion Round-up', 2006 www.blog.washingtonpost.com/worldopinionroundup/2006/09/pundits.

Morphet, Sally, 'Multilateralism and the Non Aligned Movement: What is the Global South Doing and Where is it Going?' *Global Governance* 10 (2004): 517–37.

Orlov, A., 'The Non Aligned Movement: 40 Years After', *International Affairs* 2001(?).

Pavithran, K.S., 'Non Alignment and post Cold War International System: Problams and Perspectives', *Indian Journal of South Asian Studies*, Pondicherry, 1(1)2008.

Rana, Swadesh, 'The Changing Indian Diplomacy at the United Nations', International Organization, 2001.

Sen, Narayan C., 'Mao Zedong and India-China Border Dispute',

Rabindra Bharati Journal of Political Science, pp. 18–35, vol. X, 2009.

Sen, Satadru, 'Goodbye to Non-alignment and all That', *Economic and Political Weekly*, Mumbai, 1 December 20001, pp. 4455–7.

'The Non Aligned Movement as Living Fossil', 2009. www. Ipezone. blogspot.com/2009/08/

Thalif Deen, 'Africa: Is the Non Aligned Movement Still Relevant?' 16 July 2008. www.allafrica.com.

Thomas, Raju G.C., 'What is Third World Security?' *Annual Review of Political Science*, 2003, 6, pp. 205–32.

Zopag, 'Non Aligned Movement Outdated: US', 19 September 2009, www.zopag.com/story

APPENDIX 1

Heads of the Indian Foreign Service from Independence to 1991

SECRETARIES GENERAL

G.S. Bajpai	27 June 1948 to 24 May 1952
N.R. Pillai	25 November 1952 to 1 September 1960
R.K. Nehru	2 September 1960 to 4 December 1963
M.J. Desai	5 December 1963 to 30 November 1964

FOREIGN SECRETARIES

K.P.S. Menon	16 April 1948 to 21 September 1952
R.K. Nehru	22 September 1952 to 10 October 1955
S. Dutt	11 October 1955 to 17 January 1961
M.J. Desai	11 April 1961 to 4 December 1963
Y.D. Gundevia	5 December 1963 to 18 February 1965
C.S. Jha	19 February 1965 to 13 August 1967
R. Dayal	19 August 1967 to 6 November 1968
T.N. Kaul	7 November 1968 to 3 December 1972
Kewal Singh	4 December 1972 to 31 March 1976
J.S. Mehta	1 April 1976 to 18 November 1979
R.D. Sathe	19 November 1979 to 30 April 1982
M. Rasgotra	1 May 1982 to 31 January 1985
R. Bhandari	1 February 1985 to 31 March 1986
A.P. Venkateswaran	1 April 1986 to 20 January 1987
K.P.S. Menon	16 February 1987 to 15 February 1989
S.K. Singh	16 February 1989 to 19 April 1990
M. Dubey	20 April 1990 to 30 November 1991

APPENDIX 2

Indian Ambassadors to the Soviet Union (1947–1991)

(Mrs) V.L. Pandit (1947–9)
S. Radhakrishnan (1949–52)
K.P.S. Menon (1952–61)
S. Dutt (1961–2)
T.N. Kaul (1962–6)
Kewal Singh (1966–8)
D.P. Dhar (1969–71)
K.S. Shelvankar (1971–5)
D.P. Dhar (1975)
I.K. Gujral (1976–80)
V.K. Ahuja (1980–3)
Nurul Hasan (1983–6)
T.N. Kaul (1986–9)
A.S. Gonsalves (1989–92)

APPENDIX 3

Conversation with Jagat S. Mehta, Oldest Living Foreign Secretary, Udaipur, 9 November 2009

Jagat S. Mehta was a member of the Indian Foreign Service from 1947 to 1980 and Foreign Secretary from 1976 to 1979. This unedited transcript is published with his very generous permission.

KS = Krishnan Srinivasan
JSM = Jagat S. Mehta

KS: Basically speaking, I don't think there can be any argument that non-alignment served India's purposes very well. I think I mentioned to you that I have been reading Subimal Dutt's diaries where he praises you very highly as being one of the few officers (including himself, naturally), who was, according to him, very sceptical about this very strong tilt towards the Left, and where officers were afraid of seeming to be anti-Chinese. He wrote that you were one of the few exceptions, that you were not afraid to tell the Chinese what you thought, and to tell the Indian leadership what you thought. The others were afraid. He attributed this largely to Krishna Menon although he trusted Nehru. He also particularly criticizes R.K. Nehru, K.P.S. Menon, and M.J. Desai for toeing this line.

JSM: And T.N. Kaul?

KS: Yes, Kaul should have been there but, as far as I recall, he is never mentioned.

JSM: Basically, in my view, non-alignment was right. Non-alignment meant India's ideological agnosticism. You could decide on your ideology from your domestic situation. Either you were a democracy or a dictatorship, etc., but you were not committed to being part of a military bloc. This proved correct. But in the meanwhile, we interpreted non-alignment as if it meant being anti-West. And because of the leadership of Jawaharlal Nehru, and to a large extent of Krishna Menon, it meant we were non-aligned by being non-West.

I have a feeling that every [non-aligned] summit conference had its own emphasis. In 1961, the first one, the focus was clearly non-alignment through disarmament and we should end all testing, and so we sent Panditji to Washington and Sukarno to Moscow. The interesting thing about the 1961 conference is, in 1961 nobody ever mentioned the possibility of a second conference. This was once and for all. The 1964 conference was held because in the meanwhile we'd had the conflict with China in 1962 and the Chinese wanted to have the anniversary of the Bandung Conference – the Afro-Asian conference. So that would have hurt us. So we decided to have a conference, hurriedly called, in 1964, in Cairo. Really, it was to get our act in. No conference was held after that till 1970. In 1970, by this time, so many more countries had become free, in the UNGA itself there was a majority for the non-aligned. It was at the 1970 conference, speaking from memory, when T.N. Kaul was the foreign secretary, at that conference we created something like a bureau or bloc. That was the beginning of the imitation of a bloc although non-alignment was supposed to be non-bloc. And then in the 1973 conference in Algeria, – at that time, Algeria was very pro-Soviet Union. The notion that socialism is the 'natural ally' of non-alignment arises from that 1973 conference.

KS: If we go back to before the non-aligned institution, if we go back to Suez and Hungary, do you have any comment on those? Suez is not so important, because I think there we took a right principled stand. Krishna Menon upset a lot of people, but never mind. But Hungary is a point which Dutt, for example –

JSM: Hungary was in my view, it was at a time.... The most plausible explanation for Hungary – was plausible though I don't necessarily agree with it – was that Panditji took the Cold War so seriously, he thought that we must prevent a hot war being declared, and he really thought that the Americans were preparing for an intervention in Hungary, and so he decided, let us side – maybe Krishna Menon was a more active player....

KS: Don't you think that was plausible?

JSM: Well I have a feeling.... I thank God we do not publish the records from our Embassies, because I have a feeling that all the records of our missions in Eastern Europe, particularly of Moscow, are very shameful.

KS: K.P.S. [Menon] was still the Ambassador in 1956? And Ishi Rahman was in Budapest?

JASM: He was still the Ambassador, and Ishi Rahman had just arrived [in Budapest] in 1956. K.P.S. was the supervising Ambassador; he was Ambassador from 1952 to 1961.

KS: But he had a very strong pro-Soviet inclination?

JSM: That was fashionable. This is the whole trouble. Dutt hesitated, but he didn't go along with the fashionable thing. And all those people, M.J. Desai, they were all going along with what they thought Nehru wanted to hear. Whereas Nehru, in my view, if you told him your honest opinion, he would shout at you –

KS: This has been your view all along. But people were afraid of his bark also, weren't they?

JSM: They were afraid of his bark. I have written an essay called 'Panditji Knows Best'.

KS: But isn't it a fact, sir, though, that whatever misgivings people had, they also felt that Panditji did know best? And they trusted him to work things out? Isn't that true?

JSM: I would put it this way; India generally took the Cold War as permanent and too seriously. The Cold War itself was fallacious.

KS: Was that why we were put on the wrong foot so badly, when, for example, Gorbachev was dismissed by the Gang of 7? My friend Alfred Gonsalves in Moscow made the same mistake.

JSM: Generally, India has been, I would say – we were wishful as far as the Soviet Union was concerned; we were naïve as far as China was concerned, and we were non-discriminatory as far as America was concerned. There are things wrong with America, but not as wrong as people had imagined. Only because we took the Cold War as permanent, and we took it too seriously.

KS: What happened during the Cuban missile crisis? Do you remember any statement or any attitude taken by Delhi during the Cuban missile crisis? I seem to find a complete blank here.

JSM: I have a feeling that the Cuban missile crisis and the Sino-Indian war by accident coincided.

KS: That's right. Was that the reason why we said nothing on this?

JSM: And the Soviet Union at that time was not principled. Soviet Union thought that if there is to be war with America, then they wanted China to be on their side. So during that period, 10 days period or 13 days period, the Soviet Union took a pro-Chinese attitude. And they fear, God knows, that the Americans may bomb. This has been the trouble in understanding nuclear weapons. Everybody wanted nuclear weapons because the other fellow, you never know, the other fellow may lose balance. The Soviet Union doesn't [*inaudible*] So they keep on preparing for the contingency, but in fact never wanting to use it themselves. No first strike. So assuming that the Russian decision makers thought that, you never know, they may actually bomb. The Americans have to this day, not realized, and I think I am the first person to say so, that the only ally that America had in Vietnam was the Soviet Union – except they couldn't say so.

KS: Because of the Sino-Soviet split?

JSM: Yes. You see, they didn't know whether America, in its desperation of defeat, would not actually use a nuclear weapon, and then Soviet Union would have the dilemma of whether to retaliate in order to remain the leader of the communist bloc, and risk the devastation of the Soviet Union, or to do nothing, in which case it gets exposed and the Chinese get proved right, that nuclear weapons are a paper tiger.

It's very interesting. I was in China at that time. I was the only head of mission to see off Kosygin when he was going to Hanoi. Not even the socialist countries were there, and I suppose someone in the Soviet Embassy tipped me off. Zhou Enlai was there; no ceremonial reception. Mao told him, 'you're not wanted in Hanoi', but he went all the same. The Soviet Union supplied arms to Vietnam as a matter of arms control. They did not supply aircraft.

But going back to Hungary, I think Panditji really feared that it would lead to war and would impede our development, and so he decided to side with the Russians. But he didn't understand, what none of these countries have understood, is the nature of nuclear weapons. Nuclear weapons are used as a matter of prestige. If you have nuclear weapons you are a great power. But not to be used. So Panditji thought the CIA would actually use nuclear weapons to help nationalism in Hungary.

KS: Highly improbable. But coming to Vietnam, which you mentioned, did non-alignment play any part in Vietnam? Cambodia? Any beneficial role?

JSM: I don't think so. No significance. The Americans went to Cambodia, and it made no damn difference.

KS: And in the Soviet Afghan problem of 1979–89, did non-alignment play any part?

JSM: Not at all.

KS: So non-alignment's ability to have a healing touch in any international crisis situation was almost zero?

JSM: Yes, absolutely. The story of non-alignment has been a philosophical paradox. There was incisive foresight when in the face of pressure and prejudice, the principle of dissent and non-conformity was asserted against the ideological tendency to globalization. [*inaudible*] was vindicated with the rapidity unforeseen even by its proponents when Premier Khruschev and President Kennedy in his inaugural address when they applauded the right of non-alignment which had been denounced with contempt by their predecessors only a few years earlier. In other words, we were right in non-alignment, when we didn't remain non-aligned ourselves.

KS: In that fashion we were following pretty much the rest of the non-aligned group as well, weren't we?

JSM: Well, whether we were following them or leading them on. Non-alignment became such a big group. I assert by 1970, anything you did in the non-aligned conference you could also do in the United Nations. Because we were in the majority. So there was duplication. In all the resolutions whether in non-alignment or –

KS: But many non-aligned countries took a different position in the UN.

JSM: Yes, it was covered up. And since there is no method, unlike the UN, where there is a method of saying that you dissent, or you abstain, and explain your vote. In the non-aligned conference, you enter a reservation at the bottom. There is no method by which you could record your dissent. So you kept quiet, and whoever was the host country, you went along with the host country. So in 1979 you went along with Castro. In 1973, you went along with Algeria. But in 1976 we were a little more non-aligned.

KS: Does non-alignment have any meaning now?

JSM: No, because I consider non-alignment as being universalized. So how can it have any meaning? Panditji said everyone is non-aligned.

KS: But is it worth participating in these 3-yearly meetings? Is it still something that one should lift one's hat off to?

JSM: Because in 1982 there could not be a conference in Baghdad, it was postponed by a year and held in Delhi. Uma Bajpai was the director of the IIC. So he asked me whether I would write an essay on non-alignment. I said I would write the essay, but you will have the obligation to accept it. This was for some IIC journal or some book. So when he saw it and he was consulting G. Parthasarthy senior, he said, no, no, you are too late by one week, or something like that. On that ground, he rejected it. So I showed it to Nikhil Chakravarty who was then editor of *Mainstream*. Nikhil published it.

We were so enamoured of this non-alignment. In that article I said we should declare that non-alignment has been vindicated, and then we should say, wind up the damned organization. It costs millions of dollars to hold a conference, bankrupt bloody nations, just because nobody can stop the damned thing. So we go on, and it makes no difference. Who's going to oppose it? – it's my turn next! It makes absolutely no difference. You see the last two conferences; I don't even know where they were held.

I had a backlash of the Korean War, because out of all these chaps who were POWs, some went back to North Korea, and some went to Taiwan. But there were 90-odd chaps who did not want to go either to Taiwan or North Korea. They were kept in India and when I became deputy secretary (East) which was in 1956, three or four years later, they were behind barbed wire for no sin except that they intended to go to a neutral country. So I am responsible for asking their option. So somebody went to Brazil, and few of them, about nine of them, stayed on in India, and we provided one chap some wherewithal. One fellow, Peter, became very rich – I've forgotten what his Korean name was – I got the Church to give him some land. He used to live in a tent with a lantern and keep chickens. Big cars from the Embassies came and took eggs from the chap. Fantastic story. Then he discovered that women in south India, they shave off their hair once they become widows. So he bought these and he used to grade them, and then he exported them to South Korea where they made wigs.

KS: Were these North Koreans or South Koreans? It was supposed to be a prisoner exchange, wasn't it?

JSM: They were North Koreans. They were stuck in India and behind barbed wire – that's the funny part.

KS: Where? In Delhi?

JSM: Yes, in the cantonment.

KS: Sir, Korea was the time when we managed to upset everybody due to our [non-aligned] position.

JSM: We were Chairman of the [Neutral Nations] Repatriation Commission and of the three International Supervisory Commissions on Vietnam, Laos and Cambodia. Desai was the Chairman of the Commission in Vietnam, which was the biggest, and Parthasarthy the Chairman of the Commission on Cambodia. Somebody else was in Laos. They went on for some time. Desai was succeeded by T.N. Kaul and Ishi Rahman and so on.

KS: They wound up more or less at the time of the Vietnam War. They lasted till then. If we had not tilted in our evaluation of non-alignment so far towards the Soviet Union and China before 1962, would things have been any different? That's what one asks oneself.

JSM: I have a feeling that we thought we knew, when in fact we didn't. We should have kept the superpower relationship separate, and carried on our independent policy. We could have had parallel relationships with America and the Soviet Union, and we did not – Soviet Union was not asking us to tilt with them. Or if they did, we could afford to disagree, for example on Germany. May be they understood. Hallstein doctrine was one in which we said; but, we have to get aid from West Germany so we never recognized East Germany for a long time. I have a feeling that we never realized – our missions never realized – they were never honest enough to judge how difficult, how unhappy, were the people of Eastern Europe with communism.

Today is the 20th anniversary of the Berlin Wall, 9 November. We allowed the Soviet Union – we were wishful in our attitude to the Soviet Union. We said to them, we know you are anti-imperialist; we are great supporters – they couldn't damn well deny it – in fact they didn't actually ask you to be anti-imperialist. Ultimately, –

KS: Didn't we really get any gratitude for this? From government circles anyway?

JSM: I suppose we got some gratitude from government circles. There was a certain amount of deflection of our trade in convertible currency to the West. We sent exports against rupees and they earned foreign exchange.

KS: After 1990, do you think there is any residual friendship in the erstwhile Eastern bloc, including Russia, today? For India's role during that time, or is it all forgotten? India seemed to expect that some so-called traditional friendship would continue. But I think things are much more hard-headed than that.

JSM: More hard-headed. Russia is now very Christian, and very much for the Orthodox Church. And we are hardly indispensable. Buying an aircraft carrier which they have rejected at a cost of millions of dollars to re-fit it. Something's wrong. Preparation against whom? Against Pakistan? I really think Pakistan is not worth preparing against. It is much more a challenge of diplomacy.

The trouble is that the Defence Ministry . . . that External Affairs has not really played its role. Like the Americans. Foreign policy of America has been dicated by the Pentagon through most of the period. Similarly, the RAW. Who persuaded us to send the bloody troops to Sri Lanka? RAW! And then Sunderji and 'Brasstacks'. Entirely because Sunderji wanted a field-marshalship. He thought the Pakistanis will be so alarmed there will be war, and I will defeat them. Exercise with ten divisions is something which the NATO doesn't do. Frankly it's a shame what we did at the Golden Temple.

So I have a feeling that we wasted the years of Nehru. We didn't realize that he could not be replicated. He was conditioned by what Europe believed in the 1930s. All the progressives of Europe were then sympathetic in the Spanish Civil War against Franco. [*Inaudible*. Popular?] Front. But Europe recovered from that during the 1939 War. We didn't recover.

Somebody is going to say afterwards, Panditji was wrong in 1962, Cripps Mission, in 1946 during the Cabinet Mission. Once again my feeling is that if the Cold War, the Truman Doctrine and de-colonization had not coincided exactly, and if Mountbatten had not preponed the date of transfer of power, because by December everybody knew that Jinnah had terminal tuberculosis. I was in the Ministry in 1948. I remember Panditji rushing to Birla House when Gandhiji was assassinated. The shock in Pakistan was tangible. Here was a Hindu who'd killed Gandhi because he wanted to be fair to the Muslims. Mountbatten has done such a splendid job of covering up; his own public relations that Partition was inevitable.

America cannot restore stability in Afghanistan or in Pakistan. I think we will have great difficulty, but the ordinary man both in India and Pakistan, they are coming in thousands by train from both sides. What is the source of anger? The Americans have been so stupid. They encouraged the Taliban.

KS: They made the bed; now they have to lie in it. But that doesn't excuse the Pakistanis, of course.

JSM: It doesn't excuse the Pakistanis. The Pakistanis, the stupid fellows, wanted a confederation with Afghanistan.

KS: They see Afghanistan always as a kind of surrogate ally against India: the defence in depth theory.

JSM: This whole notion that has been settled in their mind that the Muslim is on our side, and the Muslim will fight the communist. But communism and anti-communism itself is all gone.

KS: And the corollary is that Muslims do not fight Muslims, which is also not true – the Bangladesh situation makes that very clear. On China, it's been your view. . . . I was very interested in something you wrote regarding the discussions with China – there was a problem on a particular location and the Indian side tried many maps, many methods to get them to identify what the position was, and the Chinese would not identify it.

JSM: They would not give a map.

KS: They would not give a map, not give coordinates, not identify any landmarks. And to complicate it, it was called by different names by India and China, I think.

JSM: They say the only boundary which is valid is that which is formally delimited. There is only one bit of the Indian border which is 'valid' and formally delimited; that is Sikkim in 1890, but where there is no formal delimitation, generally, if there is a mountain range in between, then the water parting forms the boundary and that's so in Spain, in South America, in Africa, etc., unless you can artificially change it.

Trouble is, in the plateau of Aksai Chin, it is not so clear, so our problem on China was that where our boundary is, that was declared by Nehru, and when they drew a short communiqué of 4 lines in which they asked us to provide evidence in support of the stand of the two governments. So we were left to prove what he had already said. We did a fairly good job of it, but we had a terrible time. But what is interesting is in our. . . . I showed the draft of the final chapter which summarized our case and in that summary, there is a para we were sure to believe that this is a new claim rather than you were deceiving us from the very beginning because Arunachal is in our constitution. So Xhou Enchen [leader of the Chinese delegation] hit the ceiling. He said this is very difficult. What do you do? It was originally supposed to be ours, but you didn't say so, or we are saying you are making a new claim.

But unfortunately in the Aksai Chin area, it is all flat. It's at 16,000 feet. One year the Kashmir government had maintained a kind of post there during the winter but it was so impossible that they abandoned it in 1855, or something like that. [*Inaudible*] Zhou Enlai had been honest to Nehru in 1956, not in 1958. Jawaharlal Nehru could have piloted an exchange of Aksai Chin because we didn't need the damn thing and the road runs across it, and we would keep Arunachal.

Now the Chinese are being arrogant. This their own old notion of. . . . According to traditional Chinese notion, the boundary of China is along the southern foothills of Nepal, of Bhutan, of NEFA and North Burma. Sikkim also. All these are tributaries.

KS: I think as far as NEFA is concerned, here again like that place which they refused to define; they have not defined also the extent of NEFA that they claim. We are vaguely assuming it is Arunachal Pradesh, but the extent of their claim line is not ever made known.

JSM: I have a feeling what they want . . . most of the evidence the Chinese have given us is of Tibetan sources. . . .

KS: Of course. Monastic records, grazing, etc. . . .

JSM: Yes. If they could get Tawang, the rest would be easy. They would give up the rest. They may have a strong claim. Yellow Hat sect. But no government in India can give up Tawang. In any case now that the Dalai Lama is here, they are trying to change the demography of Tibet and Xinjiang. They have a problem with the future of having democracy. Even after fifty years, the Tibetan sense of identity has not gone. Nor is the Xinjiang sense of identity.

KS: So it's a problem of their periphery and we have a problem on our periphery as well. I don't know how this is going to get resolved. You say no Indian government can give up Tawang. If it's a question of giving up Tawang and getting the rest of Arunachal Pradesh, maybe it's a deal?

JSM: Without the consent of the Dalai Lama, that's the problem. And with the context of this kind of, with the present altercation, there is a feeling of Tibetans being badly treated. When the Dalai Lama has said, I accept to be part of China as long as you give me theological independence, that seems reasonable.

KS: But he's never going to be successful, I am afraid.

JSM: He won't be successful, but nor will . . . Chinese may suppress it.

The most successful legacy of Jawaharlal Nehru is Bhutan. That I can say is entirely due to me. Because M.O. Mathai called me: 'Sir, how can they say no to a visa for the prime minister when there's an appeal to Zhou Enlai? It has been [sent] 6 months in advance.' He said, 'You go and tell the prime minister.' I said, 'all right, I'll tell him'. 'Send a reminder.' 'We sent a reminder. But in fact they won't let you go because of the revolt in Tibet.' And I let slip that 3 weeks is exactly what we need to go to Bhutan. He said, 'ajao, let's go! What a good idea! I'll go to Bhutan.' And then the next morning, Mr Dutt pounced at me. He told me, 'who told you to make this suggestion?' I really felt bad. I couldn't say anything. My God, I've probably given a death warrant to Jawaharlal Nehru. Who knows if he has a heart attack at 14,000 feet, which R.K. Nehru had? It'd be terrible! I really was in tears. But Panditji would not hear about cancelling the trip. [*Inaudible*] 'you tell the prime minister that there's some other visitor coming, or find some excuse'. But he wouldn't hear about it. It was the only time the prime minister went on [such] a trip, it took a week to get there to Paro, one week to come back.

KS: And you went across the Chumbi Valley both ways?

JSM: Yes, there was no road.

KS: The Chicken's Neck existed, but not a road?

JSM: It was all malarial. We went across the Chumbi Valley. By going, because he went there, the King agreed to build a road.

KS: There's another fall-out of that. The point at which he entered Bhutan after leaving the Chumbi Valley is now considered to be the most authentic source for claiming the [Bhutan-China] boundary line in that area. There's a bridge or something there.

JSM: I have a picture of the bridge there across the Amo Chu. We crossed the bridge and there was a guard of honour on the other side of the bridge. The Chinese stayed on this side of the bridge.

KS: That's now a hallowed piece of ground!

THE WIDE WORLD

PAIN AND GAIN IN WORLD TRADE NEGOTIATIONS

THE World Trade Organization is vilified by many circles in in India for alleged 'neo-colonialism', domination of India, discrimination against India and generally bending India to its will. Comparisons are made with the imperiousness of the East India Company. According to these critics, we have lost our Independence, the right to our own brainpower, our natural resources and our low-cost economy, and have become subservient to the whims of this arrogant behemoth. The highly complex technical details and the subtle trade-offs that are part of these ongoing negotiations are little known or understood.

Until around the 1990s India's economy was relatively closed to the outside world, and the level of integration of our economy with the global economy was minimal. In fact, one of the explanations given for India not being much affected by the Asian financial crisis was that our economy was not interwoven with the global money markets to any substantial degree. However, with the gradual opening up of the sheltered Indian market both in goods and services, and coupled with a more liberal approach towards foreign investment, our economy is getting increasingly integrated with the world economy, and the recent fluctuations in the stock market are partly a reflection of this increasing intermeshing. It is noticeable that the Indian newspapers and electronic media now give greater coverage to events occurring in the global marketplace because these have an inevitable impact on our own economy. Today's managers are functioning in a globalized world and the distinction between domestic and foreign markets is becoming increasingly blurred. Every market in the world is slowly becoming more contestable. One of the institutions which has a profound effect on the global economy and the greater competitiveness and accessibility of markets is the World Trade Organization.

During the early rounds of negotiations under the aegis of the

General Agreement on Tariffs and Trade, there was no pressure brought to bear on India. The situation changed during the Uruguay Round (1986–94) when the developed countries started to demand the opening up of the Indian economy. Despite this, India did not have to make any major commitments in the area of agriculture, only limited ones in services, and in regard to industrial tariffs, bound only about two thirds of our tariff lines at an average of above 40 per cent. The major concession made by India during the Uruguay Round was the TRIPS agreement, and especially the obligation to provide product patents in the pharmaceutical area with effect from 2005.

The WTO came about in 1995 as a result of the negotiations in the Uruguay Round, and its main role is to frame and administer the rules, which are determined by the members themselves, for the conduct of international trade. By tradition, decision-making is by consensus, which makes the WTO a very democratic body in which every member has a veto. It is the fundamental principle of non-discrimination that has made the GATT earlier, and the WTO now, a very valuable resource for most governments. Nearly 30 countries, including Russia and Iran, are waiting to accede, and an economic power-house like China has agreed to many commitments over and above WTO requirements in order to become a member. Unlike GATT, the WTO has a dispute settlement mechanism available to all members, which has been utilized by India dozens of times, either as plaintiff or as defendant.

The current Doha Round which began in 2001 is expected to come to a conclusion in the middle of this year. Today India is considered by all foreign countries to be a strong emerging economy with competitive strengths and great potential for growth, and the major industrialized powers like the USA and the EU are demanding a substantial opening up of our thus far protected market for access for their goods and services. These countries will not offer concessions in agriculture unless countries like India are willing to reduce their agricultural and industrial tariffs and open up their services market, including the financial services sector. Developed countries have taken to categorizing India, Brazil and a few other nations as 'advanced developing countries', though no such category exists in the WTO, with a view to making these countries undertake additional commitments relative to other developing countries. This is the price of our success.

At this stage it is difficult to predict the outcome of the Doha Round negotiations and the impact it will have on the Indian economy. What is clear is that India will have to make wider and deeper commitments than ever before. This should not be a cause for concern since the Doha negotiating mandate, the July framework of 2004, the Hong Kong ministerial declaration of 2005, and the international alliances we have constructed with countries that have similar objectives, quite apart from our own negotiating stance, will give us adequate strength to defend our core interests. As the slogan goes in the fitness centres, 'no pain, no gain'. This has to be the *mantra* for previously protected markets in the WTO as well.

A vast nation like India, with its complex disparities and internal dynamics, cannot become competitive in every product in the short term. But like globalization itself, which is here to stay, a progressively contestable world in trade, investment and services is inevitable. Few of the problems faced by the Indian economy are directly attributable to the WTO, and its vociferous critics would do better to look at the various deficiencies within; at our policy failures, feudal land tenure systems, the lack of discipline, corruption, and the distortions that our internal subsidies and public monopolies have engendered.

The essence of the multilateral trading system is to provide fair competition in all markets to all members. The corollary is that to survive and grow in the global marketplace, every country has necessarily to become more competitive. It is essential to acknowledge at the same time that other markets, both developing and developed, will also become more open and accessible, and thereby enhance our opportunities, provided we are competitive enough to take advantage of them. Given our technical skills and wage structure, we are in a better position to do so than most. Only by this hard road can we achieve standing as a world power with a globally integrated economy and win the international respect to which we aspire.

January 2007

UNITED NATIONS SECURITY COUNCIL

The question of India's claim to be a fitting candidate for a permanent seat on the United Nations Security Council has resurfaced in media columns, this time in connection with President Obama's forthcoming visit and the United States' less than fulsome support to the claim. In India, the question of whether the UN needs restructuring and reform is always a loaded question. Every international organization has to change and adapt if it is to survive. Numerous international organizations are languishing, their utility long exhausted, although their constituent members for a variety of reasons decline to kill them off. It may be salutary to remember that even moribund multilateral organizations are rarely formally disbanded in the manner of the League of Nations in 1946 – in the case of the League, after it had been completely inactive for seven years.

But the United Nations shows versatility and that is why it is still relevant, even if less than effective. The UN is our only global organization, and so its reform and restructure are questions ultimately bearing on global governance. The UN has adapted its mandates and methodologies considerably over the decades, and will continue to do so. But changing and adapting is a very different matter from fundamental reform and restructuring.

No one would have imagined, even four decades ago, that the UN would one day observe elections in many parts of the world, engage in successful conflict resolution in places like Cambodia and East Timor, that there would be as many as 65 peacekeeping operations since 1948, that tribunals would be set up for crimes against humanity, that there would be an International Criminal Court, and that the UN would engage in massive relief and rehabilitation efforts in natural disasters as in Pakistan or in war-torn countries like the Sudan.

The issues raised in the debate on UN reform relate to the question of decision-making, process, transparency and accountability; and with these, the related matters of monitoring and evaluation. These are very difficult issues to resolve when it comes to dealing with sovereign states. Basically, there is a democratic deficit at the international level. In the most serious cases, the issue of peace and security, which is in the almost exclusive purview of the UN Security Council, the Charter of the UN has all too often been subverted and distorted by the influence of one permanent member; in the post Cold War era, specifically by the United States, thereby reducing the Council's credibility.

When reform of the UN is discussed, every country will agree that changes are required, but no two countries will agree on what those changes should be. The least developed, the developing, the small states, the landlocked, the industrialized and the emerging countries all have different agendas that serve their own interests. This is what makes it impossible to reach consensus. The countries making the loudest noise for transparency are the same ones that block the reform process and lobby hardest for their unsuitable candidates to find jobs in the UN system.

How effective are the WMO, WIPO, ECOSOC, UNIDO and a host of others? If these acronyms are not known to the general public, the chances are that these organs are probably irrelevant. Would there be rationale in saving money on these organizations by winding them up? Some of them have budgets only big enough to pay for their own staff salaries. It is easy to point to waste and inefficiency in many UN agencies around the world. The UNMOGIP (the United Nations Military Observer Group in India and Pakistan) has been in existence from 1949 and is the oldest peacekeeping mission of the UN – though it is not described as such. But few people even in India and Pakistan are aware of its existence, or what it is meant to do. It would obviously be a good thing to eliminate some of these agencies and establish others with new mandates relevant to the contemporary world. For example, a new UN agency to deal with energy, water and the equitable sharing of our global commons is overdue. It would be a step in the right direction to have a UN Economic Council to supplement the mandate of the UN Security Council.

There are some UN agencies that do good work. The UN Refugee Agency, the World Health Organisation, UNICEF and UNDP among others. But there is little in the way of synergy or coordination even between these bodies and it is time that thought was given to group many of such agencies under a new umbrella called UNAID (United Nations Agency for International Development), which could add value to the Bretton Woods financial institutions.

Referring to those Bretton Woods institutions, the IMF, the World Bank and GATT, now the World Trade Organization, were conceived as part of the UN family. Their governing structure is heavily weighted in favour of the industrialized countries, though their clientele has always been almost exclusively from the developing world. Only very recently has the voting power of emerging economies like India and China obtained a slightly higher quota, but both combined still total less than 10 per cent. This is clearly anachronistic and requires revision in keeping with the changed world order. The IMF had almost no role in the global financial meltdown of this decade precisely because of this lopsided governance pattern.

In India, any discussion on UN reform and restructuring seems to turn entirely around one question only, the one of expanding the UN Security Council to include India as a permanent member because of its population, its democracy, contribution to UN peacekeeping, and other arguments. India for the first time formally proposed its inclusion as a permanent member in 1994, when the writer was foreign secretary. It was in the same year that Japan made a similar claim. Both India and Japan were then, not coincidentally, in a competition at the same time for a non-permanent seat on the Council, and both still press their suit for permanent membership.

We in India see our case as self-evident, and we have expended a great deal of time, energy and financial resources on enlisting support throughout the world. When the time comes, it will come because our stature as an essential country whose opinion is required and respected is recognized by everyone. In other words, when we no longer need even to make a case. For many reasons, and several of those having nothing at all to do with India, that time is not yet ripe. But this matter still obsesses our media, for example, when the Indian president visited China recently and when China's response, whatever our wishful-thinking media may have reported, was typically ambiguous, if not discouraging.

Restructuring the UN Security Council will need an amendment of the UN Charter, which is the constitution of that international body. This is a very difficult procedure, requiring the approval of 2/3rds of the membership of the UN and the consent of all 5 permanent members of the Council, apart from the ratification by due constitutional process of all members. The process for considering amendment to the Charter itself requires 2/3rds of the General Assembly and 9 votes of the Security Council. Thus the Charter has only been amended a handful of times in its sixty-five year history, the last such occasion in 1973. Changes in structure without amending the Charter have allowed the Security Council to take decisions even if the permanent members abstained instead of voting in favour, the admission of China instead of Taipeh in 1971 and Russia taking the place of the Soviet Union in 1991. The Rules of Procedure of various UN bodies have been repeatedly modified. But there are no shortcuts to expanding the numbers of permanent or non-permanent members of the Security Council.

The fundamental point to recognize about India's prospects for permanent membership is that the outcome will have to be a package deal, not only about India but many countries covering all the continents. There will have to be give and take, bargains will have to be struck, and no country will get full satisfaction. The reality is that there is no consensus at present in expanding the Council or with which specific counties. The day will undoubtedly come when India will be a permanent member. There is no need to fret and fuss about this. We should instead build our own strength and credibility, and address our many internal weaknesses. When the time is right, we will be welcomed in; we will not have to try and force the door open.

October 2010

THE IMF WITH ROOM AT THE TOP

An international organization with a capital and lending capacity of hundreds of billion dollars will have a vacancy at its top almost immediately, as a result of its managing director's personal indiscretions and acute embarrassment to himself and the International Monetary Fund. Everyone can agree that the IMF requires a comprehensive overhaul under visionary leadership, but the race to lead the IMF is not to the most capable candidate, but confined to a narrow clique of European central bankers and politicians. This is because, by convention, the IMF's chief executive is appointed by the Fund's 24-member executive board, and to this date, has always been chosen from a West European country. The latest and tenth Managing Director, Dominique Strauss-Kahn from France, was to retire in any case in October 2011. In 2009, after a full decade of working groups, position papers and learned reports, it was agreed that the IMF should adopt 'an open, merit-based and transparent process' of selection for the top management, but this formula is not yet applied to its chief executive.

The Bretton Woods institutions, the IMF and the World Bank and the World Trade Organization, are part of the United Nations family. The governing structure of the IMF and the World Bank is heavily weighted in favour of the industrialized countries, although their clientele in numerical terms is from the developing world. At the end of 2010, India and Brazil were given additional quotas to join China and Russia among the top ten IMF shareholders, but strong economies like India and China, even with the added powers, still possess, both combined, less than 10 per cent of the voting strength. To reserve the leadership of the World Bank to the USA and that of the IMF to Europe, the two regions responsible for the global meltdown and financial panic in the first decade of this century, is patently absurd.

When this writer asked an economics professor closely identified with the discredited and now disempowered CPM regime in West Bengal whether the IMF should mark a departure by appointing a non-European at its head, he enquired rhetorically why it should matter who takes the leadership of that international financial organization. The answer to that academic is that it does matter, and it is something the developing world has been struggling to extract from the grip of the developed countries in recognition of the shift in the balance of power from the industrialized economies to the new emerging powers illustrated by the BRICS (Brazil, Russia, India, China and South Africa).

If the new managing director's credentials are such that will make him or her wary of debts and deficits, such views will be of relevance to the world, but that is hardly the full prospectus of what the IMF stands badly in need of at this time, which is nothing less than root and branch reform. The organization was shown to be ineffective during the Asian financial crisis of 1997, and its advice was resented and discounted by the affected countries in making their recoveries, especially in regard to capital controls that placed restrictions on free movement of currencies across transnational borders. The IMF also failed to anticipate or deal with the global financial melt-down of 2008, which was caused by, and afflicted most gravely, its leading shareholders, namely the Western developed economies, all of whom are still languishing in various phases of the financial doldrums. The IMF's favoured policies of free capital flows have pushed several countries into crises, such as Spain, Portugal, Greece, Ireland and Iceland. Its prescriptions are rigid and its one-cap-fits-all solutions are belatedly considered to be ill-conceived, to say the least.

The IMF has been progressively overshadowed by the G-20, a body that sets out policies for the world economy, but without any executive ability. The G-20 agreed to expand the IMF's ability to lend to countries hit by recession, but the Fund has managed to advance only about 15 per cent of the monies at its disposal, and its conditionalities remain stringent, emphasizing the restoration of fiscal balances through restrictions of wage and employment opportunities, essentially through cuts in social spending. At the same time, volatile capital movements have continued unhindered, holding the danger of creating instability in the finances of vulnerable nations. Poor and middle-income countries complain bitterly that their economies are being knocked off-course as a flood of hot money assails their markets as a result of policies adopted in the West. Whether the IMF has finally learned to slip out of its monetarist strait-jacket is debatable: it is still wedded to controls being used sparingly, in specific conditions, and only temporarily. It prefers to concentrate on capital inflows, investments, reserve requirements and lock-in periods rather than outflows which have always had a more pernicious effect. Countries that have large capital inflows are unlikely to be the developing countries, where such a phenomenon would in fact be welcomed as providing balance of payment support – in other words, nations that would have no need of advice from the IMF in the first place. Chile, Brazil, Thailand and Malaysia had instituted controls on capital outflows well before the IMF changed its traditional tune. In countries with balance of payments problems, the IMF still persists in advocating open capital accounts and further liberalization to secure investor confidence, and there is no evidence of any introspection despite IMF nostrums having made the maladies worse for several patients in the past.

What does the IMF think about high food and fuel prices, commodities futures markets, or financing facilities without conditionalities? Would the forthcoming leadership change in the IMF make any difference? At one of the most turbulent times since the Second World War, the appointment of the next IMF head acquires considerable significance. The new leader should give due recognition to the essential role of state spending in maintaining incomes and employment. Historian Trevor-Roper once wrote: 'it is European techniques, European examples, European ideas which have shaken the non-European world out of its past, and the history of the world for the past five centuries, in so far as it has significance, has been European history'. Such opinions have no contemporary relevance. The membership of the Fund has increased from the initial 29 to 187, while the Eurozone has lurched into an existential crisis. A so-called advanced European economy is as likely to apply to the IMF for a bail-out as one in Saharan Africa, and the biggest borrowers in value terms are now Greece, Portugal and Ireland. A massive change has taken place in moving the centre of gravity of the global economy away from the industrialized West, and solutions and practical examples offered by the new emerging economies will be more apposite for the IMF's role than the failed policies of the past. An IMF managing director from outside Europe will be better placed to re-position the organization. Such an appointment will also reflect a welcome and overdue awareness that history has moved on from a handful of nations in the West to a much larger group in the South and East.

May 2011

INDIA AND THE UNITED STATES: A FOREVER UNEASY RELATIONSHIP?

It is symptomatic of the perversity of the relationship between India and the USA that among the most successful periods in our bilateral relations was at a time when US policy and *modus operandi* were subject to worldwide criticism, not least from influential circles in India, and when the incumbent at the White House was either ridiculed or demonized in most parts of the world. It is for psychoanalysts and therapists to unravel the mysteries of a love-hate relationship, with the attendant emotions of obsession, expectation, disillusion, and bitter recrimination. But a love-hate description does not begin to do justice to the complications of the ties between the USA and India.

The liberties we enjoy, or aspire to enjoy, would not have come about if Woodrow Wilson and Franklin D. Roosevelt had not championed the cause of decolonization, and if the USA had not entered the Second World War in the Pacific. After the war, when the Cold War and the Indian tilt towards the Soviet Union were at their height, the American food supplies under PL-480 fed large sections of our people from ship to mouth. The amount due to the USA was written off and a facsimile was on prominent display at the Empire State Building as the biggest amount ever written on a cheque. In the USA in the 1970s, Indian representatives used to be asked at public meetings why India was ostentatiously ungrateful for this help. Fortunately, nobody talks about these awkward passages of recent history any more in either country.

Nevertheless, a predominant image of the USA in India is the unit of the Seventh fleet led by the aircraft carrier *Enterprise,* which was sent to the Bay of Bengal during the war leading to the liberation of Bangladesh. This bogey image begs the fact that the nuclear-capable weapons were unusable, and their effect as a restraint on India was zero – like the grand old Duke of York, who marched his troops up the hill and down again.

If an Indian goes to China, which was excluded by the USA from the United Nations from 1949 to 1971, or to Vietnam, which was ravaged in every possible way by the USA from 1959 to 1975, he will be surprised to find there nothing like the hostility and suspicion for the USA that exists in India – in fact, exactly the reverse. Indians love speaking about 'the Ugly American', without realizing that this person is the hero of the 1958 novel and not the villain. This is the kind of misunderstanding that bedevils the relationship.

The degree of reciprocal hostility from the USA towards India is far less, even non-existent, though there is a bemused curiosity among aware circles in that country about India's economic progress, democracy, and civilization, despite the apparent anarchy that attends every human activity here. We cannot assume that India can ever feature prominently in the public consciousness in the USA, in which the population, by and large, knows even its big neighbours like Mexico only through the Latino working class, and Canada as a part of the frozen northern Arctic. When Sarah Palin said she could see Russia from her house in Alaska, that said it all.

Is the relationship especially difficult because we are too much alike? Two big democracies that gained independence from the same colonial power, though nearly 200 years apart, should have more in common. Mahatma Gandhi gleaned many strategies of non-cooperation from Henry David Thoreau, and in turn influenced the non-violent civil rights movement under Martin Luther King. What we share in common with USA is a love of obscure team games that few other countries take seriously – baseball and American football on the one hand, and cricket and kho-kho on the other. The Americans invented records – faster, higher, stronger; and it takes a heavy dose of materialism to do that. The *Guinness Book of Records* and *Ripley's Believe it or Not* became a yardstick of earthly success. There was no concept of record-making or breaking before the Americans came on the scene. The Indian mentality is not suited to anything as finite as surpassing achievement, but has nevertheless taken lovingly to record keeping; how many minutes since the last six was hit, or which Indian has the world's longest fingernail.

Big countries usually differ on big issues, like security and arms control, the environment, or access for trade, but between India and the USA, the smallest matters are blown out of all proportion, and it seems at times as if India is searching for matters on which to take offence. Whereas the USA is supremely confident about its nationhood, which was evident from the very start and well-entrenched by the time of de Toqueville's visit in the nineteenth century, India appears still to be groping for a definition of itself as a nation. This perhaps is one of many reasons why it is so prickly and reactive to America. In a country where a proposed national health service is branded as socialism, it is hardly surprising that Nehru's and Indira Gandhi's socialistic policies and non-alignment were regarded as 'immoral' and found few sympathizers, in the same way that the US's Cold and Proxy wars against the USSR had no appeal for India. The subtlety of the Indian intellect which means maybe when it says yes, and no when it says 'no problem', found the American Manichean direct approach brash and offensive.

When the Vietnam War coined the T-shirt slogan 'Yankee Go Home – and take me with you!' this joke somehow gets near the heart of Indo-US complications. A well-known Indian actor, feeling rebuffed in the USA, swore never again to set foot on American soil – except for work, to see friends and relatives, and for holiday recreation. His personal angst may have been profound, but he knew his dilemma would leave the Americans unmoved. Would the Delhi establishment have reacted in the way it did to the Shah Rukh Khan 'humiliation' if the actor had been detained at Tokyo, Madrid or Burkina Fasso?

The Indian political leader sees no contradiction in fulminating against American policies, but resorting to by-pass surgery in Houston or an American education for his children in order to enhance their career prospects, usually by staying on in the USA itself. One prominent leftist personage from India led a party delegation to Disneyland with the stated justification of studying 'crowd control'. Those who pour scorn on the American alleged lack of civilization, culture and morals are fully aware that there is a great Indian appetite, despite the negative rhetoric, for all things American; that Bollywood shamelessly plagiarizes American movie plots and filmscores, and that a green card is a star on the cv – 'green card holding Saraswat bachelor seeks same caste soul-mate – horoscopes welcome'. The same contradiction appears in more serious aspects, such as the multiple joint armed forces exercises nowadays performed by military people of both countries without sharing any stated or presumed joint strategy in the Asian, let alone South Asian, theatre.

What of the near future? Irrespective of the diatribes of certain political circles against everything American, admittedly more muted after the arrival of President Obama, and emotional reactions against any outsiders who dare to interpose themselves in Indo-Pakistan bilateral relations, there is nothing the government of India would like more than Washington's benevolent attention and sympathetic understanding. Since the break-up of the Soviet Union, the US has treated India with caution and a minimal pressing of its point of view. In other words, it has been largely accommodating.

Various anxieties arise nevertheless. Does the US under Obama share the same preoccupation with China's rise to world power as did George W Bush? Why is it that from the US side, the only senior politician to visit India so far has been Hillary Clinton, and that too after seven months? Is the USA devoting thought and time to Pakistan at the expense of India? – a Pakistan where, incidentally, anti-Americanism is even stronger than it is in India, despite it being a client state in nearly every respect. Have the nuclear-waste enrichment and reprocessing and dual use technology access matters been finally settled in India's favour, or will mutual recriminations fly thick and fast? Will the implications of K. Santhanam's allegations of a fizzle thermonuclear explosion stir another hornet's nest? Will carbon emission controls, Iran, CTBT, fissile material freeze and protectionism, all of which Obama strongly cares about, sour relations?

In the next few years, Indian attitudes to the USA, irrational as they usually are and locked in the mindset of a bygone age, will not change. Anti-American attitudes will always find willing audiences, and not only among the left-leaning, because inherited obsessions cannot be shaken off without self-examination and a thorough mental purging. Nothing like that is likely to happen, and those who know better do not attempt to shape public opinion.

American attitudes to India, on the part of the Washington

establishment, will depend on what role is envisaged for India to further the PakAf strategy, and whether India will be compliant. The chances for this to happen are very poor. Both India and Pakistan will be unreliable allies in any US regional strategy. In the longer prospect, even by 2050, the USA will be among the world's three biggest economies, and still by far the strongest military power. India and the USA will never go to war, but neither will there ever be mutual harmony. India should show greater self-confidence and concentrate on building itself economically. As the world emerges from the present recession, India will be comparatively stronger than most countries, and will have to loom large in the future plans of every other big economy.

September 2009

THE UNITED STATES ELECTIONS: AND THE TEA PARTY

All 435 seats in the House of Representatives, 37 of 100 Senators, 37 out of 50 governors and all but 4 state legislatures have been elected on 2 November. It was not just an election, but a referendum on Barack Obama's two years in office. Neither Obama nor Sarah Palin were on the ballot, but the results could determine their political futures.

A malaise hangs over America with its optimism subdued. 60 per cent of Americans think their country is on the wrong track, 70 per cent disapprove of Congress, 50 per cent disapprove of Obama. For more than a year, the official unemployment rate has been 9.6 per cent and in reality much higher. Interest rates are so low that retirees cannot live on savings. The rate of growth cannot create jobs on the scale required. Foreclosure and bankruptcy rates are high, and the majority of homes have negative equity. Anti-incumbency sentiments are riding very high. People are looking for change and for a different breed of politicians to deliver it. Ultraconservatives have now become mainstream.

Rick Santelli of CNBC, ranting about mortgage owners bailed

out by the taxpayer, invoked the eighteenth century 'Boston Tea Party' against the British and wanted to throw mortgage documents into the Chicago River. He started a movement that unified disparate elements against high taxes, large deficits, big government, federal spending, bailouts of bankers, health care and Obama himself. Populist movements are common in USA – the civil rights movement, the anti-Vietnam War movement, and Ross Perot, who challenged the two-party system in the 1990s. It will be seen if the Tea Party movement is ephemeral or a fundamental shift to the right in US politics, but at the heart of the present Republican revival is the Tea Party.

The US is built on the power of ideas, and politicians were perceived to have undermined the cherished idea that Americans leave to the next generation a legacy more prosperous than the one they inherited. The Tea Party includes a spectrum of extreme religious, cultural and social beliefs with a merited reputation for weirdness and eccentricity. Virulent rightists are their heroes, right-wing think tanks and pressure groups the storm troopers. Huge funding has poured in from supporters of the right, including corporate America.

There is implied racism in hostility to Obama's policies that are seen as 'European' and 'socialist' – both damning epithets in the USA. Obama is vilified as communist, Muslim and born outside the US. The combination of grassroots populism, political conservatism and big money is seizing on the despair of economic distress; 'we need a new set of people to return the country to the ideas it was founded on. Since we have not been able to change the politics of people in Washington, we have to change the faces.' The Tea Party objective was to send conservatives to Congress, to abolish the energy and education departments and the Environmental Protection Agency. They also wish to abolish the United Nations.

The Tea Party did not run under its own name and is not a normal political party. It may possibly turn into a third party with its candidate, perhaps Sarah Palin, who has been bestowed with celebrity status due to her abysmal ignorance, for the 2012 Presidential campaign. Among its core beliefs are downsizing of government, cut in income taxes, national budget balanced, crackdown on illegal immigrants, and sanctity of gun ownership. It is in revolt against political establishments, including the Republicans; its success could be described as a hostile takeover of the Republican party. Its adherents call themselves ordinary citizens who could not stand idly by while the basic foundations of the USA were being eroded. They want fiscal responsibility, limited government and free markets; 'we cannot spend our way out of debt; we will be owned by the Chinese if we don't stop it'.

The Tea Party is Yankee poujadisme. It is a protest movement, a cause, a social networking site, a cultural phenomenon, amorphous, decentralized, a loose confederation of local associations springing from the grassroots with no leader and no hierarchy. The membership is white, middle aged, relatively affluent and well educated. The Tea Party is built on the anxieties of people who feel the American dream under challenge – a job, a home, secure old age, a car, the right to live without undue interference from the government. Such people feel angered that while they struggle to make both ends meet, bankers, insurance companies and car manufacturers have been rescued with taxpayer money. Afghanistan is not an issue; individual liberty is what Tea Party constituency wants, along with a return to a mythical and unattainable age. They invoke the putative values of the American Revolution. They believe in liberty but not equality; the rich can look after themselves and the poor can suffer in silence. A collection of mavericks determined to take the US back to imagined eighteenth-century roots may influence whether Obama is a one or two term president.

The election results have been the worst rout for an incumbent party in six decades. Republicans increased their tally by 60 extra seats in the House, 6 in the Senate and 10 governorships. 62 Tea Party-supported candidates are a new influence in the land, though Senate Democratic majority leader Harry Reid edged out Tea Party novice Sharron Angle in the closest, nastiest and highest profile race. The Democrats have taken a hammering, and the President is faced with a choice of legislative paralysis or having to compromise with opponents who are in no mood to compromise.

It is a far cry from Obama's euphoria days and his message of optimism. Obama's achievements are in restored dignity of the US in the world, education reform, the stimulus package, withdrawal from Iraq, health care, student loans, Wall Street regulation, clean energy and a little noticed tax rebate for 95 per cent of taxpayers. His handling of the BP oil-spill in the Gulf of Mexico compares favourably with George W. Bush's inertia over the tidal wave that destroyed New Orleans. On the explosive air freight from Yemen, Obama appeared decisive and in control – but national security is always a strong card for the Republicans.

Obama raised hopes of a different type of politics, but his timidity and inability to get things done have been his undoing. Obama embodied hope for change but did not deliver. He inherited an economic mess but did not tackle it vigorously. Most of the money Obama spent has been in plugging budgets of states like California, that has a higher deficit than Greece, but the public do not see that. The stimulus did not create jobs. Democrats are disgruntled, while Obama's personal following is unimpressed, feeling that he is influenced by Wall Street and the unions. The working class thought Obama a failure even when he had the support of both houses. His authority is gravely diminished.

Obama has relied on his wife, Chicago associates, and Bush hold-overs, and failed to connect with independent voters. The health and finance reforms did not go far enough for liberals, and were anathema for the right. And the liberals are as unforgiving as the right wing; Guantanamo was not closed, the climate change bill has been abandoned. Obama suffered from too much hype, the Nobel Peace Prize was an absurdity, and his dry intellectual style is out of touch. Obama must realize that logic can win arguments, but only emotion can motivate his followers. The great orator has failed to communicate.

What will emerge? Hyper-partisanship and inability to compromise bedevils US politics. So gridlock and crisis looms. The government's ability to raise money for health care and other causes will be wrecked by Republicans. Even with Democrats in charge of Congress, it was a battle to get legislation through; now it will be impossible. Few major legislations are envisaged by Obama, he will have no choice but to do very little. Republicans are past masters at strangling Democrat ambitions in Congress and will ensure the blocking of any major bill. But the Republicans will also do little: Obama will use his veto and Republicans will be needled by unruly Tea Party members. The odd coupling of extremists from the religious right and libertarians can hardly be a model of disciplined unity.

On the other hand, Reagan in 1982 lost the House majority like Clinton in 1994 and Truman earlier. But these presidents had great political skills, and the last two years of Clinton's first term were very fruitful. Both Truman and Clinton won a second term, and Obama will derive some comfort from that. To use a typical American expression, it isn't over till the fat lady sings.

November 2010

EUROPE IN DISTRESS: YEARS OF ANXIETY AHEAD FOR THE UNION

Since the age of European expansion, Europe has been the continent with which Indians are most familiar. The European Union, a transnational decentralized federal construct of 27 nations and nearly 500 million people, making great progress towards a common space for goods, people and services, common standards, a common currency, and espousing values such as democracy and the rule of law, was a role-model for other organizations around the world. With a combined GDP of $18 trillion it ranks above the USA and is our leading economic partner. Yet, at this time of Europe's greatest crisis, there is little attention given to it by the Indian media.

Even before the global recession, Europeans had begun contemplating the adjustments that would be needed in this century due to the rise of Asia. With the largest concentration of world population, concerns over terrorism, proliferation of weapons of mass destruction, unsolvable inter-state problems, imminent conflicts, abject poverty, food shortages and climate change, the phrase 'Asian century' is a misnomer for a continent that enjoys neither political nor commercial unity nor any common security agenda. Its few multilateral structures are weak, and governance varies from dystopia and communism to liberal democracy. Nevertheless, internationalists must note the spectacular economic growth in certain parts of Asia, with the benefits of low cost labour, large territory and resources and rapidly growing infrastructure and technology. The locus of new demand and spending power will shift to the emerging economies, especially in Asia, and per capita disparity will imply exceptional price sensitivity in the Asian market, with its implications on production, outsourcing, investment, pricing and marketing influencing the future shape of European industry.

The EU's ambitions for an innovative dynamic economy necessitate the establishment of internal economic reforms and new decision-making structures to pursue appropriate policies at a time when the Union is beset by other multiple preoccupations: ageing populations, fiscal problems including the extent of regulation, economic slowdown, ailing health services, failing pension schemes, and debating the vaguely-defined European social model as opposed to American forms of global competitive capitalism. Other challenges are the need for coherent internal governance, further rounds of enlargement, financial solidarity in an asymmetric economy, the political and military profile, immigration issues, management of diversity, use of biofuels, and normative and moral issues like biotechnology. When the current economic crisis is over, those concerns will remain, and despite being the most powerful and unified association of independent states ever devised, it confronts multiple dilemmas.

EU governments have been living on loans representing large percentages of national GDP. The amortization of these borrowings will add to the burden of public services that are too large a proportion of the total economy, which has reduced the incentives for responsible consumption. Funding the welfare state at these levels will no longer be possible unless the economy grows bigger. Despite stringent rules in principle, fiscal discipline has not always been achieved even in good times, and the next generation of governments will have to face their electorates with these realities.

Recession can no longer be considered an exclusively American problem, and the EU's recovery to growth is extremely fragile. The Eurozone was established after countries like Germany and France abandoned currencies that were expressions of their national identity, but there is now acute stress on the Euro system, focused on Greece, which after a decade of low interest rates, wage inflation, high consumption and property booms, needs to raise €50 billion in public debt this year with a budget deficit of 13 per cent of GDP (the Eurozone limit is 3 per cent) and national debt of 120 per cent of GDP. It is guilty of falsifying its eligibility criteria data to join the Eurozone, and widespread tax-evasion, but warnings are also out on Ireland, Spain, and Portugal. Iceland, not in the EU but part of Europe, is already a declared defaulter. California, with a bigger economy than Greece, has long been living beyond its means but its deficit is underwritten by the US federal government and taxpayer. Unless the Eurozone taxpayer is willing to bite a similar bullet, the EU will be revealed as having no monetary or fiscal strategy. The crisis shaking Greece and driving down the value of the Euro shows how solidarity still stops at national borders as public opposition to rescuing Greece mounts – including as many as 2/3rds of the German population, which has recently undergone salary freezes and reduction of welfare benefits. But the chaos that would occur in financial markets if Greece was expelled from the Eurozone is more frightening than the wrath of the voters. If Greece defaults, it will make lenders wary of lending to any government, and all of them need to borrow. So when Greece gets bailed out by member states, it must undergo a period of economic reforms and monitored belt-tightening that has already triggered social and industrial unrest.

It is the political dimension that will define the European Union as a meaningful international player. Its experience in Iraq and Afghanistan shows that while it may be respected for conflict resolution and peace building within Europe, it is neither an actual nor potential political or military force with geo-strategic capabilities outside Europe. Operations in Afghanistan are hugely controversial domestically, and apart from Britain, coalition members have taken pains to provide the minimum contingents deployed as far away as possible from the front line. Even so, the Dutch government has fallen on the issue of extending its Afghan commitment, and others will be anxiously watching their voting public for signs of greater unease.

In terms of 'hard' economic or military power, Europe cannot aspire to a major role in shaping world events, and the abundance of soft power generated by its various constituents has been impossible to replicate at the pan-EU level. It will have to compete in an ever-stiffer contest for raw materials in the coming decades. Its present dependence on energy imports make it vulnerable, as the extent of its self-sufficiency is steeply declining. By 2030 the production of oil and gas within the EU is expected to decline by 73 and 59 per cent respectively, and at least 2/3rds of its requirements will thereafter have to be met by imports.

The EU's fertility rate is expected to continue falling, with a drop in working age population, and no member country has the 2.1 birth-rate per female that is needed to keep the population stable. One third of the population will be 65 or over by 2050. By 2050, average EU GDP growth is likely to be around 1.25 per cent, and its share of world product is expected to fall from about 30 per cent now to 10 per cent. Contrary to current public opinion in Europe, a strategically calculated enlargement, more legal immigration, and increased flexibility in the workplace including increase in the retirement age, may prove essential for future economic competitiveness.

The labour pool in the Arab world will increase by over 100 million in a few decades and that of sub-Saharan Africa by 250 million. The consequences of these demographics cause great concern to Europe, though it will require a measure of controlled immigration to enhance productivity. Many migrant communities in Europe remain marginalized, and despite the rousing speeches of politicians extolling tolerance, are considered a burden rather than a positive contribution. The problem concerns the authority of the secular state and its impact on religious minorities in general and Muslims in particular, who number sixteen million or 3 per cent of the EU population. Only a new settlement between the member states and religion can successfully incorporate the growing religious minorities in Europe. The EU has to re-define its attitude to Islam, the Arab world and Muslim immigration, since Islam has become Europe's second largest religion.

Many nations have enjoyed rising living standards despite budget deficits, appreciating currencies, high interest rates, high wages, periods of labour shortage and limited natural resources: the stock of factors at any time is less important than the way in which they are created and upgraded. Whether the recovery is V- or W-shaped, the European Union will eventually emerge from recession to remain a major contributor to world economy, with its external relations based on normative values. But it has a packed and controversial domestic agenda to deal with first, and its biggest challenge will be to stay united.

March 2010

LIBERTY: STILL SEARCHING FOR DEFINITION

The common factor that unites the Gujarat and Maharashtra governments' actions against the books of Jaswant Singh on Jinnah and James Laine on Shivaji respectively, the *fatwas* against Salman Rushdie and Taslima Nasrin, Pramod Muthalik's hoodlums assaulting women in Mangalore pubs, and the RSS campaign against the painter Hussain, is the habitual testing of the boundaries of individual personal liberty and human rights. Democratic societies today are overwhelmed by the complex variety of conflicting claims to personal liberty.

Personal liberties are under pressure in many parts of the world and from many quarters. Nation states that are supposed to be the protectors and custodians of human rights are often the worst offenders. Israel, which sees itself as fighting for the liberty of its people, arrogates to itself the right to curtail media freedom, use disproportionate and random violence against civilians, and is pauperizing the whole population of Gaza, whereas the Palestinian population sees itself as fighting for the freedom of the Palestinian people against a foreign and oppressive military occupation. Does the right of Israelis to live safely within their own borders (presently undefined) justify the outrageous violations of human rights law for over half a century? Aung San Suu Kyi has been imprisoned in Myanmar for 21 years, solely because she threatens the perpetual military regime through the democratic process. Nelson Mandela was in a South African jail for 27 years in similar circumstances.

The concept of intellectual freedom is one that concerns us because it is assumed that a person is more fulfilled under conditions of liberty. The only limitations in theory should be the self-imposed ones necessitated by forms of collaboration, where tensions may arise between the personal freedom to think and work at one's own rhythm, and the common good of attaining a higher level of social harmony. Even the closest social interactions could constrain liberty when the freedom of the individual comes into conflict with that of others, a feature typical in any community life. Therefore society has perforce to make a choice between countervailing liberties. Civilized societies emphasize the importance of freedom for education, science, the arts and democracy itself. The basic sources of international human rights law are the Universal Declaration of Human Rights of 1948 and the various United Nations Covenants approved thereafter.

In the Netherlands, there is a 'Party for Freedom' that carries out a campaign against immigrants, in Austria a 'Freedom Party' that is part of the federal government, and in Hungary, the Jobbik Party that opposes foreigners, Jews and Gypsies. Most countries in the European Union have similar political formations. These reflect the diffuse feelings of fear due to the growing number and visibility of immigrant Muslims, exacerbated inevitably by the association of fundamentalist Islam with international terrorism, and on a more structural level, the still only partial integration of these immigrants with society due to social, religious and ethnic factors. Immigrants from less developed countries to Europe, who have not been exposed to successive emancipation movements, have problems adjusting to the cultural gap, which only supplements the challenge of different linguistic and religious traditions. Aspects of discrimination against immigrants have led to aggressive reaction. The percentage of unemployed young migrants with weak educational skills is high, and gangs and criminal acts have resulted. The law and order forces are not always free of racial reflexes, which add to the mutual divide and the reciprocal image of an enemy.

The Belgian parliament has forbidden the veil in public spaces for the sake of security, and the French are close to similar legislation. The Danish premier has declared 'there is no place for the *burqa* and *niqaab* in our society'. The debate however centers on who is discriminating against whom, and on what grounds – in France some 2000 women are believed to wear such clothes, a percentage so low that one may wonder why there should be any problem. Of this number, 2/3rds of them are French citizens and 90 per cent are younger than 40. Are European societies obsessively fixated on symbols through which small minorities are marking their collective identities, when these emblems are not shared even by the vast majority of their own ethnic and religious group? Why should the building of minarets for mosques damage the beautiful Swiss landscape more than traditional Christian bell towers?

On the other hand, it is entirely understandable that societies wish to protect their own value-systems, which may include the security of persons and property, tolerance, and freedom of expression from a minority that chooses to repudiate everything except the material advantages gained from migration to another cultural environment. But how far can such protection go without the abuse of individual liberty of expression in an absolute sense?

Since the dress code of Muslim women has been pushed to the political agendas of European countries, defendants of the *hidjab, burqa* and *niqaab* are inclined to claim that the Holy Quran prescribes this kind of attire. This argument brings the issue under the protection of the fundamental freedom to practice religious or philosophical faith enshrined by the Universal Declaration and the Covenant on the Elimination of all Forms of Discrimination against Women. But the Universal Declaration itself has been marginalized in some Muslim countries as a product of Western culture and therefore inapplicable to Islamic societies. In 1990 the Organization of Islamic Conference, which now counts 56 nations, subjected all the rights and freedoms in the Universal Declaration to the Islamic *Shariah*.

In the course of its history, the Muslim world did not develop the idea of separation of religious and secular authority. Nor did it develop any clerical hierarchy that was empowered to prescribe a unique orthodox interpretation of the holy book. Religious prescriptions have thus been interpreted through the centuries in different ways in different countries. In consequence, the reference to the *Shariah* is equally open to a variety of interpretations. The scarce references in the Quran about proper dress only concern the female gender, and without attempting any contestable exegesis, it may however be confidently stated that such prescriptions as there are, have enjoyed a heterodox observance. It was perhaps the Iranian revolution of 1979 that launched a fundamentalist reaction to women who had been laying aside the veil since the early twentieth century, and the donning of the *chador* and the *hidjab* to make a religious statement became the markers of a new order that reinvented an opaque tradition that had never been observed throughout the whole Islamic world.

Some Islamic fundamentalist groups outside the Muslim world, especially in the United Kingdom, are seeking to impose *Shariah* within their segregated communities. The imposition of a traditional female dress code is for them an expression of the rejection of the Western cultural environment in which they have chosen to live. From these circles there are calls for sexual segregation that go counter to the gradual and welcome evolution towards gender equality that has taken place in the last century, typified by universal suffrage, equal rights and pay and equal participation and benefits in education, professions, sports, medical care, birth control and the right of abortion. These are deeply-felt achievements relatively recently attained in democratic societies, and attempts to reject or retract from them will touch a highly sensitive nerve. Indeed, feminists will rightly point out that we still have a huge distance to go before women in countries like India achieve justice and equality in the distribution of social roles.

In India as in other democracies, society must be on guard against fundamentalist actions that seek to contest the gains in human rights that have been made over the past one hundred years. Obscurantists see no irony, and feel no shame, in sheltering under the very laws of human rights that they seek to subvert. Speaking of liberty, Charles de Montesquieu in his *Esprit des Lois* of 1748 wrote 'no concept has been used in a greater variety of meanings, and stuck in the minds in so many ways'. How true, even 260 years later.

August 2010

THE PAINS OF MULTICULTURALISM

Across Europe, politicians are questioning the virtues of multiculturalism, and instead urging assimilationist policies on immigrants, with emphasis on loyalty, integration and commitment to 'European values', defined as freedom of speech and worship, democracy, rule of law, and equal rights regardless of race, sex or sexuality. Multiculturalism means different things to different people, but what is clear is that there has been a recent change in many governments' approaches to immigrants, with varying solutions put forward in different countries, but uniformly based on implicit or explicit tests in language, outward conformity and citizenship.

Rejection of multiculturalism and the turn towards civic integration pre-dated 9/11 as a reaction to high unemployment and socio-economic failures among ethnic minority communities, but the rhetorical shift after the Al Qaeda attacks in USA and Europe was due to manifestations of Islamic extremism. The difficulty of fitting the practice of Islam into the European behavioural and cultural norms of gender equality, the private nature of religious belief, and conformity to secularism is the issue confronting most societies in West Europe. When the German president attempted to placate opinion by claiming that Islam had become a part of his country's culture, 66 per cent of his fellow-citizens categorically rejected his point of view, and polls show that Islam and immigration resonate as anxieties only second in importance to the slow growth in the economy. Therefore, these matters have inevitably become a matter of political debate.

German Chancellor Angela Merkel said in 2010 that her country's attempt to create a multicultural society had 'utterly failed', too little had been required of immigrants in the past, and the Germans had deluded themselves into thinking the 16 million immigrants (20 per cent of the population) would all return to where they came from at some time in the future. British Prime Minister Cameron in 2011 claimed that the biggest terror threat arose from a perverse form of Islam among British residents themselves; the authorities had been too fearful and too passive to stand up to unacceptable views and practices, such as the inflammatory and violence-inciting anti-Western public rantings by Islamist preachers Abu Qatada and Abu Hamza, despite intelligence reports about their pernicious influence. The former entered Britain illegally in 1993 on a forged passport and claimed asylum to avoid 'religious persecution' in Jordan, while the latter came to Britain as a 'student', obtained local citizenship on the basis of a short-lived marriage to a British woman, and fought for *jihadis* in Bosnia and Afghanistan. From Wikileaks it is seen that 35 of the Guantanamo inmates had been radicalized by such rabid preachers in the United Kingdom, and of those repatriated, several are still considered 'high-risk'.

Muslim spokespersons in Britain have riposted that Cameron was prey to 'hysteria and paranoia'; and to suggest that Muslims did not stand for tolerance, respect and freedom was deeply offensive. But in the London borough of Tower Hamlets, hard by the Olympics venue of 2012, Islamic extremists were ordering women to 'dress more modestly', issuing death threats to women who did not use the *burqa* or *hidjab*, and distributing leaflets saying, 'Arise and warn. Gay-free zone. Verily Allah is severe in punishment.' The Bishop of Rochester, himself of Pakistani origin, warns that certain parts of Britain have become transformed by radical immigrants into segregated 'no-go areas for non-Muslims'.

The reactions to such developments are predictable and reflect the diffused feelings of fear due to the growing number and visibility of immigrant Muslims, exacerbated by the association of fundamentalist Islam with international terrorism, and the yet only partial integration of these immigrants with local society due to social, religious and ethnic factors. Immigrants from less developed countries to Europe who have not been exposed to successive emancipation movements have problems adjusting to the cultural gap, which only supplements the challenge of different linguistic and religious traditions. Muslim emigrants to Europe have also made the error of confusing culture with creed, and tradition with civilization. They are voluntary immigrants seeking to foist their traditions on an unwilling settled population. There are no similar problems for these societies with Hindus, Buddhists, Jews or any other minorities. Two million Irish, the biggest foreign community in the UK, are considered an asset, as are the ¼ million Australians living and working there at any one time. The 'new' immigrants from the eastward expansion of the European Union, despite initial fears about job-security, are also now not considered problematic.

Taking the case of the UK, the European country with the largest Indian and Pakistani-origin immigrants, 7 million persons out of 61 million population have been born outside Britain and the vast majority of those are from outside Europe. Two-thirds of the rise in population is due to immigration; the net increase through immigration between 1997 and 2009 was 2.2 million. There were 11.5 per cent foreign-born residents in 2010, and 16 per cent of children in school do not know English as a first language. Any small boost in GDP as a result of immigration has not been matched by any rise of GDP per capita. Added to this negative profile are the sham marriages, bogus students, illegal immigrants and their dependents, benefit tourists and asylum system abusers. The stress on social services, education, health care and employment at the current time of serious economic difficulty has stretched European liberal pluralism to breaking point, while any move to restrict or reduce immigration has widespread popular appeal among voters, and consequently among politicians.

It is not only in Europe that strident views are expressed. Former Singapore Premier Lee Kuan Yew in a recent interview said

Muslim integration was failing, and 'we can integrate all religions and races except Islam'. He urged Muslims to be less 'distinct and separate' and 'less strict on Islamic observances'. Though there have been moves to ban the *niqab* in Canada, multiculturalism is not under similar pressure there, because it is viewed as a useful yardstick for differentiating Canada from the assimilationist USA. Canada and Australia are fortunate in not experiencing the socio-economic failures among ethnic minorities that occur in Europe due to their points system which has ensured that immigrants possess a certain minimum level of educational qualifications.

One result of the 'Arab spring awakening' is that thousands of Tunisian and Libyan refugees are pouring into Southern Europe, mostly by sea. Under pressure from their electorates, the French, Italians and Danes, backed by another 12 countries, are leading the rest of the EU in calling for a revision of the Schengen Agreement, a cornerstone of European unity that allows free movement between 25 nations in continental EU countries plus Norway, Switzerland and Iceland – a benefit that Indian visitors avail of provided they hold a valid visa for one of the Schengen countries.

The core belief in the West, where the Muslim immigrant issue is most pronounced, remains that individuals are free to maintain their cultural attachments provided these do not interfere with, or prevent, full integration with societal norms. But measures taken by governments to facilitate this will contribute to further alienation and anger among certain sections of the Muslim diaspora in those countries, who will resort to suicide bombings and extremism to advance their conception of an Islamic Caliphate. Thus the cycle of angst, heated debate and controversy will continue.

In the course of its history, the Muslim world did not develop the idea of separation of religious and secular authority. Nor did it develop any clerical hierarchy that was empowered to prescribe an unique orthodox interpretation of the holy book. Religious prescriptions have thus been interpreted through the centuries in different ways in different countries. It would be good, if matching the debates on Islam in Europe, the Muslim world in the wake of the 'Arab spring' would engage in an intellectual endeavour to mediate secularism and ideological differences in order to promote harmony, including by using the scholarship of distinguished *ulema*. Unfortunately, there is no sign of this happening now or in the future.

June 2011

EYELESS IN GAZA: TOWARDS INTIFADA THREE?

In this season of goodwill, there is precious little of it for the Palestinian cause. International attention to the Palestinian issue has decreased and there is hardly any media interest, except when a flotilla tries to break the Israeli blockade of Gaza, or when a presidential US peace initiative on the White House lawn heralds yet another false dawn. The choices after World War II were between a unitary state, two separate states and a federal state. India voted at the United Nations against the partition plan to create a separate state for the Jews. History may well record that a federal state on the lines envisaged by India would have been a better prospect, and that the Jews and the Arabs would learn to live together, but the Oslo accords implicitly recognized that a State of Palestine would emerge after an interim period, and this principle is now accepted by everyone. The question remains; what will be the nature of this state?

There are several related issues that arise, each burdened with immense difficulty. The first is the area of the proposed state. After the 1967 War, 78 per cent of previously undivided Palestine was occupied by Israel, leaving 22 per cent in Gaza and the West Bank. Additional problems arise with the Syrian Golan Heights under Israeli occupation, the Israeli settlements, and the thrice-holy Jerusalem, regarded by Israel as the 'eternal and undivided capital' and equally adamantly claimed by Palestine as 'al-Kuds'.

Another impediment to any settlement would be the Palestinian refugees who left in 1948 for Syria, Jordan, Lebanon and Gaza. They have the theoretical and internationally guaranteed right to return, or be given financial compensation. The Palestinians know that Israel will never allow 4 or 5 million Palestinian refugees to return, which would change the demographics of Israel, the self-proclaimed State of the Jews. So the refugees will either have to go to the envisaged new State of Palestine, or be absorbed in the host countries with financial compensation.

The whole area is water-scarce, and sharing water resources will be another major complication, which will call for regional cooperation, an aspect singularly lacking so far in every field. Security and freedom from terrorist attacks are the most important considerations for Israel, but if and when the other issues are resolved to mutual satisfaction, this obstacle could possibly be surmounted. The wall or barrier built by Israel along the Green Line has effectively contained acts of violence and suicide bombings, leaving Gaza as the main remaining source of threat to Israel.

As a result of Oslo, the Palestine Authority came into existence. Mahmoud Abbas aka Abu Mazen, the president of the Authority, was doubtful of his Fateh faction's success in any election and procrastinated, but was pressed by USA and Israel to hold them. The result was a split in the Palestine leadership, with Gaza under Hamas as an ideological and political entity distinct from the West Bank, where Abbas now has his headquarters at Ramallah. The so-called 'international community' led by Israel has placed a complete embargo on Gaza's one and a half million people who suffer poverty and deprivation, leaving Abbas in an acute dilemma. He would like to reconcile with Hamas – for which Egypt has made strenuous efforts – but Israel makes it clear that if that happens, it will terminate all contacts with Abbas or any group of which Hamas is a part. George W. Bush's roadmap went nowhere, and Obama's envoy George Mitchell has stumbled on the hurdle caused by Israeli settlements, which are regarded internationally as illegal.

On the occupied West Bank, there are 300,000 Israelis in settlements, and 200,000 more in East Jerusalem, which is a predominantly Arab area and must probably, in any eventual settlement, be awarded to Palestine. Israel, on the other hand, states that 3,000 more constructions will continue on the West Bank, whereas the Palestine Authority responds that there will be no talks unless there is a ban or at least a freeze. Obama issued an plea to Israel's Prime Minister Netanyahu to freeze settlement building, but Israel rebuffed the appeal. An initial gesture by Netanyahu to stop the construction for 10 months was absurdly hailed by Washington as 'a historic and unprecedented concession', but its resumption when the time-limit expired in September 2010 put an end to Obama's peace process. Israel has successfully obscured the issue of its illegal occupation of Palestinian land to such an extent that the matter of Israeli settlements is now being portrayed as the sole problem between the Palestinians and Israel. This has grave implications for the future.

An appeal by Abbas to freeze the settlement construction even for six months so that talks could resume has been ignored, leaving the Palestinian leader hugely discredited. Now the Americans have fallen on their knees and begged Netanyahu for a three-month freeze on West Bank settlements against guarantees of not asking for further suspensions, more security-related aid, and preventing the UN from passing any censure. Does the White House believe a two-state settlement can be achieved in three months, or is it the product of a desperate need to show some kind of result from Obama's peace initiative? Twenty years of on-off negotiations with the Israelis have produced not an iota of relief for the Palestinians despite the Goldstone and Uribe UN reports condemning Israel for its illegal blockade of Gaza and its abuse of human rights. Israel must know it will never again have the benefit of a Palestinian leader as moderate as Abbas: all his successors will be far more radical. Despite this, the Israelis have done nothing to strengthen his hand; not even token releases of any of the 10,000 Palestinians in prison, mostly without trial. This sets the stage for the third Intifada, after the first in the late 1980s, and the second in 2000.

While the Middle East question may be off the radar screen, it is linked to international concern about terrorism because it is invoked by extremists as one of their grievances, whether through sincere commitment or lip service. If the matter is resolved to the satisfaction of at least a majority on both sides, it will remove one important plank of the militant agenda. If not, it remains a festering sore, contributing inspiration and volunteers for the extremist cause. The two-state solution could be a blessing for the Israelis. The Arab citizens of Israel, now 20 per cent of the population, multiply much faster than the Jews and are expected to form the majority as early as 2035. Taken together with two and a half million Palestinians on the West Bank, it should be in Israel's interest to seek a settlement before demographics change to its disadvantage as a 'Jewish State'.

The Israelis are meanwhile content behind their security wall, and they punish the pinpricks from Gaza with impunity. They are confident they can withstand a few days of condemnation from the UN. Their opponents, the Palestinians, are divided into three groups; ½ million in Gaza, 2.5 million on the West Bank and the diaspora of 7 or 8 million.

Over the past decade, Indian spokespersons have intoned the sterile reaction, namely: New Delhi supports two states of Israel and Palestine, living peacefully side by side, eschewing violence and terror, and following the path of negotiations. Despite our friendship with both the Israelis and the Palestinians, we have done nothing to leverage this position to promote these desirable objectives. The Palestine cause has lost its emotional appeal for our Parliament, intellectuals, middle class and even the leftists. The Arab states themselves are not vocal about Palestine – what have they done to alleviate the suffering in Gaza? In its warfare against Hamas in Gaza and Hezbollah in Lebanon, Israelis smugly profess to have had the tacit support of many Arab states.

Thus, for the rationally minded, there are no prospects for optimism.

December 2010

THE ARAB SPRING: HOPE AND UNCERTAINTY

The people's revolution in Egypt was momentous, following Tunisia, which was equally game-changing. But these situations are not unique. In Asia, the first people's movement that overthrew a dictator was led by the Aquino couple, husband and wife, that toppled the regime of Philippines President Marcos in 1986. And in the South Asia region, there was a people's *coup d'état* in 1990 when the Bangladeshi people compelled the resignation of President Ershad. These were the first two indications of people's power in Asia and were marked by a scant loss of life in the process of change.

Each revolution has its own dynamics and character. In Bangladesh, political parties already existed and had earlier enjoyed periods in power. The electronic media was state-controlled, but there was a free print media, and one in which President Ershad was virulently attacked. In both Egypt and Bangladesh, a form of Parliament existed which was dominated by the deposed president's political party – respectively the Jatiya Party and National Democratic Party – and previous elections were considered fraudulent. In Bangladesh, Ershad made no pronouncements at the eleventh hour about staying on in defiance of public opinion, and the Army was never called out even in a neutral capacity. Crucially, in both countries the tipping point was not the people's determination but the unwillingness of the Army to support the position of the president, whom it was willing to sacrifice in order to protect its own interests. This aspect always turns out to be crucial in such a situation.

In Bangladesh, unlike Egypt, the president's role was passed to a chief justice who had the backing of all political groups. An interim neutral civilian administration was set up to run the country until elections took place within three months. Political parties had high profile leaders who were at loggerheads with each other, but had led the people's movement in unison. In Egypt there are no identifiable leaders, and it is unlikely that former head of the International Atomic Energy Agency Mohamed ElBaradei or Arab League Secretary-General Amr Moussa or someone from the Twitter, Facebook and Google generation will have the political staying power to garner the support of the people. Power has been passed meanwhile to a military council consisting of former vested interests.

What is likely to happen is that the Army in Egypt, as in Tunisia, will run the country for longer than the period until September that is presently envisaged. Of course, behind the scenes, they have already been running the country ever since the fall of the monarchy. It is quite probable that a new strong man will emerge from the Army ranks to assume the leadership and become the face of the revolution. It may not necessarily be the Field Marshal now in charge of the Army; it was Colonel Nasser and not General Neguib who took the reins of power after the exile of King Farouk. The Army in Egypt, if it remains united, is a *status quo* institution; it will enjoy the support of the proponents of stability such as the West, the Saudis and Israel. It will be the new establishment with no great sympathy for the Muslim Brotherhood, let alone the brand of Imamist Islam propagated by Shia Iran.

In Bangladesh, the Islamist political groups were part of the people's movement as they were in Egypt, but they did badly at the ensuing polls, winning only a small percentage of the popular vote and a handful of parliamentary seats. This is not likely to be the same case with the Muslim Brotherhood when free elections are held in Egypt, because unlike the Jamaat-e-Islami, the Muslim Brothers have a tradition of educational support and social welfare that has given comfort to millions of the deprived population in Egypt, who will be their main constituency in any election. But the cards in any polls will be stacked against them. In Bangladesh, the first election after the Jamdani Revolution was won by the conservative, nationalist, pro-Islamic party of Khaleda Zia, which beat Sheikh Hasina's pro-liberation, pro-secular Awami League. The same kind of result may be expected in Egypt, where new political parties will be formed through splits and splinter groups from Mubarak's NDP by leaders wishing to carve out a political role for themselves, and the attractions of a religiously affiliated party, other than the Muslim Brotherhood, will have obvious attractions for the new establishment and the general public.

Nurse Edith Cavell famously said, 'patriotism is not enough'. So it may prove in Egypt, where the road ahead will be long and hard towards a truly democratic state and the enjoyment of basic human rights. Building strong democratic structures from scratch can take generations. The needs of earning a livelihood and sustaining family life are always paramount, even for revolutionaries. If the Army can restore a measure of stability and progress in the social and economic life of the Egyptian nation, it can win the confidence of the people, and few will begrudge it a fairly leisurely roadmap to new and pluralist elections. Ershad made a comeback in Bangladesh politics, and his party is a member of the present ruling coalition. But he had been in power for only seven years, and not thirty; his rule had not been marked by abuse of human rights as in Egypt; he was 15 per cent autocrat and 85 per cent opportunist; and he was accessible and not a recluse sheltered within palaces and guarded by cohorts of bodyguards. Mubarak, in contrast, will never make a comeback and would do well to flee his country.

It is unlikely that the events in Tunisia and Egypt will be exemplary for the rest of the region in a domino effect. The countries ripe for revolution would be the ones where the regimes have overstayed their welcome, where politics are the monopoly of the head of state, where the population is young and socioeconomic conditions are stagnating. Among such countries are Algeria, Iran, Jordan, Libya, Syria and Yemen. They will hope to stave off the crisis by making popular concessions but falling short of political rights. Oil-rich states, like Saudi Arabia and the Gulf sheikhdoms, have cushioned their rulers from upheaval by distributing the benefits of wealth, unequally of course, but in some measure to all levels of the population despite the absence of human rights. They are helped in this by the huge presence of non-political imported 'guest workers'.

After the Bangladesh revolution and the jubilation that followed, a diplomat said wryly; 'now they are ringing the bells, but soon they may be wringing their hands'. That may be true for Egypt. The protestors comprise diverse groups with varied demands that can never be fully or quickly satisfied. Strikes and riots for better living standards have broken out and may retard the timetable for lifting the emergency, and play into the hands of hard-liners in the military council. Euphoria will give way to the reality that absolute power now vests in the military, and what the Army does with it can be anticipated by reference to the country's past history. If the Army, that has suspended the Parliament and promised a referendum on a new constitution, can proceed to fashion a democratic Egypt and hand over to a legitimately elected civilian authority, that will represent the biggest revolution of all.

February 2011

NO TEARS FOR MUAMMAR GADDAFI

The former King Idris of Libya, now long deceased, did not hide the fact that his preferred residence was in Cyrenaica, the eastern part of the country, and not in Tripolitania. Cyrenaica had been under British influence after Word War II until 1951, while Tripolitania in the west was an ex-Italian colony, where a large, mainly Sicilian, community still prospered at the time when Muammar Gaddafi and his eleven junior army colleagues took power in September 1969. Under the new dispensation of Gaddafi's, who was born in Sirte in Tripolitania, that province would attain complete ascendancy. It was hardly surprising, therefore, that Cyrenaica, the main locus of Libyan oil wealth, would be the first centre of opposition to Gaddafi's regime earlier this year. Given the separate historical traditions of the two provinces, this may well prove to be a critical factor tending towards socio-political disharmony in the country under any future government.

On the day of regime change, 1 September 1969, when Idris was overthrown in the coup, this writer was in-charge of the newly-established embassy and the only Indian diplomat in Libya. The coup architects were a totally unknown quantity to the world, and Major Abdussalam Jalloud emerged as the 'brains' of the putschists and the public face of the new order. Gaddafi's status was never clearly defined then or later, though he was always portrayed as the supreme leader. His team of twelve saw themselves as idealists, dedicated to Arab unity, the Muslim *ummah*, and people's power. Vestiges of colonialism in the form of the Italian community and the huge Wheelus airbase on the outskirts of Tripoli – the largest in the world outside the USA – were evicted. Jalloud parlayed with the oil companies with a loaded pistol on his desk, and crude prices began a meteoric rise that continues to this day. Gamal Abdel Nasser was the living deity for the Libyan revolutionaries, who offered to unite Libya with any country that would have it. Only Sudan was later tempted by the embrace, and thereafter swiftly withdrew. Undigested notions of socialism led to all commodities being available only in wholesale quantities, obliging households to band into unofficial cooperatives to purchase necessities.

As unformed as were his ideas of economic policy, Gaddafi's concept of foreign policy was no better. Oil wealth gave Libya instant status in the Arab world, but after Nasser's death in 1970, all restraints on Gaddafi's common sense were removed. Promises of financial largesse to the cash-starved Palestinians and African liberation movements were never implemented, and the would-be recipients soon became wary of what might be demanded by Gaddafi as a *quid pro quo*. The paper-trail of Libyan involvement with Muslim separatists in Philippines, the Irish Republican Army and terrorism on land and in the air, were evidence of the Libyan leader's increasingly outlandish behaviour, complete with his music-hall costumes, and travels abroad with female bodyguards, camels, tents and other paraphernalia.

Before Gaddafi became ever more eccentric and remote, I met him four times before my assignment in Libya ended at the close of 1971. He was even then reticent, a man of few words and a distant manner. He called me to his office in the Bab alAzziziya barracks, then a nondescript military compound where a single guide escorted me to Gaddafi's first floor quarters. The only decoration in the spartan office was a wall-hanging with the holy *Kalima al Tayyabah*. He had decided, he said, to send a delegation to study the conditions of Muslims in India. I declined but referred the matter to New Delhi. The ministry's rejection was absolute. I returned to convey this news, but he was scarcely put out by this rebuff; it was clear to me that he had already forgotten his earlier demarche. On the third occasion, I was summoned into his presence to receive a stinging denunciation of India's support for the Bangladeshi *mukti joddha*, whom he seemed to regard as consisting exclusively of Hindus. In passing, he also denounced the Commonwealth as a military alliance inimical to Muslims. The last time I met Gaddafi, again at the Bab alAzziziya military compound, was later the same year, accompanying the new Indian Ambassador H.J.H. Taleyarkhan, a man always given to lecturing his audience. Gaddafi was to be no exception. He fidgeted impatiently while Taleyarkhan expatiated on the glories of Indira Gandhi and the Congress party.

Gaddafi had a world-view roughly equivalent to what you would expect from a newly-recruited Indian army *jawan*. It was impossible to hold any rational conversation with him; one encountered fixed ideas and a semi-educated mind already fully made up. Pakistan not unsurprisingly was in his good books, and the Gaddafi Stadium at Lahore will ironically bear his name even after it has disappeared from public view in Libya itself. Gaddafi hugely overestimated the power that oil money could bring, though his cheque book diplomacy enabled him to press for a premature African union and won him some admirers in countries distant from Libya such as Zimbabwe and South Africa. Nearer home, his meddling and ham-handed politics in Chad, Niger, Sudan and along the West African littoral made him far less acceptable, and often a hate figure.

Gaddafi's erstwhile small band of original revolutionaries successively deserted him until he was left with just one Major at the end. Internationally, Gaddafi's Libya never had many friends. The Arab League looked askance at Gaddafi's buffooneries and was instrumental in giving NATO the legitimacy to intervene and induce a regime change. With India, there were a few commercial contracts and some thousands of expatriate workers in Libya, but there was no solid substance in the relationship. We could not, or would not, help Gaddafi with nuclear know-how, or to have the UN sanctions eased.

One of the longest serving world leaders after the Second World War, and probably the most bizarre, Gaddafi will leave nothing of an inheritance, and like Franco, Salazar, Marcos, Batista and Papa Doc Duvalier, will disappear into the detritus of history. Leaving aside his ruthlessness and cruelty, the wonder is that such a pantomime figure could strut for so long on the world stage. But we can reflect that there are some of that ilk even in the modern history of the Indian subcontinent. If you have to ask for the evidence, just look around.

November 2011

INDIA AND PAKISTAN: THE TRAGEDY OF MUTUAL MISPERCEPTIONS

There are tell-tale contrasts in perception on both sides of the border of the Shoaib-Sania marriage and Jaswant Singh's book on Jinnah. It was equally a sign of the times that at the Indian briefing in Washington on the recent Manmohan Singh-Obama meeting, there were as many as 30 direct or indirect references to Pakistan, and 11 out of 13 questions from the media related to Pakistan. If the spokesperson had rejected questions on Pakistan because the subject of the press conference was the crucial question of nuclear disarmament, there would have left only her opening statement and two questions: one about Obama's visit to India, and another on sanctions against Iran. Despite its legitimate claim to be a major regional and budding global power, India and its media have unwittingly conspired to buttress Pakistan's claims to parity and special status by making Pakistan the core issue in foreign policy.

India has multiple grave concerns with its neighbour, including Pakistan's blatant complicity with terrorism, the absence of monitoring of military assistance to Pakistan, its nuclear threats and its assertion of primacy in Afghanistan. And yet, over the decades, Indian leaders have consistently spoken of friendship with Pakistan. 'We want Pakistan to live in peace . . . and to have the closest ties with us', said Nehru in 1948. 'A stable, secure and prosperous Pakistan is in India's interest. India sincerely wishes Pakistan well', declared Prime Minister Vajpayee in 1999. 'I have stated it several times', said Manmohan Singh last year,

> that the dialogue with Pakistan is a necessity. We are neighbours and we can't choose our neighbours. I sincerely believe it is in our vital interest therefore to try again to make peace with Pakistan . . . if leaders of Pakistan have the courage, the deter-mination and the statesmanship to take this road to peace, I wish to assure them that we will meet them more than half way.

The sentiments of Indian statesmen across the spectrum of political opinion are matched by efforts for bilateral rapprochement of well-meaning individuals and organizations. There have been, and continue to be, innumerable sponsored people-to-people contacts, Track 2, back-channels both officially contrived and unofficial, the never-ending Nimrana process, and events facilitated and paid for by benefactors from the West. Pakistani diplomats in Delhi are socially lionized and cultural and sporting personalities from Pakistan are uncritically applauded, ostensibly just because they have honoured us with their presence. But the cruel fact is that all these connections have not improved our bilateral ties one whit. There are doubtless some elements of Pakistani society who desire better relations with India; their dulcet words appear on our TV screens and newsprint. But they do not count for anything, for Pakistani civil society is fully behind the army.

An academic analysis of four India-Pakistan crises which led to war or near-war between 1986 and 2002 concluded that 'for the most part, neither side . . . had a sure grasp of each other's fears and hopes . . . they are still on a learning curve in this regard'. Efforts to resolve or manage differences between India and Pakistan have foundered on mutual suspicion, and the same will apply to agreements reached through any 'back-channel' process. Commitments are not deliverable; words are not matched by deeds; the public in neither country has been sensitized to the need for concessions. India considers process to be a substitute for progress, while Pakistan has engaged in double-dealing. Each setback is characterized by recrimination and repetition of painful history. Despite this, Indian leaders persist in professing that with our shared history and culture, and living in such close proximity, each side understands the other very well. While Nehru stated, 'we have known each other too long to be indifferent neighbours', there is evidence enough to suggest that this assumption is a profound misjudgement that has led to dangerous misunderstandings. The long-standing crises of North and South Korea and Greek and Turkish Cypriots reveal that common culture and history do not open any doors to common understanding.

Pakistan's foreign policy has been dictated by issues of national identity, in compensation for a lack of a history and clearly defined sense of nationhood. Central to its identity is its confrontation with India. Having been conceived not in any anti-colonial struggle, but in opposition to the Indian nationalist movement, the attempt has been to overcome this negative legacy of identity. Based on Jinnah's insistence on the equality of the 'nations' of Hindus and Muslims, Pakistan seeks to assert itself not merely as 'not India', but a country on par with India, seeking military parity, nuclear weapons, and equality in every bilateral issue, especially Kashmir. This primordial rivalry, defying the asymmetry with a neighbour more powerful than itself in every respect, impels it to seek succour from big powers and reveals the need for external validation and recognition of its 'special status' – although such partnerships further the objectives of the great powers like USA and China and bring few benefits to Pakistan itself. Determined to free itself from a Muslim minority narrative in contrast to a Hindu majority, the desire to emulate Indian nationhood and play a role disproportionate to its actual power is fundamental to Pakistan's self-perception. It apes India's claim to regional power, especially in relation to Afghanistan, and presses its claim as first among equals in the Muslim world – a pretence that caused King Farouk of Egypt to sniff sardonically that Pakistan would have us believe it invented Islam in 1947.

Pakistan is predicated on the contrast between Indian secularism and a Muslim nation shaped by the rhetoric of Partition that contracted out of the Indian Union. Pakistan's most facile option of emphasizing its identity is to oppose India's historical precedence and Hindu identity, with Jinnah setting the tone by referring not to India, but to Hindustan. The fact that Pakistan's boundaries with Afghanistan and India are in dispute adds to the discomfiture of its sovereign identity. Conflict with India is an existential issue, with the definition of Pakistan's Muslim identity most stridently emphasized under military dictatorships. Pakistanis claim that there exists a national consensus on Kashmir because its Muslim identity acquires meaning only in opposition to India. Jinnah visited Kashmir but once and underestimated the role that it would play in Pakistan's search for national identity. As long as Kashmir remains excluded, the communal project that defined Pakistan remains incomplete, though the secession of Bangladesh in 1971 forced a re-think, and Kashmir was thenceforward portrayed as a sacred Muslim land awaiting liberation through *jihad*.

Despite wars and military stand-offs, dialogue has been kept precariously alive, and some major agreements have resulted. Yet for Pakistan, opposition to India is intrinsic to the significance of what it means to be Pakistani, since identity is dependent on obsession with, and challenge to, 'Hindu' India; the fiction that Indian Muslims, the paramount power in the region over six centuries, had achieved parity with Hindus; and the creation of two equal states in 1947 validated this contention. A further fiction is that India at worst rejects the rationale of a Pakistani state, and at best grudgingly accepts the reality. Nuclear weapons have made Pakistan more confident to pursue support for terrorists, Indian dissidents and the proxy war with India. In a demented bid for parity, Pakistan labours under the illusion that India is a fragile state rife with internal differences that will break apart, and its economic progress retarded, under the onslaught of terrorism.

Curiously, the only Pakistani leader in history who has reciprocated his Indian counterparts' appeal for peace and co-operation has been the much-derided Asif Ali Zardari. In 2008, in three interviews on the record with TV journalist Karan Thapar, he declared readiness to commit to no-first-use of nuclear weapons. He called for Kashmir to be put on the back-burner, like the Sino-Indian border, till the time was ripe for settlement, and for increased trade, which would develop greater interaction and thus greater trust. He thought every Pakistani had something of India in him and every Indian something of Pakistan, and declared, after 26/11, that all Pakistanis are Mumbaikars. Zardari broke the mould at considerable risk to himself; now his power has diminished to vanishing point and he has never again given an interview to the Indian media.

In dealing with the Pakistan succubus, India must navigate strategically between pragmatism and naiveté. It is well to have no permanent friends nor permanent enemies, but permanent interests demand that a country both recognizes and understands the inalienable characteristics that determine the perceptions, prejudices and policies of both allies and adversaries.

May 2010

PAKISTAN AFTER THE DELUGE

The millions who clung helplessly to trees and rooftops and stared pathetically at the cameras from inside refugee camps have disappeared from the headlines. It is now, only four months later, as if the greatest natural tragedy that ever struck Pakistan had never taken place. The river from which this subcontinent takes its name, which can easily be forded in the normal dry season when it reaches the Arabian Sea to the east of Karachi, wreaked havoc during the monsoon this year from Gilgit to the plains of Punjab and Sind. A tenth of Pakistan's population of 170 million were reported to be affected directly by death, displacement, injury and loss of material possessions, and the entire population by the indirect economic, social, infrastructural and medical consequences.

Since India is hyphenated to Pakistan in everyone's mind, not least in the media, military and political circles in New Delhi, it is proper to consider what might be the wider political effect of the floods on that country's future. To rehearse the background, the elections of 2008 brought back the all-too-familiar duet of national parties, the Pakistan Peoples Party and the Pakistan Muslim League, as government and opposition. An indirect election process produced a president who reneged for two years on pledges for which his assassinated wife had campaigned. The military after Musharraf beat a retreat to barracks but the newly-elected politicians were only too happy to shirk responsibility and re-endow the army with full powers to conduct the politico-military strategy against a militant insurgency that had been deliberately home-grown and was belatedly adjudged a threat to the state.

The United States, after Obama's arrival, appeared to recognize the importance of Pakistan as a nuclear weapon country with a much larger population than Afghanistan, and a huge military whose interests differed considerably from Washington's. The army suffered more casualties than the NATO forces in Afghanistan, and is in no mood to feel grateful either for the big-ticket lethal stores to feed its obsession with India, or to meet American urgings to take on the Taliban or militant extremists like the Lashkar-e-Taiba. The US will come to learn to shed its unrealistic expectations of how much Pakistan can contribute towards the American effort in Afghanistan, and how much its investments in cash and military hardware can alter the entrenched reality of widespread anti-American sentiment.

The important features of the post-Musharraf period in Pakistan have been the revival of the strength and influence of the army in all walks of foreign and domestic strategy, the ineffectiveness of the civilian body politic, the weakness and inertia of local institutions, and the growing sense of futility on the part of Pakistan's knowledgeable circles. Given this scenario, it is hardly surprising that the Pakistani state was not up to the challenge of tackling the floods adequately. Nothing captured the insensitivity of the state's response as accurately or poignantly as the images of President Zardari in his French 'chateau', or addressing a rally to promote his son in the United Kingdom. Back in Islamabad, Premier Gilani and his Cabinet were neither sufficiently agitated nor active. So it was again left to the military to step into the vacuum of disaster relief, along with its 'irregulars', namely, the militant groups masquerading as humanitarian organizations.

In the aftermath of the deluge, Zardari has lost what little credibility that he had left. Having reluctantly lived up to assurances to transfer and devolve the wide-ranging powers accumulated and handed down by Musharraf, his political importance now rests solely on his role as chief spokesman for the Bhutto dynasty on which the ruling PPP so heavily depends. No alternative to a dynastic succession shows any sign of being encouraged, or emerging of its own momentum. While Nawaz Sharif, the leader of the PML, is far more popular, his record of governance when last in power lends no grounds for optimism that he has either remembered or learned anything from his previous two periods in office as prime minister.

The army has only strengthened its already unshakeable position at the summit of decision-making in the country. Despite the army chief's three-year extension and dire warnings on the record by top American officials like Bruce Reidel of 'a very fragile, very volatile and very combustible country right now . . . we could wake up one morning and have another Zia-ul-Haq in power, a committed jehadist', the army does not seem anxious to step forward to take responsibility for whole paraphernalia of government.

Since 2002, the United States has provided $12.6 billion

of security-related equipment and opened its arms market to Pakistan for items that could have relevance only to flattering the Pakistan army's hostile obsession with India. The allocation of $7.5 billion over five years under the Kerry-Lugar legislation was intended to address Pakistan's basic civilian challenges, but the floods induced a change in plan and forced considerable diversion to direct humanitarian relief. This will enable faster disbursement than the cumbersome bureaucratic machinery would have permitted in normal times, but Washington is doomed to be disappointed if it entertains hopes that through its sponsorship of relief efforts, the current widespread animosity against the USA will be dissipated.

The terrorist organizations and their parent bodies, such as the Jamaat-ud-Dawa, will capitalize on the grass-roots goodwill earned through their relief efforts in the same way that they did five years ago after the Kashmir earthquake. This will stimulate the flow of volunteers for *jihad* to these extremist groups from the flood-affected regions. Even if the government showed any inclination to discourage the credit flowing to such groups, it would be impossible and unpopular if any counter-measures were taken, especially since the militants enjoy the patronage of their main protectors and promoters, the army. The huge disparity between the lack of adequate relief in the areas most affected in the tribal belt, in contrast to the greater emphasis of relief activity in the feudal-landlord plains of Punjab, only highlights the distorted priorities that are designed to serve the vested interests.

Much has been made of the resurgence of Pakistani civil society and the media, but it would be rash to expect them to be the agents of any major change. Whatever Asma Jehangir, the newly-elected head of the Bar Association, may claim as a fearless agenda of checks and balances spearheaded by the Bar, no new dawn is breaking on the efforts to curb the incompetence of the political class, the extra-constitutional powers of the army, or the vice-like grip on society by the feudal and business-related political leadership and robber barons. None of the non-governmental, non-militant-related spokesmen connected with the flood relief has succeeded in developing a national voice, and there is no publicly expressed opinion to challenge the relevance in Pakistan of a military policy that aspires to compete with India's rising power both domestically and internationally, at a time when palpable distress prevails at home, and when the priorities should be, after immediate relief and rehabilitation, employment for the youth, education, primary health, improved water management, better managed power supply and stronger democratic institutions. The plight of those seventeen million Pakistanis rendered dead, homeless and impoverished by the floods has changed nothing, and seems to have been forgotten already. It is the mark of a failing state when an ill wind blows no good.

December 2010

AFGHANISTAN'S THIRTY-YEARS WAR: END GAME IN KABUL?

Foreign interventions were habitual during the process of Afghan nation-formation in the nineteenth and twentieth centuries, were usually resisted by the people, and contributed nothing to the welfare of the Afghans, who harbour a well-merited aversion to foreigners. The present Afghan war has been going on for more than thirty years and during those years, several million Afghans were killed and more than 10 million have fled, leaving 28 million in the country. Almost all the great powers tested their military hardware there, promises of peace and democracy degenerated into more war and devastation, and uncountable fruitless operations resulted in bloodshed, hatred, horror, and an upward spiral in drug production.

The Taliban ruled Afghanistan from 1996 to 2001, and are best remembered for barbaric Islamist practices and the wanton destruction of the Buddha monoliths at Bamiyan. From 2001 onwards, under unanimous UN Security Council resolutions, an International Security Assistance Force was set up, initially to protect the government of Hamid Karzai, and then to eliminate Al-Qaeda and combat insurgents. 100,000 US troops and 40,000 from 48 other countries are in ISAF in what is already the longest military exercise in US history. But there is no international consensus on the objectives of intervention, and it seems the Americans themselves hardly know why they are there. They assert they have no quarrel with the Afghans; it is only the Al-Qaeda that is the enemy. Speaking to me at the time of ISAF's creation, Jaap de Hoop Schaffer, then NATO's secretary-general, envisaged an early withdrawal when democracy and rule of law were established in Afghanistan. That type of nation-building did not succeed in Kosovo or Albania or Bosnia in Europe: how was it ever possible in Afghanistan?

Afghanistan is portrayed as the most acute security problem in the world, and the Taliban as a threat to regional and global peace. Is terror contained because ISAF/NATO is in Afghanistan? The answer depends on how to define the Taliban. People everywhere have heard of these Afghan 'students', but to describe their aspirations in any detail, apart from the removal of foreigners from their country, is problematic. Despite the presence of ISAF, 65 per cent of Afghanistan is under Taliban sway. The Talibs are now vastly different from the pre-2001 variety, being younger, more skilled at propaganda, and closer to Al-Qaeda, Wahabis and Salafis. They have better tactics, use guerrilla methods and are entrenched even in urban areas. They obtain widespread Afghan respect because they are seen as fully opposed to foreigners. Karzai himself describes the Talibs as 'disenfranchized brothers', thereby confusing the people and the army.

The Karzai government's control continuously shrinks in the face of the Taliban, and security deteriorates every year. Al-Qaeda has been disrupted by the US offensive and the death of Osama bin Laden, but *jihadi* terrorism will continue for as long as it has the support of the Pakistani state. The Taliban are far from degraded, due to their safe havens in Pakistan. Calling Pakistan the 'epicentre' of global terrorism, Admiral Mullen, chairman, US joint chiefs of staff, has said that America cannot succeed in Afghanistan unless terrorist safe havens in Pakistan are shut down. So the prime obstacle to removing the threat of terror is clearly identified.

ISAF's aim to 'disrupt, dismantle and defeat' Al-Qaeda and

its principal backers, the Taliban, has been modified more realistically. This year, according to President Obama, the US will start transferring out of Afghanistan and 2014 is the timeline to shift authority to Kabul. This is made easier by bin Laden's demise. The immediate goal is to secure an agreement with the Taliban because the Afghan army and police cannot cope with internal and external threats unless the level of threat is reduced. This exit strategy is only about exit and not strategy, according to Henry Kissinger.

Afghanistan must prepare for the reality of US military withdrawal. There is wide disapproval of the Afghan campaign in the USA and all NATO countries, making it politically impossible to stay on. The US military budget, at this time of economic strife, is higher than rest of the world combined, and the ratio between the highest and the average incomes in America is an unacceptable 120:1. US troops may remain in Kandahar and former Soviet-era bases, not for the sake of Afghanistan, but to maintain surveillance over Pakistan's nuclear facilities that are vulnerable to terrorists. Washington will never make this public, unless it is obliged to by domestic political considerations.

There is some developmental progress in Afghanistan; it is not a medieval or broken state. There have been advances since 2001 in respect of the media and civil society, roads, rail and power. Six million children go to school, of whom 38 per cent are girls. In 2001, only 1 million were in school and they were all boys. There is primary health in 2/3rds of the country as opposed to 10 per cent in 2001. But there are setbacks in economy and security, the rule of law, corruption and narcotics, and human rights abuses are perpetrated both by government and the insurgents. Reconstruction in Afghanistan needs prolonged engagement with the West and the UN since it will need huge funding. The US says it is committed in the long term to Afghanistan's development but, as by far the largest donor, its aid has so far been too closely tied to counterinsurgency strategies, with the blurring of humanitarian and military objectives.

In politics too, there have been serious errors. External controls over the governance process have weakened moves for Afghan self-government. The Afghans have a tradition of decentralized authority, whereas the USA stresses a strong centre, though it simultaneously undermines it by dealing directly with warlords and local power groups. Sub-governance is probably the right answer, but all Afghans will oppose American think-tank proposals of balkanization into quasi-sovereign provinces or seven administrative units that correspond roughly to ethno-political divisions. There is a culture of corruption at all levels, with ISAF itself guilty of paying protection money to local warlords. Counter-narcotics policies are not succeeding, and NGOs are acting like parallel authorities. Polity is a hybrid between the traditional and modern, and the debate goes on about a presidential or parliamentary system, and the role of *shuras* and *jirgas* in any future dispensation. Despite the problems in determining legitimacy, the West will have to relax its control over outcomes. Elections have failed to produce an Afghan voice, and the traditional forms of consensus-building like the *shura* and *jirga* have also not succeeded.

In the search for a solution, various regional approaches have been mooted, especially since diverse ethnicities in Afghanistan need reconciliation. The ethno-linguistic complexities are immense, with Pashtun, Uzbek, Tajik and Hazara majorities living outside the country, and only the minority within Afghanistan. The neighbours pursue competing and conflicting interests, to say nothing of outsiders like Saudi Arabia with its profound and malign links with the Taliban. Pakistan wants to exclude any Indian influence in what it regards as its backyard; Iran cannot accept Shias being treated as apostates by Wahabis; China fears Uighur contamination by Islamic extremism; Central Asia fears narcotics and terrorism. The US refuses to involve Iran, while any armed action against Iran by USA or Israel will hugely increase radicalism in the Middle East and Central Asia, with unpredictable consequences. Pakistan can be a deal-maker or deal-breaker, but a Pakistani-brokered peace will not be acceptable to its neighbours, or to all the Afghans.

There is no such thing as a card-carrying Taliban. Pushtuns and Talibs are not synonymous, and the Taliban are not monolithic. The Talibs are in at least three formations – Mullah Omar's Quetta *shura*, Haqqani in North Waziristan (strong Arab element and attached to Pakistan's ISI) and the Pakistani Taliban. Each Taliban group has a different leadership with different agendas. The Taliban are therefore more of a 'movement' intending to defeat ISAF/NATO and re-claim Afghanistan. Ethnicity and Islam are not cementing factors, Hekmatyar, the *mujahid* of anti-Soviet vintage, is a constant spoiler, and the Taliban will not cohere after any settlement and once the NATO troops withdraw.

Despite all this, moves for a settlement are constantly afoot and will now accelerate. Karzai is moving closer to viewing Pakistan as essential for his continuation, and Rabbani, a former Afghan president, is acting as his intermediary with the Quetta *shura*, though the US does not want Mullah Omar in the peace and reconciliation process. The process is highly opaque between all the various players. There are whispers of future talks, perhaps in the Gulf, perhaps in Turkey. The broad principles could comprise: no partition, no single outside power to be dominant, no hand-over to Pakistan, no reversion to the *status quo*, no imposed neutrality, the Afghans to own the process, and Afghanistan's independence and sovereignty to be guaranteed by Pakistan.

It is unlikely that any talks will be fruitful unless there is a prior end to combat operations, and in addition to the insurgents, any negotiation must include formal and informal power holders, and should ideally include obligations to human rights and accountability – though enforcement will be impossible. But there is a saying in Afghanistan: 'In principle, no compromise; in compromise, no principle'. And that, finally, is likely to be the untidy and unsatisfactory outcome.

May 2011

LOOK EAST, BUT LOOK HARDER: INDIA, CHINA AND SOUTH-EAST ASIA

The attributes of an influential power are never precise, but would certainly imply that India's impact must spread to its neighbourhood beyond South Asia. India's prominence in West Asia is impeded by the religious factor as well as the blocking abilities of Pakistan, Iran and Saudi Arabia. South-East Asia is one of the few remaining areas for Indian cultural, soft power and economic expansion, which could not materialize during the Cold War period.

After India realigned its position with the post Cold War order, engagement with East and South-East Asia had to be one of its priorities. India had first to convince ASEAN that it had seen the light, and would befriend countries with which relations had been cool over previous decades. India had been perceived by ASEAN as close to the Soviet Union, and neither really fully Western nor Asian, and India's cultural uniqueness was not considered a positive element in facilitating its integration with ASEAN. The 'ASEAN way' rests on personal relationships, gradual consensus building and skirting contentious issues, whereas Indians are seen as legalistic, bureaucratic and impersonal. In other words, India was a very late starter, and had to catch up with the established presence of other big countries both from within and outside the region.

The Indian 'Look East' policy accorded with the market model in place in South-East Asia. China's involvement with those countries had already witnessed strong momentum, helped by people of Chinese origin who had long dominated business in at least half of the ten ASEAN countries. India had fallen far behind in the movement for regional integration, although the political and strategic situation on India's south-east flank affected its security, even more so after the admission of Myanmar brought ASEAN adjacent to India's land border.

India had showed no inclination for political leadership in SAARC, but paradoxically now wanted to go beyond South Asia and the Bay of Bengal to extend its influence towards the Pacific. India's new emphasis on the East was motivated by the China factor, its social, cultural, religious and linguistic links with ASEAN, and the persons of Indian origin who had a presence in the socio-political life of the region. As Indo-ASEAN ties increased, the role of these communities became more salient.

In general terms, compared with the caution of the early 1990s, India is now a reasonably confident participant in the Asia-Pacific political and strategic domain. However, in the economic sphere,

India is yet to make any notable headway. The recent conclusion of the Indo-ASEAN free trade agreement exceeded all timelines and it remains to be seen how it will operate in practice. The leverage exercised by Indian protectionist lobbies on political circles in New Delhi should never be under-estimated. In terms of intra-regional trade, in comparison with China, Korea, Japan and the ASEAN members, India has been insignificant. There are several shortcomings in the Indian economy, where the market is quite closed, the average tariff level high, investment environment poor, and the level of infrastructure development and external trade low, with the result that India is not a highly regarded commercial partner. India's partnership with East Asia will crucially depend on its capacity for making a distinct contribution towards the progress for closer economic integration in the region.

While India's economic and political contacts are formal rather than functional, its bilateral defence arrangements with individual ASEAN countries have assumed greater relevance. India has never clarified what genuine interests it has to defend in the region, but in general terms, the Indian presence is welcomed by ASEAN, an attitude premised on the balance of power. ASEAN welcomes all major powers to participate in the regional security architecture, but in its view, no single power should be permitted to dominate the area. This is to India's advantage. Because India has greater military resources to share with ASEAN than vice versa, defence cooperation has occurred to some degree with almost every ASEAN country – in fact more so, in most cases, than with India's neighbours in the Indian subcontinent. In contrast, there is little Chinese military involvement with ASEAN, other than Myanmar.

The ASEAN Regional Forum is the first multilateral security forum ever to be joined by India. It had been India's traditional approach to keep security issues out of the scope of regional groups such as SAARC and the Indian Ocean Rim Association, in both of whose formation it had played a key role. But with the ARF, the objective of 'containing' China influenced India to reverse its historic position on such groupings. Competition between India and China in the region is predictable because the two countries do not enjoy mutual trust, and there are overlapping perceptions of their historical spheres of influence and interest. They have made efforts to address bilateral problems with some progress recorded, but given the inherent rivalry and geopolitical interplay, the nature and degree of friction between them is a constant concern for the members of ASEAN.

There is therefore a competitive edge in India's policy, to achieve some kind of equal footing with China. But it will be necessary for India to draw China closer into discussions on cooperation and security in the Asia-Pacific region. The approach of 'containing' China by aligning with some individual powers whose strategic goals and military practices do not necessarily complement our's, nor share the long term vision of India's relationship with its northern neighbour, will be most unwise. India's strategic engagement with ASEAN should not be dependent only on the China factor, and military means cannot be considered the preferred method of asserting a regional role in preference to the more valuable soft power assets like culture, technology, IT, trade and investment. India has taken the initial steps to being regarded as a serious partner in emerging Asia, but it has now to enhance its economic and strategic relevance that are both largely in the potential rather than the actual sphere.

India may already see itself as an influential factor in the ASEAN economic and security space, but this self-perception will not be shared by other major actors. ASEAN has differing levels of consensus on many issues including security, and many among its ten members regard India only as an Indian Ocean power and not an Asia-Pacific one. Being part of the Asia-Pacific is a necessity for India's pursuit of world status, and its friendly ties with USA can boost that strategy, but in matters critical to ASEAN like the Korean peninsula, the Taiwan Straits and the South China Sea, it remains to be seen whether India has the capacity and will to be involved; for instance, it has given no significant opinion on Pyongyang's nuclear and missile ambitions. In security conclaves like the six power talks on the North Korean nuclear issue, India is not included, and if the six member *ad hoc* body eventually morphs into an embryonic Asian security construct, Indian relevance and participation might become a subject of contention.

India will be prepared to play a more energetic role, along with the West, in maintaining the security of international sea-lanes, and its ambitions may be on the right lines, but it has incrementally to enhance its economic integration with other Asian countries. India has to make much greater efforts towards the objective of making ASEAN an important stake-holder in Indian prosperity. India is still far from being an indispensable country, and the reality is that the gap between China's and India's levels of engagement with ASEAN remains huge: no number of summit photo-opportunities for our prime minister with East Asian leaders will redress this imbalance.

Military contacts are not nearly as important as economic interdependence, because without such integration, it is premature to talk about any possible role for India in the security architecture in Asia. At this time when the level of acrimony between India and China is disturbing and even reminiscent of the 1950s, it is sobering to keep in mind that in the unlikely event of a clash of arms, such international support as India receives will again come, as it did in 1962, mainly from the West, for the West's own purposes, whereas the so-called non-aligned group of countries will at best sit on the fence, or far more likely, tilt towards our northern neighbour.

November 2009

MYANMAR, AND THE PROFIT AND LOSS ACCOUNT

In the vast numbers of books on India's foreign relations, Myanmar is a country that has almost remained off the radar screen. In part, this is due to the reclusive nature of that country, in part because Myanmar is not regarded as an important player in the international arena, but mainly because relations between the two countries were virtually non-existent in the three decades between the military coup that deposed U Nu in 1962 and the mid 1990s.

Burma was the largest province in British India, and in 1937 was acknowledged as an independent unit within the British

Empire. Indians were drafted in large numbers into the colonial army during the three Anglo-Burman wars of the nineteenth century, and about 4 lakh Indians migrated there to run several public services. Added to these were the Tamil-speaking Chettiars and agricultural workers. The number of persons of Indian origin on the eve of the Japanese invasion was probably underestimated at 1.1 million or around 8 per cent of the total population, mainly in urban centres. These people became a bone of contention, being treated as resident aliens and discriminated against, even though they had lived in Burma for generations. Despite these privations, the Indian government estimates – mainly guesswork – show that there are nearly 1 million persons of Indian origin in Myanmar today. Better relations between the two countries would improve the lot of these people.

In the late 1980s, India supported the pro-democracy uprising and offered sanctuary to Burmese dissidents, but a few years later New Delhi settled for constructive engagement with the military regime in Yangon in the context of its 'Look East' policy, to counter growing Chinese influence, and the desire for closer ties with ASEAN. The need for new sources of energy played its part, and a powerful ingredient in India's thinking was the imperative to develop the north-east without the disruption of insurgencies.

The first border trade agreement was signed with Myanmar in 1994 involving points in Manipur and Mizoram, and the next year a joint military operation against insurgents took place. High-level military to military contacts began in 2000. Heads of state visited each other and accords were concluded on security, culture, hydro-electricity, petroleum, remote-sensing, and Buddhist studies. Indian loans of $40 million were offered to Yangon.

The rationale for India's policy shift to befriend Myanmar despite that regime's ill-treatment of people of Indian origin and the ruthless repression of its own citizens may be understandable, but the lack of concrete beneficial results from the new orientation is harder to comprehend. Not only has the new strategy failed to even partially open a closed polity, but insurgency in the Indian north-east has not diminished; India and Myanmar have varying types of problems with different sets of insurgents and do not share the same priorities in addressing them. Therefore cooperation against the cross-border militants has tailed off. It was hoped that greater border trade with Myanmar would lead to regeneration and help to quell narcotic and arms trafficking and AIDS. However, only one of the two border posts is open, for which India blames Myanmar, the road on the Indian side to Moreh is sub-standard, two-way trade is constrained by the small list of tradable goods, excessive regulation and restrictions, and is negligible compared to trade across the Myanmar borders with China and Thailand. The north-east region is swamped by goods of Chinese origin, but there is hardly any movement of Indian exports in the other direction. The benefits of economic prosperity seen in other parts of India have not yet touched the region.

India interacts with Myanmar in several economic forums – the ASEAN, the Bay of Bengal Initiative, the Kunming Initiative, and the Mekong-Ganga Cooperation Initiative. Apart from China, Myanmar is the only one of India's neighbours that exports more to India than it imports, and India does not even rank among Myanmar's top five import sources. Trade is hampered by both countries not accepting direct payment methods such as telegraphic transfers or letters of credit, forcing the involvement of third parties, such as Singapore. Transaction costs are high, and the disparity between the actual and official rates of exchange is another disincentive, as is the difficulty in obtaining export credit and insurance. Many Indian companies are even disinclined to reveal they are operating in Myanmar.

India has given \$100 million credit for Myanmar infrastructure, while \$57 million has been offered to upgrade Burmese railways. A further \$27 million in grants has been pledged for road and rail projects, but there is little of significance to show for this approach in terms of concrete benefit. The Tamu-Kalemayo 160-km road in Myanmar has been built by India, but there is reluctance by India to rebuild and reopen the Stillwell road, on which the Chinese work has started from Yunnan. The Kaladan river project to link a newly constructed Sittwe port to the Indian north-east involves dredging the river to create a transhipment terminal and will take several years. A proposed railway from Hanoi to Imphal, and a 1,500-km Trans-Asian highway from India to Bangkok, are being talked about. ONGC is working three offshore blocks off the Rakhine coast, but the debate continues on whether the energy extracted would be transported to India by pipeline or LNG, while Bangladesh blows hot and cold on the use of its territory for transit. Meanwhile China has predictably moved faster; it is building pipelines to Yunnan, a deep-sea port at Kyaw Phuy, and a road linking that port with Kunming.

China looms large in every aspect of India's Myanmar policy, but after the barren years since the 1960s, India is destined to play catch-up with a weak hand. India's desire to regenerate the north-east is matched by China's wish to develop Yunnan and Sichuan and integrate the economies of autonomous Burmese border regions with Southern China's economy. Large numbers of Chinese investors and traders, and the large Chinese diaspora in Myanmar estimated at 2 million, are assisting actively in this process.

New Delhi takes comfort from the view that Myanmar wishes to balance the preponderance of China with relations with India and ASEAN, but in the jostling for influence in the spaces along India's frontiers, India is faltering in Myanmar; departments in our capital blame each other for the loss of momentum; and no one is prepared to drive forward the agenda without a clear directive of priority from the political leadership, with adverse consequences for the 'Look East' and north-east strategies.

India's maritime strategy focuses on threats in the Indian Ocean. New Delhi is not reassured by Burmese promises that its territory would not be used for military purposes against any third party, and the Indian military is concerned about China modernizing naval bases at Hanggyi, Cocos, Akyab, Mergui and the port at Kyauk Phuy. This has become an unequal partnership, where one party is reaping all the benefits. New Delhi was reluctant to condemn Myanmar during the monk-led fuel and food protests of 2007, and quick to send relief after the recent cyclone, but while this was noted positively in the new capital of Naypyitaw, the realistic assessment is that had India not responded in the way it did, there would have been a negative fall-out.

The outcomes of all the energies expended by India over the past two decades have been chalked up to Myanmar's benefit. The situation calls for a re-appraisal designed to turn the tide in our favour.

November 2008

MYANMAR: CHANGE FOR GOOD?

Myanmar is of great strategic and economic importance to three major powers of this century – the United States, China and India. With the first signs of a thaw in Myanmar after 60 years of self-imposed seclusion, it is an open question if India can benefit more from the potential opening up of our neighbour than from being one steed in a two-horse race for influence in that country, as has been the case for the past twenty years.

Even twelve months ago, any prospect of progress in Myanmar appeared utopian, but winds of change are now in evidence, with hopes of movement towards a pluralist political order. The electoral laws for the elections last year to the national and provincial legislatures had mandated that political parties could not have convicts as members, which constrained Aung San Suu Kyi's National League for Democracy, since its chief was under house arrest and other senior leaders in prison. The outcome was a boycott by her party that had overwhelmingly won the free, but later annulled, elections of 1990.

Amid allegations of widespread malpractices, the 2010 elections brought the military-backed Union Solidarity and Development Party to power and former Prime Minister Thein Sein to the presidency. There were few expectations that the new government would be any more responsive to human and civil rights than the previous army junta. Yet, Suu Kyi was swiftly released from detention and allowed free movement, and some political prisoners were released, with credible indications that many more could be released soon. Restrictions on accessing online media sites are being eased, and state-run media have refrained from criticizing the press abroad. Legislation permitting the right of workers to unionize and strike and the right of people to demonstrate peacefully is being considered, and Burmese in exile are encouraged to return. Citing environmental concerns and popular protests, the Thein Sein government has halted construction of a giant hydro-electric project on the Irrawaddy in northern Myanmar that was being constructed by Chinese companies mainly to supply electricity to China.

Moreover, there are indications of rapprochement between the NLD and the government. Suu Kyi has said; 'I have met President Thein Sein, and I personally believe that he is very genuine in his desire for change.' The electoral law has been amended to allow people convicted for crimes to join political parties, and political parties henceforth will only 'respect and abide' by the constitution and not be obliged to 'safeguard' it. Such developments have prompted the NLD to decide to re-register itself and contest some forty upcoming by-elections. Suu Kyi has hinted she may be a candidate herself.

The imperative of economic growth and the desirability of breaking free from total dependence on China seem to be motivating the Burmese actions, and both will require the regime's interaction with regional and global powers. The government seems confident that it can control the pace of political reforms by virtue of the USDP's absolute majority in parliament. Twenty-five per cent of seats in legislatures being reserved for defence personnel, and with constitutional amendments requiring the approval of three quarters of the members of Parliament, there could be no reform possible without the military's concurrence. Given these provisions, the pace of political reforms in coming years could become contentious between Suu Kyi and the authorities in power. The pace of political reforms will also be impacted by the ongoing ethnic conflicts in Myanmar. There are multiple armed ethnic groups demanding greater autonomy, and the cease-fires between the military and these rebels have come under severe strain due to differences on the proposed integration of the rebels into the border guard force. There are, for example, reports of clashes between the military and the Kachin Independence Army on this issue. If Suu Kyi's NLD and the government cannot find common ground to address these ethnic conflicts, this too may result in acrimony.

For the moment, despite the prospect of such future challenges, the steps taken by President Thein Sein have received international approbation. The Association of Southeast Asian Nations decided to make Myanmar the host for the 2014 ASEAN summit, which implies that all ten countries are reasonably confident that the reform process will maintain its course and not be reversed. An ASEAN summit in Myanmar will receive delegations not only from ASEAN but also from the USA, UK, Japan, Australia and others who have been highly critical, and for a country treated as an international pariah until recently, this would constitute a significant change. A British cabinet minister together with a BBC TV team has just visited Myanmar and met Suu Kyi, while President Obama has announced that Secretary of State Hillary Clinton will be there next month – the first visit by a senior American dignitary since Dulles in 1955. If that trip proves fruitful, then economic sanctions imposed on Myanmar by the Western industrialized nations may be lifted, and Myanmar's engagement with the outside world will fundamentally alter the geo-politics of the region.

It would be premature to come to the conclusion that China is losing its prevailing supreme status in Myanmar. These are early days in the reform process and if there are renewed strains in its relationship with Suu Kyi, the Myanmar government will once again invoke Chinese assistance to balance and fend off any pressure in bilateral and international forums. While it is true that Myanmar has halted construction of a hydro-electric mega-project that would have benefited China, local considerations seem to have played a significant role in that decision, and the fact that the authorities are responsive to the concerns of the populace is regarded as a welcome sign of an awareness of, and respect for, human rights. While the West had turned its back on Myanmar, Chinese businessmen had a free run to develop strong networks with the élite in Myanmar, and such alliances will play an important role in ensuring that China continues to be highly influential.

China has a past record of supporting insurgencies such as the Communist Party of Burma's uprisings in the 1960s and 1970s. The Myanmar-China border is extremely porous and China has close ties with a significant number of armed ethnic groups operating in Myanmar, such as the United Wa State Army. Therefore, in the event that relations with Myanmar descend into a tailspin, China has the capacity to encourage armed rebels in Myanmar aggressively to protect its interests. To borrow an evocative phrase from the Burmese author Thant Myint-U, 'Myanmar is a place where China meets India'. So much so, that any increased insurgent activity there will prove to be extremely disadvantageous for India, and specifically for our troubled and unstable north-east.

In the coming years, Myanmar may achieve a measure of plurality in political decision-making. This will present an absolutely novel and challenging environment for New Delhi. Instead of only engaging the military leadership, India must immediately make fruitful contact with various national political parties and the regional ethnic parties. Because of the economic and political sanctions against Myanmar by the USA and the European Union, India had found it relatively easy thus far to attract the attention of Myanmar's decision makers. When sanctions are lifted, this advantage will disappear, and India will have to compete with many other powerful countries to promote Indian interests in Myanmar. On the other hand, the opening up of Myanmar to global intercourse could equally prove a blessing in disguise, because India by itself is not in any position to stop the Chinese juggernaut from making huge in-roads into Myanmar's politico-economic space. And if economic sanctions are eased, then the foreign investment pattern will be diversified and Indian companies could collaborate with regional and global companies to participate more vigorously in Myanmar's economic opportunities.

It is accordingly the right moment for India to scale up its politico-economic and cultural engagement with Myanmar dramatically. Democracy always requires robust institutions in the political and economic realms, manned by citizens with adequate training to staff these institutions. Given India's democratic experience, it can and should play a significant role in human resource and capacity building, which in turn will facilitate the speedy and sustainable political reform process. Now that Myanmar is on the move, there is no time to be lost.

(With co-author Sanjay Pulipaka)
November 2011

CHINA THE DOVE OR DRAGON?

Whether because American recovery from recession may be more fragile and long-lasting than expected, or because Obama's policies towards Islam, Palestine, Iran and Af-Pak are foundering, or a Dick Cheney mindset returning to the American forefront, the acrimony between the West and China seems to be growing sharper and more frequent. Washington blames China for opposition to additional sanctions against Iran, and for obstructing a more ambitious conclusion at the Copenhagen climate change conference. Google, which is backed by the US and is set to leave China in April, has accused China of censorship and cyber attacks, while the American Chamber in China finds that 38 per cent of its members feel unwelcome.

The US has criticized China for mercantilism and currency exchange manipulation, saying the yuan is undervalued by 20–40 per cent. But China has a huge trade surplus of $450 billion this year and reserves of $2.4 trillion including a large proportion of US debt, and Washington is acutely conscious of China's clout as a creditor, with an economy that grew at nearly 9 per cent in 2009 and budget deficit at only 2.2 per cent of GDP despite a big stimulus package. So the US does not dare apply a surcharge on imports from China as was the case with Japan and Germany in the 1970s. China has recently unloaded some $34 billion in US securities, a move that has political significance in both countries and caused concern in America, since Sino-US interdependence is at an all-time peak, with global politics and economy increasingly reliant on cooperative Sino-US relations.

Ties between Australia and China have soured with China warning Australia against politicizing and interfering in its trial, which was partly behind closed doors, of four Rio Tinto executives for corruption and spying. But China is Australia's chief trading partner, a vital customer for Rio Tinto, and Rio Tinto has just signed a $3 billion joint venture for iron ore in Guinea with Chinalco of China. Therefore, like USA, Australia finds that its reprisal options are highly constrained.

There has been a surge in cyber attacks originating in China that have significantly increased over the past year; the US Congress and government agencies reported 1.6 billion attacks every month. The software security firm McAfee has raised the future prospect of mass Chinese cyber attacks, during which India will be especially vulnerable, not only because of its 'lowest rate of security measures', but because it can be used as a gateway to cripple services in the industrialized world, particularly USA, from where 85 per cent of Indian software revenues are derived. Security is expensive, and being low-cost outsourcing providers, Indian companies cut costs on security to remain competitive.

China's relations with exiled Tibetans, never cordial, have come under greater stress. The Chinese-selected Panchen Lama Gyaltsen Norbu has appointed to the Political Consultative Committee, while the Dalai Lama-recognized divine Gedun Nyima remains anonymous in Tibet. The Tibetans in exile have responded sharply to Beijing claiming the right to approve any reincarnation of living Buddhas or lamas, asserting that this was an internal matter for the Tibetan people and will take place according to traditional procedure – though the Dalai Lama himself has offered several alternatives to the traditional religious rituals and divinations; there could be an election, or his appointment, even of a woman, as successor. He has further incensed Beijing by claiming the Chinese are trying to annihilate Buddhism, that there is a serious problem in Tibet, and expressing sympathy for the people of 'East Turkestan', the name given to Xinjiang by Uigur separatists.

The Chinese, for their part, have hit back, professing they are the injured party. They strongly object to the latest US $6.4 billion arms sales to Taiwan and threaten action against the exporting companies. They condemn Obama's meeting the Dalai Lama as interference in their internal affairs. They accuse Google of spying and thwarting China's indigenous technology. As for Copenhagen, Premier Wen Jiabao suggests he was humiliated by not being invited to a meeting with EU leaders and Obama. Beijing says exchange rates have little to do with imbalances, Chinese surpluses soared even when the yuan appreciated 20 per cent between 2005 and 2008, and the present fixed rate of 6.8 to the dollar is an important ingredient for stability. On Iran, China states that it supports the NPT and is opposed to any nuclear weaponization, but that the proposed sanctions against the Revolutionary Guard, shipping, banking and insurance may force Tehran into a position of no retreat, and Iran deserved to be treated as an equal rather than be subject to threats. Beijing gratuitously advises Washington that the rhetoric of Obama's speech to Muslims in 2009 must be translated into concrete actions since Arab enthusiasm has cooled, and the Israel-Palestine issue lies neglected.

Demonstrations of belligerence by authors belonging to the Chinese military are grist to observers who see menace in Chinese intentions. Perhaps to gauge military opinion, test public reaction, or reflect concern over North Korea's nuclear testing, a number of serving and retired officers have recently been permitted to recommend an assertive policy beyond their country's borders. Three army officers have urged the selling of US debt, increase in defence spending and expanding deployments of forces. Another calls for China to abandon modesty and hasten to displace the USA as a global champion: 'we need a military rise as well as an economic rise, and the strongest military force to deter the USA'. An Air Force General's observation that 'competition has shifted towards space' underscores that China's space programme is entirely military-dominated. Chinese academics echo such sentiments, noting that national interests extend across borders, and it was necessary to enhance the ability to protect them, including by a blue water navy with carriers and overseas bases.

China has widened its anti-piracy effort in the Red Sea by offering to escort UN food shipments to Somalia, which will necessitate more than the three vessels (two frigates and a supply ship) there since 2008, the first time in centuries that the Chinese navy has operated beyond home waters. A retired Admiral opines that growth in submarines operated by ASEAN countries could pose a threat – although China has the world's biggest submarine development programme – and advocates a naval base in the Middle East. An Air Force Colonel also urges overseas bases for China to shoulder its international responsibilities, to provide support facilities for China's economic interests, ship escorts, and disaster relief in the interests of, needless to say, world peace. A prototype base could be started on Mischief Reef in the South China Sea, and other ports where China enjoys friendly relations in Asia, East Africa and the Indian Ocean. Gwadar, Hambantota and Chittagong which are among those envisaged as 'access points' or 'friendly locations' to support long-range naval deployment. The same Air Force Colonel writes that China is surrounded by hostile nations, predicts war in 10–20 years and identifies the enemy; 'if the US can light a fire in China's backyard, we can also light a fire in their backyard'.

The Chinese authorities wish to contain the mounting international concern, and have no desire to jeopardize ties with their key trading partner and the world's biggest military and economic power, the USA. Till some years ago, the Chinese were adamant that they desired 'no places and no bases'; the 1995, 1998 and 2000 White Papers re-stated that China did not seek military expansion, military bases, or stationing troops abroad. Now 'places' to handle the needs of non-war military operations without pre-positioned munitions and a large-scale military presence are apparently seen as potential assets enabling China to project power without alarming USA, India or Japan, and making it easier for host countries to accept.

China's rise implies it is more self-confident, assertive, and as a global player, bound to come into conflict with strategic interests led by the USA. As China's trade minister bluntly told *The Washington Post*, 'America is the one that needs to adjust'. Washington has come to acknowledge that China is no new version of the USSR, but a far more formidable adversary. If Copenhagen is any guide, there will be greater pressures on China, but Beijing will insist on reciprocal satisfaction and its leverage will apply to the extent that the world community is prepared to accept more strident and demanding Chinese behaviour.

Indian analysts are equally divided between viewing the rising China as a dove and a dragon. Relations between the two neighbours, both major economic and nuclear powers with differing political and cultural traditions, are unlikely to be uninterruptedly calm, and it is reasonable to expect periods of a costly state of tension. These will need to be acceptably contained, and will give our diplomats, theoreticians and military planners some continuous intellectual exercise.

March 2010

JAPANESE DISASTERS IN THE WORST OF TIMES

Since March, Japan has been reeling from a 9-point earthquake and the resulting 25-foot tsunami that struck 250 km north-east of Tokyo, leaving 11,000 dead, 17,000 missing, and 250,000 evacuated from a 25 km radius due to a possible catastrophic meltdown of over-heating fuel rods at the Fukushima Daiichi nuclear power plant, from which radiation leaks have been detected up to 19,000 times higher than normal. The two banks of nuclear reactors at Tokyo Electric Power Company's plant add up to some 6 per cent of Japan's electricity generation capacity and their shutdown affects the greater Tokyo region that houses 35 million people. Twenty thousand acres of agricultural land have been inundated by saline sea water, 30 per cent of Japan's fisheries were located in the region, some industrial units, including hi-tech companies, have been destroyed, five million households were without electricity and two million without water. A quarter of a million people are in shelters. The Japanese government estimates the cost of the disaster at $300 billion. The whole world has looked on with horror and sympathy, but also with great wonder at the stoicism, self-sacrifice, discipline and civic consciousness of Japanese society. There has been no panic, no breakdown of public manners, no riots or disturbances despite unimaginable privation. Notwithstanding one false alarm originating from TEPCO, official statements and warnings are willingly acted upon. All evidence points to the opinion that Japan will recover its equilibrium faster than any other country could have in similar circumstances.

But this tragedy has struck the country at the worst of times. Japan rose after World War II, under a democratic constitution and without regular armed forces, to become the second biggest economic power after the USA, with its security assured by a nuclear umbrella in an alliance with America. It increased its real GDP by eight times between 1955 and 1985, had 15 per cent of the world product, became the largest provider of credit and aid, and the yen appreciated by 300 per cent against the US dollar. Japan had effectively organized the 'Greater East Asia Co-prosperity Sphere' that it had identified as an objective, but had not been able to achieve, in the Second World War. It aspires, like India, to being a permanent member of the UN Security Council, and shares with India the implacable opposition of China.

When Japan should have been enjoying the fruits of the post-Cold War period, it fell into economic stagnation. With a population of 128 million and a GDP of $4.3 trillion, now the third after the USA and China, it is trying to adjust its systems of government guidance, regulation, education, management and social stability to the compulsions of globalization and the 'new economy'. Japan's readjustment to the globalized epoch has been difficult because it has the vulnerability of a trading nation that is resource-poor, and its ethnocentric culture militates against the generation of soft power. The Japanese sense of national identity is based, with good reason, on the conviction of its country's uniqueness. Reluctance at using the Roman alphabet, for example, is resolute, although objective experts agree that it would suit the language well. While the rhetoric of East Asian fraternity and cooperation is often expressed, Japanese uniqueness is still regarded as precious and exemplary, and the absorption of western technology has left traditional Japanese values comparatively uncompromised.

A conservative élite is the source of Japan's distinctive style and strategy in dealing with the rest of the world. This élite was pragmatic and opportunistic, and ensured that the nation would organize itself internally to succeed externally. Each major change in strategy has been in response to a new configuration of world power. The rise of China, threats from North Korea, terrorism and piracy in sea-lanes are now inspiring another reassessment of strategies, and have already led to a tighter alliance with the USA. Japan has responded by taking a more active stance in East Asia and expanding its naval forces. It wants eventually to amend Article 9 of its constitution to enhance the quality and reach of its armed forces. Chinese incursions into Japanese waters are the latest threat, especially to the Senkaku (Diaoyutai to the Chinese) islands. In addition, Russia and Japan have a dispute over four islands, the Northern Territories (Japan)/Kuriles (Russia), and Takeshima/Tokudo is also disputed between Japan and South Korea.

Nearly 20 per cent of Japan's exports go to China, while China is the biggest exporter to Japan. Japan employs 9 million Chinese in various enterprises in China. But the relationship between the two countries is always fraught and volatile. China continues to see Japan through the optic of Japan's violent past, whereas Japan perceives China in the context of its own constitutional pacificism, and worries deeply about what kind of neighbour the rising China will turn out to be. The result is an uneasy balancing act, with Japan courting better relations with Beijing, but at the same time seeking security assurances from Washington. With the end of the Cold War, many of the self-binding restrictions adopted by Tokyo to preclude entanglements in foreign commitments have been unravelling. The famous eight 'Nos' – no dispatch of the Japanese self defence forces abroad; no collective defence agreements; no power projection; no more than 1 per cent of the GDP for the defence budget; no nuclear arms; no sharing of military technology; no arms exports; no military use of space – may all be revisited, and only the ban on nuclear weapons will remain sacrosanct. Because these restrictions are self-imposed, Japan can change them at its own speed and volition.

Japan has revived its Ministry of Defence after sixty years. No US strategy in the Pacific rim will be possible without Japan's cooperation, and the Japan-US agreement of 2005 for Mutual Cooperation and Security seemed to anticipate a revision of Japan's constitution. On the Taiwan issue, Japan is faithful to the American position, and whether the ambiguous reference to 'surrounding areas' in the US-Japan Security Treaty of 1997 includes Taiwan or not, Japan and the USA share acute anxieties about China and North Korea's missile capabilities. In a Theatre Missile Defence arrangement, Japan plays host to a US radar system to intercept missiles, and the US will deploy Patriot and Standard missiles. With 119 warships, Japan is a formidable asset to the Americans at sea. In the defence budget, Japan sets aside a sum of about $50 billion for an active force strength of 250,000 and a reserve of 50,000. Nevertheless, its military and security arrangements with the United States prevent it from exercising wholly independent strategic choices abroad.

Japan is a world leader in many fields – science and technology, robotics, digital electronics, alternative energy, computer games, and nanoscience. But there is widespread dissatisfaction with old-style politics, its average life span is 82, the yen is weak, and energy prices are high. Its service sector has lagged, and it suffers from a lack of domestic competition. It is inefficient in many domestic sectors, and its professional services are considered backward by pace-setting standards. It has been highly efficient at exports, running an approximately $90 billion surplus in trade account each year with the USA, but now there are many more competitors in the export trade. The compelling need for energy security has lately obliged Japan, like China, to enlarge its scope of economic interest to Central Asia. Japan has to rebuild its domestic economy to eliminate a culture of rules and rigid ideas, women who do not work, resistance to change, opposition to immigration, non-acceptance of outsiders, preference for large organizations, and traditional collective decision-making that is slow. Japan is fortunate in that it has no large peasant class and no smokestack sector side by side with knowledge-based industry, but in the first decade of this century, manufacturing output was less than it was in the previous decade, and its share in both world output and exports was shrinking.

After the trauma, an aversion to generation of power through nuclear energy has manifested itself globally, with immediate political outcomes like the Green Party causing an electoral upset in Germany. Whatever governments and societies decide on the future of nuclear energy after prioritizing questions of energy security and climate change, it can only be on the basis of relative risks, because nothing in this field comes with certainties. Back in Japan, the radioactive contamination from Fukushima will take months to be controlled. The Japanese public has voluntarily embraced an austere lifestyle thanks to admirable self-restraint and community spirit, and the previously weak government of Prime Minister Naoto Kan has been strengthened, because people feel he has performed creditably and transparently in adversity. When the Japanese have overcome the setback of a cruel act of nature, they will revert to the even greater challenge of re-asserting their nation on the world stage.

March 2011

THE SECRET OF INDIA'S UNHAPPINESS: DAMNED LIES AND STATISTICS

In an attempt to provide the basis for a more rounded picture of human development, Amartya Sen and other like-minded economists put forward the view that GDP and GDP per capita were inadequate measurements of a nation's genuine progress. Nevertheless, South Asia hardly benefited from the new formulae. The newly constructed human development index used the yardstick of GDP per capita together with the supplements of life expectancy and a composite measure of education, including literacy and school enrolment. With this revised approach, India climbed from the rank of 132 out of 174 countries in 1999 to 127 out of 177 in 2005. It only fared slightly less well even by the old measurement of GDP per capita, by being ranked 131 out of 177 in the United Nations Human Development Report of 2005.

The constant search for new measurements to assess the quality of life continues. Politicians in the West espouse such efforts as an aid to governance. David Cameron, the leader of the British Conservative party, says that 'improving society's sense of well-being is the central political challenge of our time'. Well-being may not be quite the same thing as happiness, but the concept obviously owes a great deal to the work of another economist, Labour peer Lord Layard of the London School of Economics, with his views on happiness in society and what promotes it. This has led all political groupings to toy with originating some newly-fashioned felicific or hedonistic calculus, which would serve to show that their policies are working, even if subliminally. A national happiness audit would clearly be able to inform and judge a government's performance and social policies.

It comes as little surprise that statistics on this subject, based on life-satisfaction, life expectancy, and an ecological footprint (namely, the extent to which the ecological demands of human economic activity are within, or exceed, the capacity of the biosphere to supply goods and services to that community) show that Canada, Denmark, Iceland and Switzerland are, or should be, the world's happiest countries. And India? According to the Happy Planet Index, it ranks as low as 14th just in the Asia region, behind Bangladesh, Bhutan, Maldives and Sri Lanka.

The happiest societies are shown to be the most equal ones while unemployment and ill health make the largest contributions to unhappiness. Creating paid employment opportunities and a level social playing field is therefore good policy both for the economy and to spread individual happiness. High levels of individual income by themselves will not generate overall happiness, especially in a country like India, where 10 per cent of the population accounts for about 40 per cent of the total income, and the next 10 per cent might own products like cell phones, TV sets and two-wheelers in the next five years. This will still amount to only one-fifth of the population whereas 60 per cent will have to get by on less than Rupees 100 per day. India's economic growth, with the nation's attention fixed on the annual percentage growth of GDP, has been largely job-less, with the much-vaunted IT and BPO industries employing less than 1.5 million persons. When one adds to unemployment the malnutrition, illiteracy and social and economic disparities and discrimination so widely prevalent in India, there can be little expectation of a higher grading on the happiness index.

India also scores very poorly on various other global databases. Transparency International's Corruption Perceptions Index of 2006 ranks India in joint 70th position out of 163, equal with Saudi Arabia, Egypt and Senegal, but below countries like Croatia, Cuba, Belize, Jamaica and Bhutan. The Human Poverty Index in 2003, which is based on the probability at birth of reaching the age of 60, functional literacy skills, the percentage of children undernourished, and the percentage of the population without access to safe water, rated India in 127th position after Equatorial Guinea, Gabon and Mongolia. In the Pilot Environmental Performance Index 2006, India is ranked 118 out of 133 countries, after China, Pakistan and Sri Lanka.

In the recent Mercer Human Resource Consultancy's Urban Quality of Life Index, Delhi and Mumbai share 150th position after Colombo and Dakar in Senegal, while Bangalore and Chennai fare even worse.

Notwithstanding Manmohan Singh's ability to secure honorary degrees from the many universities he attended by virtue of his reputation as a prophet of economic liberalization, the league tables tell a different story about the success of Indian governments in this century. The World Bank's 'Doing Business 2007' index rates India in 134th position out of 175 countries, and for the enforcement of contract second from bottom at 173rd. Nevertheless, influenced by the élite 10 per cent who own and read the newspapers and the TV stations, and despite a warning from Manmohan Singh himself that only a small minority of Indian citizens could aspire to Western standards of living, our media only reflects the bubbling overconfidence of the high-consumption class. Thus we read and hear each year about callow graduates of the IIT/IIMs gloating about their job offers along with, in Indian terms, obscenely high remunerations from multi-national companies. We cannot expect anything better from the media with its well-known lack of social awareness and sensitivity, but would have at least thought that the bright sparks of our youth would have shown a more appropriate degree of modest equilibrium at their privileged opportunities when compared to the vast mass of their fellow countrypersons.

We may ask, in the words of Lenin; 'What is to be done?' Whereas Lenin provided some answers to his own question, our political leaders since independence have failed to find any responses suitable to our circumstances. Even the Indian states ruled for many years by parties professing the politics of secularism, egalitarianism and pro-poor policies, have not shown any markedly better economic indicators than the rest of India. The usual excuse is the constraint of our democratic structures and coalition governments, but these are the very aspects which are praised to the skies when it suits us to proclaim our democratic credentials. We cannot have it both ways. There has been no Reformation in India, no Peasants Revolt, no political revolution, no Industrial Revolution, nor an agrarian revolution. The main characteristic of India, namely, that what does not change is more important than what does change, will continue to hold true. Our country, that designs the software for some of the fastest and most highly cutting-edge technological railways on this planet, is apparently unable to produce an adhesive that will stick down postage stamps and the flaps of envelopes, leading to the absurd, ubiquitous and environmentally unfriendly use of staples. Indian citizens are accustomed to such paradoxes.

January 2007

SO NEAR, YET SO FAR: THE INDIAN NORTH-EAST

The Indian north-east region, comprising about 5 per cent of the land area and 8 per cent of the population of the country, is one of most complex in Asia, with about 200 ethnic groups, languages and dialects. These societies have lived in isolation not only from the rest of the country but from each other, and both legal and illegal migration has created new fault lines in traditional societies. The whole area, where parochialism transcends nationalism or even regionalism, is in painful transition, to learn tolerance with other ethnic groups and adjust to the concept of planned development.

There is a tendency to assert that the north-east is not 'integrated' with India because of ethnicity and insurgency, but this is only partly true. Arunachal which has the biggest number of tribes, is peaceful, while Manipur, which is prey to secessionist groups, is otherwise well integrated in terms of arts, culture and sports. Nagaland is the only state where militants are not reconciled to their tribal space being part of the Indian Union, though even there, many people see benefits when compared to neighbours like Myanmar and Bangladesh.

There is another aspect to human integration: 90 journalists from Assam alone work in Delhi, 10 per cent of the IT-sector people in Bangalore are from the north-east, hospitality sectors all over India look for and employ youth from the north-east because they speak better English and are more sophisticated.

5,000 young persons from the region each year go to other states to find employment.

The north-east comprises eight states with only 1 per cent of their boundaries adjoining India – the rest is with Burma, China, Nepal, Bhutan and Bangladesh. India's trade with the countries bordering the north-east has gone up five times, but no impact is seen in the north-east because this commerce is through the sea ports. The five-nation BIMSTEC was supposed to help the north-east, but there is a lack of connectivity that precludes the opportunities transforming into results.

Our import substitution economy after 1947 deprived the north-east of its natural markets, as did the 1971 Bangladesh war. There are massive imports into the region, and Chinese consumer goods are to be seen in every market place. The exchange rate is unreasonably low for Chinese imports, and these goods have obviously not come through established channels. Illegal trade and smuggling exist because there is no trade facilitation.

There are three points for border trade with China at places where there is no dispute on the boundary; Lipulekh in Uttaranchal opened in 1993 and Shipkila in Himachal Pradesh in 1994. I led an Indian delegation to Beijing in 1994 that proposed the opening of Nathula to the Chinese. It then took nine years for the memorandum to be signed, and a further three for the border point to be open for trade. For 58 years after the Younghusband expedition of 1904, Nathula had been the main artery between India and China and constituted 80 per cent of the trade between the two countries. The expectation was that by 2010, trade at Nathula would represent 10 per cent of the total Indo-Chinese trade, namely 1 billion dollars. Why 2010? Because the Border Roads Organization said it would take as long as that for the one-track road to be made two lanes. Considering that India and China are among the two fastest growing world economies, and with Tibet itself growing at 12 per cent, Nathula should improve prospects for the whole north-east which trails behind at about half of India's growth rate. Though Indo-Chinese bilateral trade has exceeded expectations, the optimistic prospects envisaged for Nathula trade and its beneficial effects have never materialized, and now do not look as if they ever will. If the north-east opens up, would it be primarily for our exports or only for imports of cheaper Chinese goods? This question seems to obsess the decision makers in New Delhi who always want to play safe.

North-east progress depends on the creation of assets in power, infrastructure and opportunities. India may be looking East but evidently not to our own north-east. The shocking fact is that 97 per cent of the natural resources in the north-east like hydro-electricity, biodiversity and minerals are not exploited. There is practically no private sector involvement. The entrepreneur does not need tax breaks and incentives from the state. What he looks for first are raw material sources, the potential market and logistics.

Tourism could transform the north-east. Ethnologically and linguistically, the north-east has historic links with south west China and the Mon-Khmer peoples in Myanmar and Thailand. The structures for tourism are poor, but infrastructure is equally poor in parts of south-west China, Tibet, Nepal and Bhutan, which are all also landlocked. Yet those countries and regions attract manifold numbers of tourists; Bhutan, Nepal, Tibet and Myanmar by far surpass the tourist numbers to the north-east. There has been no use of specialized promotions, like adventure, veterans of World War II, wild life, spiritual, nostalgia (for tea planters and missionaries) or eco-tourism. Air connectivity to the neighbouring countries does not exist, and the permit raj of inner line, restricted area, and protected area permits are a serious obstacle.

The North-East Council was established as early as 1971, and has been revamped many times since. Health and education are identified as priorities, along with employment, good governance and food security. The public's interest in participating in development is high. But while multiple recommendations are drawn up, little or nothing is seen on the ground.

The centre's response has characteristically been, as in Kashmir, to throw money at the problem with no consideration of outcomes or accountability. In addition to the allocations in the state plans, there are funds from the NEC, and central ministries since 1998 have allocated a non-lapsable 10 per cent of their budgets for the north-east. There is re-imbursement of expenditure incurred by north-east states on security-related issues, funds for modernization of police, border areas development grants and other sources of funding too numerous to mention. Yet the minimum identified needs have not been met, despite the massive funds poured into the region. With this cornucopia of funds, there has been great seepage and massive corruption. Effective measures to prevent this have neither been devised nor executed. Pumping in funds leads to distortions in the economy unless there are investments in real assets. The shift from agriculture to industry and services is at a snail's pace even compared to the rest of India.

There are legitimate fears of loss of identity, and the demand by various ethnic groups for more and more autonomy continues and has to be addressed. The need to protect the socio-cultural and religious practices of the various ethnic groups, and to give them an effective say in running their own institutions has often been underlined, but there is no adequate devolution to the minority tribes in the autonomous areas and funds are not released directly to the autonomous councils. The various ethnic fractures prevent cooperation in anti-militancy. The Union government deals with combating the thirty-odd active militant groups both because of reluctance by the states to get involved due to alleged lack of financial and human resources, and suspicion by the centre of the state governments' ability to keep intelligence reports confidential. Even to resist illegal migration, HIV-AIDS and drug trafficking, there is little cooperation between the states. In other words, there is a 360° lack of trust and faith. This is the reason why so many aspects of governance in the region have been left to the supervision of the army, and the prolonged deployment of the military, which is unfamiliar with the local terrain, language, culture and social ethos, has led to serious recriminations and alienates the local people. After fifty-years experience in the north-east, the Armed Forces Act is viewed as tyrannical and inspires hatred.

The Union government might want to look East but most of its bureaucrats in the region look West. Admittedly, life is difficult, and education facilities are limited. There are restrictions in the acquisition of property by 'outsiders'. The result is that there is no long-term commitment to be found on the part of the civil service. An administrative and police service for the region composed exclusively of officers from the north-east is long overdue.

November 2007

THE BJP: THE BOOK AND THE BAN

The serious aspect in the long-running comedy of the BJP committing *hara kiri* by stabbing itself in both feet with its *trishul* is the expulsion of Jaswant Singh for his book on Jinnah, and the banning of it by the BJP-governed state of Gujarat. The author must have known that his party had 'form' in such matters, and he should therefore hardly have been taken by surprise. The BJP was only acting in character: it is no stranger to the banning and burning of books.

An unflattering article by *Time* magazine in 2002 about Prime Minister Atal Behari Vajpayee's physical infirmities resulted in the burning of the magazine by party activists and a volley of criticism from most of the same politicians and journalists who now deplore the action taken against Jaswant Singh. The reporter concerned was probably saved from expulsion from India by the fact that the prime minister's limitations were common knowledge, and a widely-held suspicion that the article was instigated by a pro-Advani lobby that wanted Advani to replace Vajpayee.

Speculation about Shivaji's paternity – that too, by a foreigner – provoked the BJP prime minister in 2004 to 'warn' the author, caused an oriental research institute in Pune to be looted by party loyalists, the book to be banned India-wide, and the Maharashtra government to ask for the author's arrest through Interpol. The same state government, apparently on a legal complaint by a Shivaji descendant, banned yet another book by the same author in 2006. Jaswant Singh, along with Arun Shourie and others who have now apparently discovered the merits of free speech, was complicit through association at the time, and has been hoist on his own petard.

Despite the arguments of Amartya Sen and others, Indians are a far from tolerant people; the discriminations of the caste system are sufficient manifestation of that. But the Congress party, being a big tent and unburdened by any obligatory ideology, can afford to show much more latitude than the BJP. Its record is by no means free from intolerance of the written word, allegedly on the grounds of 'public order' as in the case of *The Satanic Verses*, but it has prudently not resorted to bans on many works strongly critical of the lives and actions of Pandit Nehru and Indira and Rajiv Gandhi, and the critics have been quietly rehabilitated in the bosom of the party.

A welcome discussion of the meaning of history has arisen as a consequence of Jaswant Singh's predicament. History is the transmission of ideas about identity and common experience through the interpretation of the past in which perception and myth can play just as important a role in the construction of identity as do literal fact and reality.

It is argued that with 70 per cent of the Indian population under the age of 40, it is the future and not the past that should be of pressing concern, but this is gravely missing the point. History is now; we are all affected by incidents, stories and images of the past that, consciously or not, we carry over into our lives, and these perceptions may be disturbing or exalting. Nations, like people, are wounded or inspired by incidents at birth and early life, and reshape and enrich them as inherited myths to serve as warnings or exemplars. In this transmission of information and its interpretation, we learn not only about the past, but about the present and ourselves. The past is not a dead subject but a continuum, a memory to which all of us belong. That is why revolutions have ultimately to rewrite history, because history has not only to make sense of the past but also of the future. This is what makes the events and personalities attending the Partition of India especially reverberative; and even more so, to those whose ideological *raison d'être* rests upon a specific interpretation of such personalities and events.

However, in evaluating events and personages, there can be no room for nostalgia. In the historian's retelling of even familiar episodes, there will be change, and nothing can ever be the same as it was before in the reinterpretation of our received assessments – otherwise there would be no purpose in the retelling. India over the past millennia has not been a solid unchanging entity, and it is good to revisit the interpretations of the past, however painful the exercise might prove. The English still debate the nature and extent of progress (as defined in modern terms) in landmark events like 1066 and the 'Norman yoke', Iranians deplore the Arab conquest which introduced Islam but destroyed their former civilization, and the French subject the 1789 Revolution to repeated analyses and reconstructions.

Among the key elements in the formation of national identity is a sense of the achievements of a shared past, not necessarily of a literal past, but often one that is at times selective and structured to serve a purpose. In such renderings, each new era sees itself as a reflection of the active mythology of the past. History written with this purpose is teleological and constructed with a view to invoking patriotism and continuity, which are its main themes. There is, sadly, a long tradition in the subcontinent of leaders rallying followers around historical symbols that unify adherents of one group in order to set them in opposition against another. To such leaders, political consensus resides in a shared and unquestioning sense of history, which lies at the core of allegiance. The BJP would have been more than happy if Jaswant Singh had stuck to this script.

As is the custom with myth and legend, our attitude to history is Manichean; the heroes are unblemished and the villains are irredeemable. So our political hero can do no wrong. To impugn his qualities is to commit heresy and betray the ideology. To show any sympathy for his antithesis is unacceptable. Indians associate political power with kingship, divine right and absolute authority, leading to infallibility and the hereditary principle. How else can one explain the legions of followers and hangers-on, who wait patiently in corridors and lobbies for a glimpse of the *neta,* wishing for nothing except a *namaskar* or just a glance in their direction, or not even as much as that? Just to be in the presence is sufficient; to participate in a *darshan.* Our politicos know better than to turn them away. That is why there is no popular outrage, and on the contrary, perhaps some political mileage to be made by the Maharashtra government in deciding on a giant statue of Shivaji at a cost of Rs. 350 crore and taller than the Statue of Liberty during a critical time of drought and farmer suicides,

The line between history and mythology in India is drawn too fine. The past is consciously invoked to legitimize aspects of the present and to strengthen the forces of cultural nationalism. History is used to promote ideology, and the more the ideology is drafted into the service of myth-making, the less relevant becomes the scientific approach. Totalitarian instincts need to harness history in their support, and to rewrite it according to the canon to serve their purposes. Non-specialists and politicians have intervened in a field that should be purely academic, not understanding that there is no such thing as 'correct history'. There are only opinions based on evidence and analysis. History should not be written in the context of narrow nationalism; it is not intended to teach patriotism, loyalty or morality. If historiography in India is to be a rational study, its status must break free from hagiography and the malign influence of political interference.

History has to be contestable, but not in political party conclaves nor the law courts. Nor should it ever be determined or influenced by state violence, mob assault or government bans. Arbitrarily closing down proper historical debate is tantamount to closing down the mind. What would be the public reaction if the characters and careers of iconic figures like Rabindranath, Maulana Azad or Subhas Chandra Bose were to be deconstructed and demolished? Will India be forever prone to emotional convulsions, and could our enemies be tempted deliberately to use historical biography to divide our society?

September 2009

MISCELLANY

INFLATION AND INDIA'S GLOBAL STANDING

Quality Breakthroughs Needed to Protect Export Services

INFLATION is threatening India's economic growth. Apart from aggravating social tensions, diminishing our shopping baskets, affecting the stock market and scaring away foreign investors, it will also seriously damage India's reputation as a global information technology power centre, which foreigners regard as India's unique selling point. The fact that visiting dignitaries like Obama and Cameron head for the techno-city of Bangalore speaks for itself. Inflation may be a worldwide phenomenon as the Indian government alleges, but with domestic prices rising and having a knock-on effect on wages, a higher salary bill will have a negative impact on Indian aspirations to play a larger economic and political role on the world stage.

India's service industry accounts for 57 per cent of the country's GDP, and information technology and business process out-sourcing contribute 25 per cent of the country's exports. Over the past two decades, exports of services regularly grew between 30 and 50 per cent annually, but rising production costs now threaten to constrain this sector severely. Until a short while ago, Indian information technology professionals were paid one-sixth of the salaries drawn by their counterparts in the USA or the European Union: today they are paid about one-third and this gap is steadily dwindling, nullifying the cost advantage previously enjoyed by India in global markets. Once cost competitiveness is no longer assured, the Indian services sector will have no option but to compete on the strength of quality of performance alone.

Indian service providers claim that they are going up the value chain. British Telecom awarded a US $1 billion contract to Tech Mahindra, Wipro received a $300 million contract from General Motors, and ABN Amro gave a $500 million contract to TCS, Infosys and Patni. These would have been unthinkable even a few years back, but authorities representing the industry still cite lower costs in India rather than quality of services as the country's main comparative advantage in doing global business. This implies that Indian companies will start regressing down the ladder as soon as there is someone else who can do the same work cheaper. Some Indian companies are aware of this, and are trying to secure their low-cost future by setting up companies in China, Philippines and Bangladesh. This tactic will protect their profitability in the short term, but the adverse impact on India's global reputation and services exports will be considerable.

History has examples of countries that made economic breakthroughs when they were under severe pressure to find new approaches to quality. The 'Made in Germany' label, far from being the result of any promotional strategy crafted in Berlin, came into being in response to protests from blacksmiths in Sheffield against cheap German imitations. The British Parliament made it mandatory in 1887 for imported items to carry an identification of the country of origin. Only then did the Germans take note of advanced technological developments and embark on new standards of quality. Similarly, at the start of the last century, Japanese cars were first assembled in bicycle repair shops, and later made their international debut purely on the strength of their low price. The pressures of the global marketplace, however, soon compelled Japan to shed its image of inferior quality. Companies like Toyota then introduced methods like Total Quality Management, Kaizen and Lean Production that lifted manufacturing to a totally new level. The concepts behind the world's renowned quality management approaches, like Lean SixSigma, have their origins in the Japanese manufacturing revolution.

Can India consolidate and advance its export reputation by doing in services what the Germans have done in engineering and the Japanese in manufacturing? To achieve this, the service industry has to regard the present challenges as an opportunity. It must shed its traditional low-cost focus and reposition itself as a symbol of quality. Some may argue that this has already happened, citing that the number of Indian companies with top quality certifications from globally reputed organizations is the highest in the world. But a collection of certifications does not establish any country as a global quality leader: the idea behind quality certifications is standardization of processes, and does not *per se* reflect any guarantee of all-round quality. And while the philosophies originating with TQM have a more holistic approach, they nevertheless remain rooted in a time of manufacturing, and an environment when many repetitive tasks needed to be optimized.

Innovative approaches to quality led to breakthroughs when craftsmanship turned into engineering, and engineering into high-end manufacturing. In the same way, the change from manufacturing standards to quality services will require major transformations in thinking. The pressures of losing its cost advantage, and the key role it has been playing in global sourcing, should make India an ideal candidate for the creation of a new hallmark of quality for this people-centred industry. A few first steps towards integrating human resources with quality management are being attempted, and some Indian software companies have started speaking about 'controlling visibility' in the context of employee-client interaction. Unfortunately, all this means in practice is that companies hide their less competent employees, and prevent clients from seeing the shortcomings.

Inevitably, competing companies in other countries are already moving on: in the USA, for instance, HumanSigma has gained some recognition as a quality management system specifically designed for services. Surely the time has come, if India is to be a force in this sector, for there to be an Indian certificate that is even harder to obtain than one from USA or Europe? Our IITs and IIMs need to bend themselves to this task. It will be a pity if India, from being a world leader, now has to play catch-up.

It is instructive to note how Indian professionals compare with counterparts in other countries. Of the 350,000 engineers who graduate from our universities every year, only a quarter are considered employable by recruitment agencies. Google in India finds it 'a challenge trying to hire engineers as compared to other parts of the world', and Microsoft states that 'Indian computer engineers are more into theory and less into managing businesses, building businesses or writing source codes, the key to software development'. Among the legion Indian engineers, there may be some brilliant minds, but few are working on quality services.

And for this, the senior management and our education system are to blame.

Meanwhile, the effects of rising costs are already ominous. The history of the Indian offshoring industry was not only about successful multinational companies and large contracts coming to India from abroad. From the beginning it also had a darker side, with companies closing down or failing in offshore attempts, when quality concerns were the problem. Lately, such cases are on the increase, and several companies are shutting down operations for cost reasons; the shrinking difference in salaries no longer justifies the expense of employing staff here. With China and several Latin American and Southeast Asian countries now aggressively pushing into the global market of low-cost off-shoring, the question is whether a 'Made in India' label can stand for quality in services when the cost advantage is gone. Steps beyond accumulating certifications are necessary, and having a large number of engineers at the company's disposal is not the answer.

An economic policy by New Delhi that successfully controls inflation is nowhere to be seen. When it happens, it will buy time to secure India's position as a permanent leader in services before the cost advantage runs out. In the interim, human resources and quality management need to be inter-connected in original and imaginative ways. That is the current challenge confronted by the leaders in the fields of Indian business process offshoring and information technology. If they fail to rise to the occasion, the goose that laid the golden eggs will have flown away and the Indian image could revert to what it was in the pre-globalization period.

(With co-author Andi Pueringer)
March 2011

CASTE AND THE CREAMY LAYER

There is no accepted view about the origins of the Indian caste system. The word 'caste' itself derives from *casta*, the Portuguese word used from the sixteenth century to describe the segregated groups the Portuguese sea-farers encountered in Indian society.

Some assert that the Indo-Aryan migrants established the caste system to situate themselves at the top level, but the nature of Indo-Aryan migration itself has come into dispute. Though many Hindu scriptures contain passages that can be interpreted as sanctioning the caste system, there are as many indications that the system might not be essential to Hinduism and may not have been hereditary: it may even pre-date Hinduism. The Vedas give little importance to it, mentioning it rarely and cursorily. Ancient Hindu texts divide human society into four 'varnas' that define a person's social standing and occupation: in order of status, Brahmins, Kshatriyas, Vaishyas and Shudras. The laws of Manu of the first century BC asserted, 'it is better to do one's duty badly than another's well'. Every 'jati' or caste and sub-caste belongs to one of these groups, but excluded from society altogether were the 'untouchables', now called Dalits. These people were the poor landless labour, servants and those at the bottom of society who were not even given the dignity of a caste name, were mentioned in Vedic texts only in terms of pollution, and were to perform the humiliating tasks that other humans would not consider. They suffered discrimination of all kinds, religious, occupational and social; were not allowed temple worship with others, nor water from the same source, and were denied interaction with other castes. Not very dissimilar is their situation today.

Dalit is a generic term. In practice there are hundreds of such groups who live separately and do not intermarry. Some regard themselves as descendants of some divinity or sage, and seek revenge for having been cheated of their rightful place in society. The British started to classify people by caste in census, but this practice stopped before the Second World War, so all the statistics now are largely theoretical and speculative. It may be noted that there is social and other discrimination even among Dalits – sub-groups among them do not interact with those they consider inferior, no caste sees any merit in any other caste, and each higher group wants to keep the lower ones down. They are as bitterly divided against each other as they are against the upper castes, and many feel more aggrieved by the attitudes of the lower caste just above them than by the more remote Brahmins and upper castes. Every section in society in India seems opposed to everyone else, and in this melange, unexpected hostilities and alliances are common-place, especially in the political arena, where the Dalits will ally with Brahmins or Muslims or anyone else who can assist them to power.

Some historians claim that the hierarchy of the caste system was more fluid prior to the British imperial era. According to this view, the British rulers accepted caste as an indicator of social standing and intellectual ability, which stratified the system and made it rigid, especially when castes were enumerated in the census. This view asserts that in earlier times, rankings could change according to circumstances, and could rise or fall depending on economic or political prominence; that caste is not a Hindu doctrine but merely a social practice. Other social scientists say that caste is a system of exploitation of the poor by prosperous, mainly landowning classes, who degrade the landless labourers and poor artisans with ritual emphasis on their allegedly God-given inferior status.

The spread of Islam with its militant egalitarianism inspired the Indian *bhakti* devotional movements stressing equality before God. Christian missionary activity created greater access for education and health, pastoral care and dignity. These were the same reasons that prompted Hindu conversions to Buddhism, Islam and Sikhism – that is, release from the existing social order. But over time, many converts too were absorbed into the traditional hierarchy by the assimilating character of India's societal culture, and the caste system is so all-pervasive in Indian society that it came to be observed, *mutatis mutandis*, even among followers of egalitarian religions, especially in respect of marriage and management of worship.

The caste system may be gradually decreasing, especially in the urban areas and the organized economy. Provision of civic amenities and public services, information technology and the growth of civil society movements have blunted some discriminative practices. Urbanization and information technology leads to the anonymity that makes it easier to escape caste taboos, but people still marry customarily into, and live among, the same-caste members. In villages, however, you may be born into a job or caste function from which you will never escape. Caste is a major element in India's society structure and private sphere, and is strongly adhered to in most rural areas. Groups of lower castes have tried to elevate their status by emulating the practices and rituals of higher castes in a process called 'Sanskritization', but regardless of education and economic power among some members of lower castes, their social mobility is restricted. In rural India, where caste discrimination is as rampant as ever, hundreds, perhaps thousands, die of caste-based violence each year, some at the hands of the police. The world media has recently written about a Dalit millionaire in Agra to show that opportunities in India are available for anyone with entrepreneurial flair, but the person himself gave the lie to this, stating that the 'economic boom is only enjoyed by the high-caste people. I feel real despair . . . the gap between the scheduled castes and the higher castes is increasing . . . they stay poor and everyone else gets richer'.

Untouchability has been abolished by law, and India's Constitution in 1950 outlawed caste-based discrimination, but the challenge of eradicating the prejudices of thousands of years engages all governments and enrages all sections of the population – both the higher and the lower castes. India has the most extensive programme of affirmative action in the world, but it is less than effective. It perpetuates the caste system that was intended to be abolished within ten years of the 1950 Constitution, although no democracy can accept that its citizens be perpetually divided on the basis of accident of birth. To a great extent this is due to Dalit leaders themselves, who consistently reject the defining of what is meant by a 'creamy layer'; in other words, the affluent and well-educated Dalits, whose families have used affirmative action to prosper and have no further need for it to enable upward mobility. Those persons want such benefits to continue indefinitely into future generations, even though this reduces the opportunities available to other Dalits.

The quotas or 'reservations', on which the government's affirmative action is based, protects about 50 per cent of government jobs at the point of recruitment for Scheduled Castes (about 15 per cent of the population), Scheduled Tribes (about 7 per cent), and Dalits/Other Backward Castes (50 per cent). Reservations are now proposed to be extended to them in higher education institutions, and also for Muslims (15 per cent). A few months ago, the Supreme Court stayed *ad interim* a law that provided a 27 per cent reservation in higher education for other backward castes, on the ground that the 1931 census figures could not be regarded as a yardstick today. Each state in India can formulate its own reservation policy, and in Tamil Nadu, for example, the reserved quota for government recruitment is as high as 70 per cent. Non-Hindu Dalits do not benefit from any reservations, except by very recent legislation in Tamil Nadu, and Hindu Dalits strenuously oppose reservations for any other religious communities on the grounds that Islam and Christianity reject caste. In reality, the opposition is because including other religious communities in reservations will reduce the opportunities for Hindu Dalits.

In politics, the lower castes have the numbers that count. More than 50 per cent of the population consists of lower castes, and together with large minorities like Muslims, they can easily form the majority in any election when they exhibit solidarity. The day will come when a Dalit will be the prime minister of India. Rebels in other lands and other times have fought against authority, invoking egalitarianism and universality of human rights, but most Dalit leaders appeal only to their own sub-caste and ignore others in the same or worse straits. They emphasize their own lower-caste status to focus on what divides and differentiates. Thus backward-caste Yadavs will ally with Muslims or Rajputs against the Brahmins, who are only a small fraction of the population everywhere in India. Expanding and taking advantage of the reservations is the main political policy of the lower castes, who project no special platform for foreign policy, economics, good governance or anti-corruption. They are hostile to the privatization of the economy and seek to introduce reservations in the private sector. Social justice for them translates into more jobs for the Dalits. There is no emphasis on performance; only on caste identity.

Some writers, even with a strongly humanitarian background, abhor caste discrimination but urge re-thinking on the caste system as such. They make three points: firstly, that the system is a strong stabilizer. As a result, India has suffered no peasants revolt, no Luddite movement, no evils attributed to an industrial revolution, and no signs of any political revolution either. In a country as large and diverse as India, the virtue of social stability is obvious, and the point is made that if the system was infirm, it would have collapsed long ago. That it has not done so, makes its value self-evident. Secondly, to the lower castes, it makes great sense to believe that a better deal awaits in the life hereafter, whereas such presumptions have less relevance in the contemporary material world. Lastly, reference is made to India's affirmative action policies, especially now that politics in India is dominated by the lower castes and this will be the case for the foreseeable future.

Prime Minister Manmohan Singh has recently compared the caste system to racial apartheid in former South Africa, though only a few years ago, the Indian government made fevered efforts to stall any discussion of caste at a United Nations Conference on Racism in 2001. The allegation that segregation and oppression of peoples in terms of their descent and occupation constitutes a form of apartheid was rejected in India on the grounds that there is no racial difference between the various castes, whether Brahmins or Dalits. It is good that Premier Manmohan Singh has broken the shackles of Indian sensitivity on this debate, and by implication has acknowledged the validity of the criticism of the caste system from outside India.

November 2007

CHARITY BEGINS AT HOME, BUT NOT IN INDIA

The end of the year is the traditional time to exchange gifts and goodwill. Gifts are an essential aspect of the spirit of charity. Paul in his first Letter to the Corinthians spelled it out: and now abideth faith, hope, charity, these three; but the greatest of these is charity. Aeschylus had earlier coined the word philanthropy from a combination of love and humanity.

In March 2010, according to Wikipedia, the Indian dollar billionaires numbered 69, compared to 52 last year. India is second only to USA, which has 403. The recent economic fortunes of India have brought untold wealth to certain individuals who, unlike the *panwallah* millionaire of popular legend who conceals his riches and continues his humble occupation, are not shy in flaunting it – like Mukesh Ambani's Mumbai house 27 storeys high and worth $973 million, ostentatious mega-cost weddings, Bollywood extravagances and the Indian Premier Cricket tournament. The 'brand value' of sporting celebrities who earn over a crore of rupees per commercial photo-shoot is gleefully reported in our media, as is the soaring market value of IIT graduates and IT personalities. On 28 October 2010, the launch in India took place of the Bugatti Veyron 16.4 car at the cost of Rs. 16 crore each, and the company aims to sell 60 of these vehicles here in the first year alone.

According to Forbes, the combined net worth of India's 100 richest people rose to $300 billion this year from $276 billion last year, driven by the country's booming economy and a rally in the stock market. Mukesh Ambani tops the list, followed by the steel baron Lakshmi Mittal, who retained second position with a net worth of $26.1 billion. Premji's wealth increased to $17.6 billion from $14.9 billion last year, taking him to the third spot. Fourth on the list were the Essar Energy brothers Shashi and Ravi Ruia with a net worth of $15 billion, bolstered by the company's IPO in the United Kingdom that raised $1.85 billion. Mayawati, who owned next to nothing when she launched herself into politics, now admits she is worth Rs. 88 crore. Much lesser known Indians are buying assets abroad – for example, Venky's Chickens, hardly a name to trip off the tongue in India, purchased Blackburn Rovers, a premier division football club in the United Kingdom, for $37 million and debts of $30 million. Hardly chicken-feed.

Diego Forlan, the Uruguayan footballer with the 'Golden Boot' in the last World Cup was brought to Calcutta only a few weeks after the World Cup, and Baywatch star Pamela Anderson appeared for a few fleeting days in an Indian reality show for Rs. 2.5 crore. This is just a glimpse of the huge amounts available in India in the entertainment industry. And yet, with all this loose change sloshing about in India, where is the support for education, the arts, the theatre, music and other good causes? We admire the love of their fellow-men shown by people like Steve Waugh who come rarely to our country, but take the time and trouble to raise money altruistically for a good cause here. To stave off the implied criticism of our own celebrities, we are told that they are also in the habit of doing good works, but prefer to do so anonymously, presumably not for reasons of modesty but to avoid the attentions of the tax authority. So we are never told where and what are their charitable involvements, though we are vaguely aware of their lavish donations to temples, gurus, and hospitals that bear their name and collect fees from patients, though they have charitable windows of access, probably again to avail of tax benefits.

Yes, our dignitaries and celebrities participate in runs, walks and other fund-raising events, but nothing as exhausting as the (so far) twelve long-distance walks of Ian Botham, including one of a 900 mile one-end-of-the-country-to-the-other, to raise £12 million for leukemia and lymphoma research. Nelson Mandela, who has no shortage of invitations, chose to celebrate his 90th birthday in 2008 as the main attraction in a star-studded concert for charity in London's Hyde Park. Former World Cup Italian footballer Roberto Baggio commands nothing like the income of Bollywood stars or Indian cricketers, but he has been voted the winner of an award in 2010, not just by Italians, but by former Nobel Peace Prize winners, for his personal efforts for charity, for Aung San Suu Kyi's freedom, for hospitals, Haiti victims of earthquakes and to combat bird flu.

Funding by charitable donation is taken for granted in the USA, whether in politics or academia. It is interesting to observe that the contributions of Indian capitalists to educational institutions outside India, especially in UK and USA, such as Oxbridge, Stanford, Cornell and Harvard in recent years is hundreds and probably thousands of times higher than their donations to universities and centres of learning in India. One Indian corporate giant has given $50 million for a building in an Ivy League University. This obviously betrays a lack of confidence in the educational structure in India itself, and reveals false priorities. It is also galling when leading Universities in the West come calling cap-in-hand to India seeking donations, to this country that is the poorest low-income country in the G-20. It is a shameful irony for the West when it seeks a bail-out for its tertiary sector from poverty-stricken India. It is equally shameful, this time for India, that there are still hundreds if not thousands of Western 'volunteers' working in India, often with irregular visa status, in our educational and non-government organizations, which seem to look abroad for both manpower and money, when there is such abundance of both in India.

In the UK, about 1 per cent of the GDP is spent in charitable donations, and in USA this figure rises to about 2 per cent. In the USA, households with an income of $200,000 a year or above give 7.4 per cent of their money to charity, and in the UK, 1.2 per cent. Comparable figures for the Indian well-off are not available, but would make them ashamed if they were capable of any feelings. Andrew Carnegie gave $7 billion in today's money to build the Carnegie Hall in 1901. The Sainsbury family donated the magnificent Sainsbury wing of London's National Gallery. Warren Buffet has made the world's largest individual donation of $31 billion to charity; Bill Gates and his wife Melinda are busy spending their money on fighting malaria and river blindness far from the shores of the USA. Leonard Blavatnik gave £75 million to Oxford University. J.K. Rowling, who once lived on welfare benefits in Scotland, and Elton John, of very humble origins, are leading British philanthropists, betraying none of the insecurities and family concerns that apparently prevent Indian first-generation millionaires from reaching into their pockets for charitable good causes.

Mr Gates and Mr Buffet recently launched a 'Giving Pledge' to get their fellows in the league of the wealthy in the USA to donate half of their fortunes to charity. One may well conjecture what would be the outcome of such an appeal to the Indians who figure on the rich list. But before they hasten, led by the Reddy brothers, Madhu Koda and Lalit Modi to convey their regrets to Messrs Gates and Buffet, they would do well to remember the advice of Francis Bacon; that money is like manure – it is only useful when it is spread around.

December 2010

GUPTA'S MONOLOGUES: A SHORT STORY

HE smoked incessantly, an aggressive look on his broad brown bull-face, daring you to interrupt or contradict. He spoke without using his hands, no expressions, no gestures. He had a hacking smoker's cough, and in the middle of a severe bout, was usually bent double, holding up a warning hand to caution his listeners not to use the interruption to interject or change the subject. He hadn't finished speaking. Let me talk! he would urge when he was able to straighten up. And breathlessly, sometimes gasping, he would carry on. He drank either Black Label whiskey or wine; no cognac, no cocktails, nothing frivolous. He was always in deadly earnest. When he said something amusing and his listeners laughed, he would pause, stare at them suspiciously to check if his leg was being pulled, and then, having assured himself that it was not, would laugh briefly and boisterously himself.

I sat with him in his orchard, under the fruit trees, as the sun set. He was a passionate gardener in active correspondence with soil and irrigation experts and seed dealers across the world, and took justifiable pride in the exotica he was able to grow for his table, even leaving a reasonable surplus to be marketed. He was incongruously dressed that evening in a well-cut tweed suit, very much the armiger on his estate. He rattled the ice-cubes in his empty whiskey glass, a signal to his steward to re-charge it, and looked at me dubiously when I remarked on his excellent tailoring.

Let me tell you. Can you believe where I bought this suit? You'll never guess. Will you listen? Listen to me! You will never guess how much I paid for it. Of course, I'm now speaking of the 1950s. There's the shop Chester Harris near Austin Reed in Regent Street. That's where I got it. I went there again this year and was strolling around. Would you believe it, my steps strayed towards Regent Street and I was drawn towards the store window as if pulled by a magnet! I immediately realized that I needed another suit. This one I had bought at Chester Harris still fits me like a glove – you can see that for yourself. And guess how much

I had paid for it in 1954. Ninety-five pounds, and it was then almost more than I could afford. I had to think twice before buying it. Well, I did, and I've been delighted with it for over forty years. So here I am at the shop window of Chester Harris after all these years, rubbing my hands in keen anticipation! And thinking about the whopping five hundred quid I had kept until the end to spend on my new suit. Let me tell you. Well, you can guess. I saw a suit just like the one I have on now and like so much. I loved it. I wanted it. How much did it cost? Come on, guess. You'll never guess. Seven hundred pounds. I couldn't believe my eyes. I went inside and asked them, just to make doubly sure. Seven hundred pounds and a knocked-down price for a sale at that. Ninety-five pounds to seven hundred pounds, I ask you. So I didn't buy the suit after all. If I was going to buy something, it had to be as good as what I had before, or not at all.

We progressed into the house for dinner, a modern bungalow full of art treasures, kept immaculately clean by his wife Rekha. In the sitting area were dozens of Persian and Indian miniatures, ancient bronzes, and thousand-year-old sculptures of Hindu deities made of black basalt stone. His father in his time had been a great collector, and he had built on that inheritance. Rekha, with old-age short white hair and pursed lips, passed around hot bread rolls to go with the soup but when she essayed some comment on the statues, he raised a broad palm to pre-empt her.

You're speaking of Hindus? Gurus? Swamis? I wouldn't tolerate those people in my house. They won't be allowed to cast their shadows on my front door. No, thank you. And I'm not a bigot. No one can tell me I'm not a Hindu. Of course, I'm a Hindu. I'm as Hindu or not as the next Hindu. You can tell a Muslim or a Catholic or a Protestant – that he is one, or he isn't one, but you can't tell a Hindu that he is or he isn't. Let me tell you, there's no such thing as a Hindu fundamentalist. There just is no Hindu fundamentalism, it's a contradiction in terms. And I'm no Hindu chauvinist, you mark my words. Those religions, they were solidly based on sound principles. No beef – you've got to think of your herds, the procreative cow, without which the nomadic tribes would have starved to death. No pork – not hygienic in hot temperatures. The sacrifices of Lent and Ramadan – excellent to fast for physical good health. Wrap the common sense around with religion if you must, but essentially it's good for you.

There were photographs in the sitting room, in silver frames. There always are in the homes of the retired Mandarins. One of them showed him as a young man accompanying an older, stooped figure, perhaps his Ambassador, to a ceremonial function. He found me looking at it and wagged his finger in my face to compel my attention.

You should have seen my first Ambassador, Mohan Singh Kapoor, in his Austrian costume. Green trousers, leather jacket with green pockets, alpine hat with a chamois skin plume of some kind, looking vulgar and ridiculous. And then he had the nerve to sit in my drawing room swilling my whiskey and telling me what he considered to be my faults. He wanted my wife Rekha to be there too, because he thought I might explode and man-handle him. And I might well have done so. I heard him out without saying a word and then I fixed him with a stare and I said; 'Mr Ambassador, if you are saying this as my sister's father-in-law, it goes in through one ear and out through the other. If you are saying this as my Ambassador, I just will not have it.' That shook him.

I told him:

> Let me remind you, Mr Ambassador. I have been taught the Consular Code in 1943 in Chungking by the British Empire. I was then a young 28, and looked younger than I was. I was the first and only Indian Consul in the whole of the British Consular Service worldwide. I will remind you, Mr Ambassador, that I am therefore more senior than anyone in the Indian Foreign Service, including yourself!

The ambassador's wife used to offer silk scarves to all the female guests at their cocktail parties, and during the office hours, the old idiot used to sit with all the young countesses and baronesses and the other locally-recruited ladies of the embassy – you used to be able to find an impoverished noble lady looking for a job at every street corner in Vienna in those days – well, as I was saying – will you listen to me? – they used to sit there with him in the Chancery, all very cosy and domestic, chatting and making his tea. After some hours, I couldn't take it any more. I would burst into his room and cry, 'Sir, they may be countesses and baronesses, but they are also typists and telephone girls and without them doing their normal day's work, my Embassy cannot function.' And that's how I would break up his little gatherings. It did not endear me to him, of course.

He made a visit to the bathroom. His wife and I exchanged some news about relatives and common friends, some of whom had just been on a museum tour of Europe. He returned and resumed his seat, and pausing only to strike a match and light another cigarette, he effortlessly wrested the topic from us. Rekha's eyes met mine briefly as she rose to supervise the clearing of the table.

And how did the British Empire become the biggest Empire in the world? My dear, let me tell you. Will you listen? What happened to the Portuguese, who were much bigger in the initial stages? Why did they fade out? Listen to me. The British knew the people they ruled over. They mixed. The Company people made copious notes. Who? Why? Where? They had a keen eye. They noted every jewel in the turbans of the Indian rulers as they moved from the fourth circle to the third and from the third to the second. You know that in the Great Mughal's court, that was the protocol. You moved closer only at the pleasure of the monarch, the Shahenshah. Then came the British administrators. These were the younger sons because primogeniture gave the noble titles to the eldest sons. The younger ones had the choice of the Church, the Army or the Empire, and India was the biggest catch in the Empire. These people were not the carpet-bagging types of foreigners you find in India nowadays. They came from noble stock. They came and they observed. The District Gazetteer, a kind of Domesday Book, was written not with love, but with dedication and inspiration. After three days hard march from Musafir Sherrif in Afghanistan, a district officer would write to the Home Secretary saying there was an illuminated Koran in the village he had arrived at, even better than the one at the Asiatic Society in Calcutta. Then in the Third Afghan War, someone would remember. Now you see, that's the point! Someone would remember that dispatch! After sacking the biggest covered market in Asia at Kabul, a company would strike out for that village to recover that very Koran. Let me tell you; know your garden, know your people.

After dinner he continued to drink claret. The house steward, well-trained, left a bottle of Chateau Prevost beside his glass. Rekha told the servant in a low aside to go; that was enough work for the day. My host stopped talking abruptly to glare at her with glowing round pigs' eyes, and then continued my tutorial.

Now listen to me. Will you listen? The real lessons in life don't come from books. The real lessons come from your father, perhaps your teacher, usually from strange and unpredictable sources. In my case, my main instructor in the art of living was a man called Tajuddin, a North West Frontiersman from the British Empire's Gulf Administration Service. He was not an officer – he was what I would call a ranker, a man emerging painfully from the clerical ranks. He was an accounts man. By several strange and uncanny quirks of fate, this Tajuddin found his way into the consular service at the same time as me at the British Consulate at Chungking. The Agent General in Chungking being absent from the headquarters on the day I arrived, this man Tajuddin met me at the railway station. The first thing that this estimable Tajuddin confided to me was that Zafarullah Khan, later to be the Governor-General of Pakistan and the President of the International Court of Justice and with innumerable other high and mighty distinctions, had run away from his post because of the pork that was commonplace with every Chinese meal and the pork fat with which the Chinese habitually cook. You must remember that at the time I was both young and fastidious. No, listen to me! He gave me my first important lesson in life – never enquire into what you are eating. I've stuck firmly to that advice ever since, as you well know.

Now Sir Kenneth Ashton was the British Agent General. Tajuddin was the accountant. Although I was a diplomatic officer and Tajuddin a mere clerk, we were soon to become fast friends. The man spent hours and days poring over the accounts and every month huge fat ledgers of them were dispatched by us with my signature to Delhi. Then out the blue comes a letter from no less than Sir Olaf Caroe, the Foreign Secretary himself. 'My dear Ken', he writes,

> My dear fellow, I am informed by my Accountant General that your monthly accounts just don't add up! I am quite aware that you have a small office, but isn't that young feller Gupta with you? Can he not be made to add up two and two? I would dearly appreciate it, my dear Ken, if some efforts could be made by him to get the totals right.

Now let me tell you, that reference to me could easily have been the end of my career. Frankly, I didn't know a thing about accounts. I had heard that the reprimand had arrived, and I waited in some dread as you can imagine. At length, Sir Kenneth Ashton called me in. He gave me a dauntingly huge set of accounts books and asked me if I would like to take charge of them. What could I say? I carried them with difficulty to my room and opened them out. The pages rolled out like a concertina, full of minute figures in black ink like ever so many thousands of eels. I looked at them dazed. Just looking at them made my head ache. I couldn't make head or tail of it at all. I didn't even know where to start. There was nothing for it. I had to call for Taj. In he came and took one look and said:

> That *haramzada,* the son of a bitch, when I go to see him in the morning, he doesn't even say good-morning to me. He just grunts when I wish him. So I have deliberately fouled up the accounts every month, hoping that he'd get it in the neck. I wanted to pull him down, but I have no wish to do you any harm. Let me have them, Mr Gupta. Leave everything to me.

Three days after that Ashton asked me to bring him the accounts. Taj still hadn't returned them to me, and you can imagine how I was sweating. The diplomatic bag was due to be closed in two hours time. Then with thirty minutes left to go, Tajuddin came in smiling with fat wet lips and laid the accounts ledgers reverentially on my table. He then took up a paper knife and pointed here and there on each page like so, like so. Taj said, 'sign here, sir, now here, initial there, sir, sign here. Full signature here, name in block capitals there. Initials on the top here.' So it went on. I followed his orders blindly. There was nothing else I could do. I didn't know what I was doing. Then he suddenly closed the accounts books with a sly smile, and I took them in to Ashton. 'Have you checked them?' he asked me severely. 'Absolutely,' I replied, 'I have done so to the best of my ability.' Which was, of course, entirely true. So these accounts were dispatched to Sir Olaf Caroe with a suitable covering letter from Ashton. Two months later came the reply, which complimented Ashton on the vastly improved quality of the accounts. Taj took me aside and said, 'let this be a lesson to you, sir. Always respect your staff and especially your accountant.' I never forgot that lesson in life either.

On another day, we strolled side by side in his garden. He was in a reminiscent mood. A hunter's rifle crackling in the valleys took him back to his days in the uniform of the King's Commission during the Second World War.

I was a young lieutenant, Bengal Sappers, based in Chungking. How and why is a long story, and I will tell you about it later. Will you listen? Let me talk! You know, I've been up and down the Burma Road but I never saw Peking. I never saw North China. It was one of those things. But I know the whole of the South like the back of my hand. I've seen 2,000 miles of the Silk Route, the path of Marco Polo. I have seen the lantern sails on the Yellow River and the cormorants flying with their long necks thrust out.

There I was in the Second World War. To the south of me, Vinegar Joe Stillwell was harassing the Japs. When the Japanese were closing in on Chungking, we had to strike camp and move out the headquarters. So there I was with a group of diplomats,

Dutch from their exile government, British, American, – I can't remember all their names now. We went to the Outer Tibet area, the land of the Lo-Lo tribes. Whether Third Secretary or Ambassador, we were all one, and just before leaving we tried to get someone, anyone, to buy out all our personal possessions. Like the rest of us, the British Ambassador, Sir George Seymour, sent circular letters to everyone else. I recall that he described his shirts as silk and slightly worn at the neck. Anyway, they still got sold.

The entire Chiang Kaishek army was supplied by air. But as for us, one measly Dakota a month hauled our stuff in from Calcutta to Chungking. Needless to say, the Yanks were the suppliers to Chiang. Their squadrons flew from Calcutta to Dinjan in Assam and then on to Kunming. Whatever one may say about the Americans, and I have a great deal to say about them at all times, they were great young boys. They used to fly in droves, steering through the 'hump' between two sheer cliffs, the one break in the mountains, at 16,000 feet. That is, if they could see it. On the days that they couldn't, and there were plenty of those – mist, fog, cloud – they had to go up to 19,000 feet. The crew wore oxygen masks and there were no passengers. They would radio to the control tower in Kunming – 10 minutes fuel in the tank, 8 minutes flying time, 5 minutes, and when there was no room on the runway to bring a plane in to land, ground control would point it at Magnetic 20 north or whatever it was, and ask the crew to bail out. Only 50 per cent of those poor boys were ever found.

Later, the three of us were inside the house, drinking tea. Rekha's face, slightly flushed, intense but resigned, wanted to tell me how her husband's merits had been overlooked throughout his career. He stared at her intimidatingly with bulbous eyes and presently held up his broad traffic policeman's palm. She mumbled into silence and looked away.

Being an army man myself, I spent the war poring over maps. I found the safer route to Yunnan, and tracked the path of the Long March. In fact, I nearly made it there myself, but Sir Olaf Caroe said no, young Gupta has years of adventure left before him, and he can sit this one out. And that was that. Sir Olaf wanted me to stay and learn something from Richardson, as he put it. Richardson was from the ICS, the Indian Civil Service, the steel frame of the Empire, the iron men. Exactly the same thing happened when my name was put forward to accompany Gould from Darjeeling to Lhasa in Tibet. Sir Olaf Caroe said no again, and that, again, was that.

The thought that he had trumped the idiots at headquarters, or his recalcitrant colleagues in Embassies abroad, filled him with the greatest retrospective delight. He regarded the people he had to deal with at the Ministry as either incompetent or intriguers, or both. He chortled as he recalled the good fight he had fought, the thousand unequal skirmishes he had won.

In Kabul when I was the Ambassador – will you listen? Let me talk! – when I was the Ambassador, I asked the Foreign Secretary to let me have as my number two man, a person from the Muslim faith. The Indian Ambassador's place was always traditionally near the King. That is, on all but one occasion, which was the Id, the main Muslim feast which culminates the month of sacrifice, Ramadan. Not being a Muslim, I had no place at those religious observances. I got the usual pompous reply from Delhi that we are a multi-religious state, and it would a wrong principle to introduce sectarian considerations when it came to appointments, etc., etc., But I held absolutely firm and in the end I prevailed. I was bent on seeing our First Secretary, a Muslim, praying next to the King, along with the other Muslim Ministers and Ambassadors. I told my headquarters that the seating of our First Secretary at the Id ceremonies would be the acid test – we would see whether our number two man would be equated with the other Ambassadors, and pray in proximity to the King.

After many an acrimonious argument, the Mandarins in Delhi finally agreed. Arif Jehangir, with impeccable Muslim credentials on paper, duly arrived. So did the King's invitation to Id prayers arrive almost simultaneously. Of course, addressed to myself. I passed it on to Jehangir. He returned it to me with a demur. It appeared that he did not, by conviction, believe in outward conformity. I insisted that he nevertheless attend. Then we resorted to minuting each other on the file. Jehangir recorded, 'Perhaps the Ambassador is unaware of my background. Since my childhood I have not attended organized prayers.' My plans for a diplomatic masterstroke were thus being unravelled by this idiot. I sent him back my terse minute. 'There is always a first time.' In the end I had to lay down the law of the Embassy, as painful as it was to invoke my authority to issue an unequivocal order. And Jehangir went to the mosque to join the King and his co-religionists at prayer. Jehangir was properly placed in consideration to his position in the Embassy, and the importance of the country he represented, and my point was made. I made no further efforts at enforcing religious conformity among my recalcitrant Muslim underlings.

I pressed him to leave something to posterity. He eyed me balefully. 'Memoirs? An autobiography?' he asked contemptuously. 'That's for idlers and megalomaniacs. I have no time for such trifles.'

Indeed he didn't. Shortly thereafter, he was found in his garden shot dead with his own service pistol. The police took first the steward and then Rekha into custody. The steward was quickly released. At her trial, Rekha said nothing in her defence, and her lawyer complained that she had told him nothing either. 'Any one would think she was a deaf mute!' he protested. The prison doctors who examined her confirmed that in no way were her faculties impaired; she could hear and speak perfectly well, but she chose not to do so.

But I understand her silence. After all, she is my mother and I am the one who shot my father stone dead in mid-sentence.